PRAISE FOR
Discover Your Child's Learning Style

"Only about 5% of the population has the conviction that they are capable of going for their dreams. Encouraging talents, interests . . . in childhood is the best way to draw out each person's unique abilities. . . . This book is the tool that can make the difference for your child."

—David D'Arcangelo, chairman, Entreport Corporation and author of *Wealth Starts at Home*

"There is no greater gift you can give your children than to help them realize they don't have a problem—that they are very special just as they are. Mariaemma Willis and Victoria Kindle Hodson show parents and teachers how to do just that—to educate and encourage children with many differing learning styles. Children are worth that effort."

—Jane Nelsen, Ed.D., coauthor of the POSITIVE DISCIPLINE series

"As parents we know that sometimes school or even a particular teacher is a better fit for some children than others. Often children (and adults too!) take the poor fit as a negative message about who they are and that makes a difficult environment even more of a challenge. This book celebrates the fact that we are all unique and can contribute and learn in our own ways and offers very specific suggestions for learners who feel like they don't fit. It is very encouraging!"

—Jody McVittie, M.D., family physician and parent educator

"Our work with parents and children all over the world (as well as with our own kids) convinces us that each child has his own unique set of intellectual and emotional gifts, and thus learns and develops in his own unique way. Parents who understand the principles in this book will be better parents!"

—Richard and Linda Eyre, authors of *Teaching Your Children Values*

"*Discover Your Child's Learning Style* is the most helpful information I have found both as a parent and a professional. I immediately understood how each of my children are best able to learn and used the ideas in the book to create the best learning environment to support each of them. It has relieved so much of my stress with homework and helped my children excel in school that I always share this information with the parents in my parenting classes. Every parent of school age children should read this book!"

—Deborah Critzer, PositiveParenting.com

"I believe that every parent and every teacher will find this book an invaluable tool in the greatest task confronting us: educating our children."

—Clayton C. Barbeau, M.A., MFCT,
author of *How to Raise Parents*

"This book is a necessity for homeschoolers. It goes much deeper than other learning-style philosophies and offers field-proven insight and knowledge resulting from the authors' work with hundreds of real families. The material in this book changed our family's life!"

—Michael and Mary Leppert, authors
of *The Homeschooling Almanac, 2000-2001*
and publishers of *The Link*, a homeschool newspaper

DISCOVER YOUR CHILD'S LEARNING STYLE

DISCOVER YOUR CHILD'S LEARNING STYLE

Children Learn in Unique Ways—Here's
the Key to Every Child's Learning Success

Mariaemma Willis & Victoria Kindle Hodson

THREE RIVERS PRESS • NEW YORK

Published by Three Rivers Press, New York, New York.
Member of the Crown Publishing Group, a division of Random House, Inc.
www.crownpublishing.com

THREE RIVERS PRESS and the Tugboat design are registered trademarks of Random House, Inc.

Originally published by Prima Publishing, Roseville, California, in 1999.

All of the characters in this book are based on real persons, but in some cases, names have been omitted or changed to protect the privacy of the people involved. Therefore, any resemblance to actual persons, living or dead, is purely coincidental, unless authorized by the actual person mentioned.

Interior photos copyright © Tony Stone (pages 1 [left], 41 [left]), copyright © Photodisc (pages 1 [right], 66, 209 [right]), copyright © Comstock (pages 41 [right], 209 [left], and copyright © Corbis (page 66 [far left]).

Printed in the United States of America

Library of Congress Cataloging-in-Publication Data
Willis, Mariaemma.
    Discover your child's learning style: children learn in unique ways—here's the key to every child's learning success / Mariaemma Willis and Victoria Kindle Hodson.
        p. cm.
    Includes bibliographical references and index.
1. Learning, Psychology of. 2. Cognitive styles in children. 3. Education—Parent participation. I. Kindle Hodson, Victoria. II. Title.
    LB1060 .W55 1999
    379.15'23—dc21

ISBN 0-7615-2013-9

18 17 16 15 14 13 12 11

First Edition

To all the children
who are waiting to be heard.
To all the parents and
teachers who are listening.

Mission Statement:

*Promoting experiences that allow
learning-success for every child.*

Rekindle or Fuel the Self-directed, Eager Learner in Your Child.

The Key to Success in Learning
The Learning Style Profile

DISCOVER YOUR CHILD'S
• Disposition • Talents • Interests • Modality • Environment

The Benefits
Creates an individual who:

Knows his or her
strengths and goals

Knows what s(he)
loves to do

Is an eager,
self-directed
learner

The Steps: Get on the Team • Do the Profile • Coach for Success

CONTENTS

ACKNOWLEDGMENTS

Victoria:

This book has been possible because of the support and inspiration of many people: my husband, Stan Hodson, who contributed his knowledge of the writing process and encouragement based on his deep belief in the importance of books to help people have powerful encounters with ideas; my son, Brian Hagoski, whose learning style first took me to uncharted areas of education and whose ability to take on challenging learning tasks delights and inspires me; my mother, Pauline Kindle, who encouraged me to pursue my interests even when it was a financial hardship on our family; and who, along with my sisters, Kathy La Lone and Ginger Desy, and their families, has read my material and listened to my ideas about education for 30 years.

In memory of my father, Douglas Kindle, to whom I had hoped to be able to give the first copy of this book. His stories about his school experiences moved me deeply and gave me courage and conviction to find a voice as an advocate for the individual learning needs of children.

In memory of Dorothy Jayne Wright, the teacher in my life who most epitomized the relationship with a child that I'm talking about in this book—she saw me as competent and treated me as if I were.

Mentors and friends—Patty Van Dyke, a gifted therapist who read the manuscript at different stages of progress to give advice from her experience working with individuals and families; Ellie Pope, therapist, who has been sharing her invaluable understanding of individuals and families with me for more than a decade; Susan Hansberry, good friend as well as a remarkable teacher and administrator who has been advocating for the needs of children in public schools and creating innovative materials and programs for 25 years; Sonia Nelson, dear friend and teacher, who has provided unwavering encouragement and support; T.K.V. Desikachar, mentor, who helped me realize the significance of the learning style work and encouraged me to accept the challenge of writing this book.

Mariaemma:

Ron Willis, my husband, without whose love and help my work would not be possible, and whose expertise is continually called upon when I feel like throwing the computer out the window.

Michael Pelullo, my father, who always told me I could be anything I wanted and my mother, Josephine Pelullo, who responded to my learning style needs by teaching me to read and write when I was three years old.

Peter Krasucki, who, nearly 30 years ago, when I was sick of playing the "school game," told me I would be nuts to quit college—thanks for getting me back on track! Because of you I love what I am doing today.

Nancy Chaconas and Jood Lee, for your continued belief in me—you have been a source of inspiration through the years; Rose Marie Helling and Valerie Kahle, for your behind-the-scenes enthusiasm and encouraging words; Joyce and Lee George, for 10 years of testing materials, proofreading, scanning pictures, collating and binding, and tons of moral support!

Sister Mary Noel, SSND, my 8th grade teacher, who made sure that the "poor students" got their shining moments by acknowledging and putting to use their individual talents—though she probably didn't know it, she was the first to teach me that everyone is "smart" in his own way.

My own gifted coaches, Dr. Barbara R. Bishop, Chuck Bauer, Charlo Stuart, Bunny Vreeland, and Chellie Campbell, who changed my life in many ways.

And my dear Aunt Lina (Carolina Scelso) who in her 80's continues to model daily the life-long, eager, self-directed learner!

Joint Acknowledgments:

Linda and Christopher Selvey, for reading and proofing, for their enthusiasm and encouragement, and for being our biggest fans! Marilyn Mosley, Lynn Nelson, Mary Noren, Patricia Flanigan, and Patricia Funchess, who recognized and supported our work before we, ourselves, realized its full importance; John Whitaker, Richard F.X. O'Connor, Suzanne Lopez, and Vivian and David

Moore, for their encouragement, advice, and generous giving of time.

Mary and Michael Leppert for providing the springboard for our work and for cheering us on! Jamie Miller at Prima for recognizing the potential in our work and seeing it through to publication. Libby Larson and Rosaleen Bertolino, our editors at Prima—we so appreciate their incredible skill and sensitivity for our work.

Teresa Andrade, who daily teaches the children in her classroom with love, in spite of incredible obstacles—what's in this book is already in her heart—she can never be thanked enough; Dee (Linda) Gardner, Sharon Fleur, Francine Burns, and countless other teachers who genuinely love their students and strive to bring out the best in each of them.

The parents and families who have trusted us with their children and the numerous children who have taught us lessons far beyond any textbook.

And, we gratefully acknowledge all of you who have acknowledged us with your endorsements of our work.

A Collaboration of Styles

Finally, we would like to comment on our own Learning Styles and the collaboration which made this book possible.

To Victoria—I continue to be in awe of the visual and artistic element that she brings to our work. Of course, at times, this gift can cause chaos for a person of my learning style! It is her creative abilities, however, that bring a meaning and depth to our work that would not be possible without them. And it is because of her that I have a greater understanding of the Thinking/Creating person. I am so grateful for the "coincidence" which brought us together over 10 years ago.

To Mariaemma—I am thankful for her indefatigable attention to details, organizing, and planning—aspects of the writing process that drive me crazy. I can't imagine where this book would be right now without her well-practiced Producing skills. I also thank her for keeping our philosophy of education alive year after year in practical, daily ways and always believing that we would find an audience for this work.

INTRODUCTION

"I love this, I can do this." "Taking notes in science class was easy." "School is so much fun now." These are just a few of the testimonials from children (and there are even more from parents and teachers) who have used the method of learning you'll discover in this book.

Children are born with an incredible eagerness and ability to learn. Our purpose is to provide tools to help you keep that motivation to learn alive in your child. You might be thinking that that's not your job because you're not a teacher. However, after fifty years of combined experience working with students, we are convinced that *parents are the most important teachers in a child's life*. If anyone has the power to affect how your child learns, it's you. In the book, *Awakening Your Child's Natural Genius*, Thomas Armstrong talks about the positive influences on a child's learning process as determined by research in education, "One of the most consistent research findings is the important role that parents have in educating their children. In program after program where parents are closely involved in their children's learning process, there has been a dramatic improvement in student motivation and achievement."[1] A Swahili proverb says, "The greatest good we can do for others is not just to share our riches with them, but to reveal their riches to themselves." And, as Dorothy Corkill Briggs says, "When children know uniqueness is respected, they are more likely to put theirs to use."[2] Each child has unique ways to interact with the learning process. It is our job, as parents and teachers, to discover what their uniqueness is and nurture it.

> **A**fter fifty years of combined experience working with students, we are convinced that parents are the most important teachers in a child's life.

Schools have traditionally provided one curriculum, one teaching environment, and one teaching methodology to fit all learning needs. This structure has favored some learners, left others out, and over the years created a population of learning "misfits." Everyday we work with young people and adults who are living with the effects of one-size-fits-all educational experiences. From these people, we've learned that helping kids find out *who they really are*—what they are good at and what they love to do—is the most important way of maintaining natural curiosity and eagerness to learn. We need to stop drawing attention to what kids *can't* do and start emphasizing what they *can* do. When it comes to increasing learning-success, a young person's interests, talents, expectations, hopes, and goals for herself are better motivators than a parent's or teacher's goals

> **We need to stop drawing attention to what kids can't do and start emphasizing what they can do.**

The "school" world has known these principles for many years—since the 1890s in fact! John Dewey was among the voices of the time proclaiming that schools should meet the needs of each child, not the other way around. In 1896 he established a school at the University of Chicago that inspired and cultivated the interests of individual children. Educators took note of its successes, while administrators apparently ignored the implications. David Guterson writes, "The status quo was rote memorization and recitation in classrooms thronged with passive children who were sternly disciplined when they expressed individual needs."[3] Although Dewey is known as the father of modern American education, our educational system was not modeled after his ideas.

One hundred years and many research studies later, not much has changed in our schools, even though now we know even more about how the brain learns, how different styles affect learning, and what teaching methods work best. Many more voices, including Howard Gardner, Thomas Armstrong, Priscilla

Vail, and Rita Dunn have declared the importance of respecting each child's learning needs. Yet, for the most part, schools have not responded. So now, we bring this information to you and ask *you* to provide your children with the personal attention they need to become self-directed, eager learners.

We are excited to introduce you to our Learning Style Model of Education. We have researched and refined this method over many years of experience in teaching and educating. Various factors influenced our desire to investigate new ways of motivating children to learn. For each of us, they were both personal and professional.

Victoria:

My son was not doing well in the public school system, although he was obviously bright and talented. Rather than feeling encouraged to learn, he was becoming unmotivated and discouraged. I began searching for learning environments, methods and materials that would help him thrive as a student, which he did by the time he was in junior high school. His renewed eagerness for learning took him into honors English in high school, to compete in a physics contest in Chicago where he placed 11th in the nation, and to study architecture 3,000 miles from home at Pratt Institute in Brooklyn, New York. As an adult he continues to be an avid learner pursuing a career in aviation and developing many diverse interests and talents in skiing, photography, furniture-making, and designing and building homes.

In addition to my son's situation, I also tutored children who were having difficulty learning. When I defined goals specific to each child's skills and needs, the children performed well; in fact, I saw no disability at all.

Eventually I set up a Learning Style "laboratory" in a private school where I was able to experiment with materials, curriculum, and classroom arrangement. The students eagerly participated in all subjects in new and different ways; they conducted their own research projects and often taught each other the facts and processes they had just learned. Many ideas from the "laboratory" are in this book.

Mariaemma:

I spent 11 years as the director of a school for children with learning problems. My speciality was testing, diagnosing, and setting up programs to "fix" these children. Soon I realized that most of what I had learned in teacher training and special education courses didn't work, so I began experimenting with different materials and methods to find the ones that worked best. Meanwhile, I learned so much from my students. I was amazed at how gifted the students were in different areas.

When I went into private practice, I began researching the subject of learning styles and came across the works of Myers-Briggs, Golay, Gardner, and Armstrong and began to apply their recommendations. After a great deal of success with my students, I began teaching workshops for parents and teachers. It was at one of these workshops that I met Victoria.

We both saw the need for an easy-to-use and easy-to-understand assessment system that would be accessible to children, parents, and teachers. Each of us had had years of experience in a variety of educational settings, including the regular classroom, special education, private tutoring, home school consulting, curriculum development, adult literacy, parent/teacher conferences, and workplace seminars. We wanted to develop a more complete learning style assessment that included five aspects of learning style. The result was a *A Self-Portrait* ™ Learning Style System. Later, we expanded this system into the Learning Style Model of Education presented in this book.

Over the last 10 years this system has been used by thousand of families. It encourages you to accept a central role in supporting your child's unique Learning Style. When you help your child identify and respect his own learning strengths, interests, talents, and needs, you give him roots in the gifts he was born with. When you help your child discover his dreams, passions, and goals, you give him the wings of motivation and purpose for becoming an eager, self-directed learner. In both cases your efforts result in a more successful learner.

The Learning Style Model has three components:

1. Get on your child's team.
2. Do the profile.
3. Coach for learning success.

You might be wondering what the words "team" and "coach" have to do with learning. Sounds like sports, right? Actually, people in sports make use of many wonderful principles of learning that never make it to the classroom or the homework table. The sports approach says that everyone needs a coach. Athletes understand this principle. Even those of us in the general population who are not interested in sports grasp the concept that if you are a serious athlete you need a coach. People training for the Olympics wouldn't dream of doing it without a coach. Nowadays, there are also personal trainers, lifestyle coaches, weight-loss coaches, organizational coaches, and money-management coaches. Why not *learning* coaches?

Part I of this book introduces you to the idea of getting on your child's team and prepares you for discovering your child's Learning Style. In Part III this idea is expanded upon and you are taken through the process of becoming your child's learning-success coach. In between, in Part II, you are introduced to the Learning Style Profile, an assessment which will give you the Learning Style information needed to successfully coach your child.

Throughout this book you will encounter our philosophy that *all* children can learn successfully if taught through their learning styles. We wish to explain here that we are not including children who are developmentally delayed or brain injured. We realize that these children have special needs that cannot be addressed simply by looking at their learning styles. However, you will find that, with some adjustment, the concepts and principles in this book can help with the education of these children as well. Every human being has a special genius inside each of them, waiting to be noticed and drawn out.

THIS BOOK IS FOR:

Young People

The Learning Style Profile asks young people to speak for themselves; we provide the questions and listen respectfully to what they tell us. Our experiences have shown us that genuine acknowledgment of how kids see themselves unlocks a treasure trove of interests, concerns, dreams, hopes, and passions—which provide the real reasons and motivation to learn. If we expect young people to behave responsibly and competently in society when they leave high school, it is unrealistic and unwise to wait until they are seventeen or eighteen years old to discuss goals, ask their opinions, and encourage them to make decisions based on their own talents and interests. Recently, a college admissions director commented in an article, "This is probably the first time in their school life someone is asking them, 'Where do you want to go? What do you want to do?'"[4] High school graduates will be better equipped to make intelligent choices if we ask these types of questions as they are growing up. Gradually, during the school years kids need to:

1. learn about their own strengths and weaknesses
2. set their own goals for the future
3. practice more and more complex skills that help them meet their own short- and long-term goals
4. take daily, active responsibility for their choices so that they can mature into competent people who are on their way to being productive, responsible adults

The Learning Style Model of Education believes that students are capable and that their potential is unlimited. It *expects* differences in individual students—different learning readiness, different rates for learning, and a need for different teaching methods. For most children, learning the content of different subjects is not a problem when they are taught in ways that work with their learning styles. Higher standards can be met when programs are individualized, because eagerness and ability to learn increase. The more success and accomplishment young people experience based on their unique styles of learning, the better equipped they are to deal with learning and life in general. The thousands of families we have come into contact with have proven this to be true.

Parents

This is really a parenting book, although not in the usual sense of the word. We are encouraging you to take charge of your child's education journey—to accept the job of being your child's foremost teacher, to become your child's learning-success coach! Whether your child attends a traditional school, an alternative school, or you are homeschooling, the learning style information presented in this book will help you to become more closely involved with your child's learning process, to change learning attitudes and behaviors, and to encourage learning-success. To do this you will need a solid, supportive, nurturing working relationship with your child. In addition to the Learning Style assessments, we give you the parenting techniques that support learning-success, techniques that have already worked for thousands of parents.

> **The more success and accomplishment young people experience based on their unique styles of learning, the better equipped they are to deal with learning and life in general.**

Because we are emphasizing the learning style needs of the child, you might get the idea that we are advocating a completely child-directed approach to learning. That is not the case. For most children, the world of school and learning is weighted on the side that takes into consideration very few of their needs. This book helps restore balance. We recommend that you keep in mind your own fundamental beliefs, values, and family rules as you balance your personal needs, your family's needs, and your child's learning style needs.

The Learning Style Model of Education presented in this book is applicable to all age levels—preschool to adult. If your child is just beginning school, you can implement this model right from the start. If your child is already older, you can still use this information to increase learning-success—it's never too late to apply these principles.

Teachers

If you are a teacher, feel free to administer the Learning Style Profile to your students and use the information for your classroom needs. You, too, are invited to help students achieve learning-success with the learning style information presented in this book. Please check with your school to find out if this assessment would fall under the district's testing policies, which might require you to obtain parental permission.

Other Adults

You might be reading this book for your own self-knowledge. Perhaps you have returned to school, or are a volunteer tutor in a literacy program, or teach adults at the college level. The learning style information in this book applies to adult learning as well. The Learning Style Profile, principles, and concepts presented here have made a significant difference in the lives of hundreds of adults we have worked with.

 ## For Our Picture Learners

In keeping with our belief that people learn in different ways, we felt it was appropriate to provide not only for the Print Learners but for the Picture Learners as well. Along with the traditional table of contents, we have included a picture overview of the book (which follows) to guide you through the reading, exercises, and assessments. You will also find other ideas and concepts presented in picture format.

 ## How to Use This Book

We recommend that you read this book in sequence, doing the exercises and filling out the assessments as they are presented.

Please note that all teaching materials and resource books mentioned throughout are listed in alphabetical order, as well as by subject, in Appendix II. After you've finished reading the book, you can review individual chapters as needed. When in doubt about where you are or what to do next, consult the Flow Chart. We hope that you will continue to use this book as a reference throughout your child's school years.

> *The finest possible curriculum is precisely the one that starts with each child's singular means of learning.*
> —*David Guterson*

We hope that this book will give *you* the knowledge, inspiration, and courage to become involved in your child's education, both at school and at home. We know that we have helped numerous students through their parents and teachers, by starting them on a new road of self-motivation and confidence in their own abilities. We are delighted to be a part of your family's learning-success journey. Through this process you will unlock the eager, self-directed, successful learner in your child!

The stories in this book are true, although the names have been changed. They involve situations that we have each experienced separately, with family, friends, and clients. In order to make the telling of the stories more personal, we decided to combine both of our voices into one. Beginning in Chapter 1, the narrative voice becomes "I" instead of "we."

Keep two questions in mind as you read the book:

1. What is a successful learner?
2. How can I help my child become a successful learner?

How to Use this Book

Part One
Get on the Team

A. Read Chapters 1–3

B. Do Exercises

Assessment

Part Two
Do the Profile

A. Read Chapter 4—

B. Make Copies
- Assessments
- Forms

C. Take the <u>Assessments</u>:
- Talents
- Interests
- Modality
- Environment
- Disposition

D. Transfer Scores to <u>Summary</u> Form

E. Read Chapters 5–11

F. Do the <u>Plan</u> Form

Plan Form

Summary Form

Part Three
Coach for Success

A. Read Chapters 12–15

B. Do Exercises

C. Fill out the <u>Portraits</u>

Portrait

PART 1

Get On the Team

Chapters 1 to 3 give you the information you need to get on your child's team. Chapter 1 takes you back to the eager, self-directed learner your child was before he began school. You'll explore the reasons your child may no longer be an eager learner and what's needed to rekindle his motivation for learning. In Chapter 2 you'll learn the difference between the traditional School Model and the Learning Style Model of Education and discover the true learning-success that is possible for every child with the Learning Style Model. Chapter 3 discusses how to care for and nurture your child's learning endeavors, and introduces you to the idea of forming a learning team.

Let's Get Started!

- Read Chapters 1–3
- Complete the simple exercises in Chapter 3

The Eager Learner

There is a self-motivated, eager learner in every child. You might be thinking that I can't possibly mean your child—the one who is more interested in video games than homework, who hates to get up in the morning, who lost a science book last week. You might think that I don't mean your child who is labeled ADD or ADHD or LD. Yes, I mean your child, too. I mean all children. From birth until the time we enter school we are all eager learners. We crawl, stand, walk, run, and talk with great purpose and urgency without teachers or grades. Figuring out how things work is a fundamental imperative—like learning to walk and talk. It's your child's natural curiosity that keeps her investigating the CD player in spite of the fact that you've told her twenty-three times not to touch it again. School is a major part of a child's surroundings, and most kids are excited to find out what it's about.

After a short time in school, however, something drastic happens to too many children. Their excitement wanes. Their curiosity turns to discouragement and fear, and they realize that school is not a place they want to be. Even one child losing his curiosity is too many, especially if it is your child. As a fourth-grade "A" student I remember wondering how many more years

I would have to endure the endless repetition I was faced with every day. I was disheartened when I realized that I had eight more years to go. For some students, interest wanes sooner. The day after the long-awaited first day of school a kindergartner said to his mom, "Do I have to do that again? I did that yesterday."

WHAT ARE WE DOING TO OUR EAGER LEARNERS?

We know that all children pass through the same stages of growth. We know that all children accomplish developmental milestones at their own pace and in their own way as if governed by an internal clock set just for them. Jane crawls a month before Elizabeth. Wayne slides along the floor in a sitting position and isn't crawling at all. Jeff could say Mama, Dada, and dog at ten months old. Patricia made lots of sounds until she was two years old, then spoke in whole phrases. We don't expect infants and toddlers to develop at the same rate or to do things in exactly the same way, so why do we transport all of our vital, lively, distinctly different children to uniform environments, teach them all in one way, expect them to progress at the same pace, and call them below average if they don't?

> *Avoid compulsion and let early education be a matter of amusement. Young children learn by games; compulsory education cannot remain in the soul.*
> —Plato

Of course programs exist that use individualized instruction for the "gifted" kids and kids who are called "learning disabled." The "learning disability" programs promise a lot and often end up teaching the same material over again using the same methods that didn't work in the first place. At both ends of the learning spectrum, kids are stigmatized and left to reap the social implications of being superior or inferior. For the "average" kids, alternative, individualized learning programs are sometimes set up in isolated schools by a few teachers who realize that one-way-fits-all methodologies don't work. For the most part, however, no matter how many in-service trainings teachers take on the importance of learning styles and individualized methods of instruction, teaching "outside the box," that is, actually using techniques for individual learning styles, is not the policy for most schools or for the school system in general.

RAISE YOUR HAND IF YOU HAD A POSITIVE SCHOOL EXPERIENCE

If we took a poll asking how many Americans had positive school experiences and how many had negative experiences, how do you think it would turn out? I don't know the answer to the question myself. What I do know is that the overwhelming number of people I've met in the last ten years at workshops, in private consultations, and at conferences sum up their school experiences as negative. Many members of my family, many of my friends and associates, many of the parents of children I work with had discouraging school experiences.

A startling fact I've discovered is that by the end of first and second grades many students actually see themselves as failures. It is estimated that 95% of kindergartners feel good about their learning potential. However, 98% of seniors in high school have lost their creative, inquisitive spirits.[1] So, what has happened to all but 2% of these seniors? The astonishing number of stories of school

> **W**e don't expect infants and toddlers to develop at the same rate or to do things in exactly the same way, so why do we transport all of our vital, lively, distinctly different children to uniform environments, teach them all in one way, expect them to progress at the same pace, and call them below average if they don't?

discouragement and failure that I've collected over the years provided the motivation to write this book. The following are some of these stories.

Scott's Story

A second grader came to me expressionless and slumped, as if he were carrying a heavy burden, and told me he hated school. His mother explained that as a three-year-old he had looked forward to attending preschool. At first he enjoyed meeting the other kids in preschool, playing on the playground equipment, riding the trikes, finger painting, growing a garden, and so on, but when he began to fall behind in basic skills, teachers told him he wasn't trying hard enough and that he was lazy. He became discouraged and didn't want to go to school anymore. By second grade he had a reputation for being shy, withdrawn, and "not working up to his potential." In spite of remedial classes he was failing in math and reading. How can an obviously bright child fail second grade? How can a school tell a seven-year-old that he is failing at anything? What kind of motivation is provided by telling an eight-year-old that he is a failure? Furthermore, why do we as parents accept so readily what the school system tells us? Why do we accept the labels? Why do we accept the remedies that are offered? Why do we stop believing in the spirited, active learners our children were as three-, four-, and five-year-olds?

> *If you add up the amount of undivided individual attention most students get during their twelve years in school, it probably comes to about three to six school days' worth.*
>
> —Peter Kline

Mark's Story

Mark had a wonderful experience in a Montessori school for two years. He was accustomed to choosing his own learning activities, playing with other students frequently between work times, painting at the easel, and hanging his own pictures up to dry. He had learned to read phonetically and was well on his way to being a competent reader. He was curious, confident, and active. When he transferred to public school in the first grade, he was excited to be put in the top reading group with three other students considered to be "readers." He was happy to meet new friends, to have a new teacher, and to be learning to write. It wasn't long, though, before Mark's mother was invited to school to talk with the teacher. Mark already had a reputation for being disruptive in class. When people knocked on the classroom door with messages for the teacher, Mark jumped up to answer the door. He forgot to ask to be excused to go to the bathroom. He couldn't sit in his chair for more than ten minutes. He talked to other kids in class and didn't want to come in from recess. In addition, he wasn't catching on to the sight-word-based reading program, and he would have to be put back one or two reading groups. After only four months in the first grade, Mark's interest in studies was gone. Now, seeing his friends was his primary reason for going to school. He was sullen and withdrawn in the classroom, and he refused to read. At this point he was brought in for help.

What happens to shut down a child's natural curiosity? Does it make sense to set up learning hierarchies in first and second grades? Should a child be labeled disruptive and punished for wanting to move around the classroom? Does learning occur best when a child is seated at a desk? Can we afford to turn children off to learning at age six?

What Happens When Scott and Mark Grow Up?

For some kids, school is a place they *cope with* every day. It is a place that reminds them over and over again that they are not measuring up. How many times do you have to hear that you are failing before "failure" becomes your definition of yourself? How many sad faces stamped on your first-grade papers do you have to see before you lose your desire to try? What does it mean when for years and years a child receives primarily negative messages in spite of the fact that she is actually doing her best? Where does the eager learner go in children stigmatized as failures?

Lifelong self-images are formed by how successful we are in school. The word "failure" often echoes in a person's ear well into adulthood and undermines marriages, parent-child

> **Lifelong self-images are formed by how successful we are in school.**

relations, and careers. I wish I had the space to tell my adult clients' stories about the negative consequences of having been labeled a failure in elementary school. Perhaps you have a story of your own to tell.

ANOTHER KIND OF FAILURE

My experience shows that another kind of learner is not being served well in the "school world." This is the person who gets the A's and B's and is considered successful by school standards. Gina's experience is an example of how getting good grades doesn't always tell the whole story.

Gina's Story

Gina was a straight-A student all through school. She followed all the rules, filled in all the workbooks, did all of her homework, and turned everything in on time. She liked getting a list of assignments, with specific instructions and due dates. She liked knowing exactly what was expected of her, doing it, and getting the stars and 100s. What she did not like was repeating the same work year after year, since each grade spends the first few months reviewing things learned in the previous grade. She told me that sometimes she "thought she would scream" if she had to do one more grammar worksheet or practice multiplication one more time. She wondered why she had to do pages of addition problems in seventh grade. She had been proficient in adding since the second grade and was a whiz at fractions, decimals, percents, and all other math! Gina also didn't like having hours of homework every night. Sometimes when she went somewhere with her family after school she was miserable, because she was worried the whole time about finishing her homework. Usually she took it with her, so there would be no chance of it not being completed.

It was even worse in high school. She claims that she missed out on a lot of fun—spending hours every evening and weekend writing papers and memorizing facts for tests. Once the test was over, she promptly forgot everything to make room for the next set of "useless" facts for the next test. Her mother was alarmed by the amount of homework Gina was assigned.

What Gina found especially irritating was that people were certain that she loved school because she got such good grades. Furthermore, people equated her good grades with being a good girl. Gina says, "As if choosing an abnormal life, curled up on the couch surrounded by textbooks, is the equivalent of being good."

What we consider a reward can turn out to be a punishment.[2] Good grades are the rewards we give kids. Not getting A's then becomes their greatest fear. In Gina's own words, "I remember realizing early on in elementary school that people thought I was smart because I got A's." She claims that she was continually anxious—fearful that she hadn't studied enough and the next test would show that she wasn't smart, after all. Kids who get good grades can carry a big burden, too. Perhaps the worst thing about it is that people expect them to "be smart" in *everything*! This expectation sets the stage for disappointment, feelings of failure, and an unwillingness to risk trying new things.

Yes, Gina was "smart" as defined by the traditional School Model of Education. She had the Learning Style that made reading, spelling, writing, math, and rote learning very easy for her. She knew how to do well on tests. But in order to get the good grades, she had to do hours of busywork assignments that she considered meaningless. As a result, she did not like school; sometimes she hated school. In fact, she was so burned out by the time she reached college that she almost quit school to get a job as a secretary (an excellent job for a person with her Learning Style!). If not for the reaction of a good friend who challenged her decision and told her that she was crazy not to develop her academic talent, she would not have continued beyond high school. The day she finished her last college exam, after nineteen years of continuous school, she shelved the textbooks and didn't pick up another book for a year, not even to read for fun.

Having talked with many adults who were "driven" students like Gina, I have found that they usually agree on one thing: they knew that other kids in their classes who were getting C's, D's, or even failing, were actually smarter than they were in many ways—these other kids often understood a subject better, but they weren't good at memorizing information and taking tests. As super-students, the driven kids are often too busy cramming to ever really learn anything or even to pursue what is most interesting to them.

"I think it is a miracle that I was able to discern a direction for my life and choose a career that I've ended up really loving! *Nothing* I ever did in school helped me in making these kinds of decisions," Gina exclaimed.

I would not call Gina an eager, self-directed learner. She failed in a different way from Scott and Mark. She succeeded in the system, but failed at developing herself. The dozens of people I've met like her sum up their school experience by saying, "I got straight A's, and I didn't learn a thing." They often feel a great deal of resentment because they weren't encouraged to explore and discover more about themselves and the subjects they were studying. Because they are so used to following instructions, these people often say, "I don't even know what I think or want."

THE DISINTERESTED, THE BORED, THE AVERAGE

Unfortunately, we haven't yet exhausted the categories of students who fail in school. If you haven't found your child in the stories already told, perhaps you will find him here.

> " *Children are taught what they should do, but few are helped in the discovery of what they can do.*
>
> —Marti Eicholz "

How many kids are just hanging in until graduation? In some ways that describes all young people; however, the students I'm thinking of are barely passing. School is a routine they've learned to cope with. They aren't good at studies or sports, and they don't belong to the "in" group, so school is not a place where they can do well academically, athletically, or socially. These kids associate school with many punishments and few rewards. They are just putting in their hours, punching the time clock, biding their time until the ordeal is over and they can get on with their lives. I wonder what kind of life they are prepared to "get on with" after practicing such passivity for so many years?

Another group of students that is not served well by our schools is the academically "very bright." Regardless of the grades they are getting, low or high, these students are like jet aircraft that can't get off the ground. They never get their academic engines revved up enough to feel the exhilaration of academic challenge. It isn't necessarily for lack of knowledgeable teachers that these kids aren't challenged. It isn't because teachers don't want to teach these students. It is, as my good friend who is vice-principal of a school explained to me recently, because classroom management (discipline) takes up so much class time, that there is less time for in-depth instruction. Teachers are recommending homeschooling to some of their brightest, most serious students because of the discipline problems in some junior and senior high schools. Classes for the "gifted," as mentioned earlier, can be helpful, but they often don't take sufficient numbers of the students who need or want the academic challenge.

The "just average" student is probably the most underserved. The squeaking wheels at each end of the spectrum get special services—the very high highs and the low lows. In the middle, students are left to do the best they can with overly crowded classrooms, a shortage of materials, and overworked teachers under the pressure of unrelenting curriculum demands. In the current conservative climate

> **How will the voices of the "just average" students ever be heard?**

of education, additional pressure to bring up achievement test scores will soon be added to a teacher's duties. How will the voices of the "just average" students ever be heard?

TAKE CHARGE

It takes *personal attention* to discover and nurture the self-directed, eager learner in any child. Unfortunately, the majority of our schools do not have enough time or sufficient numbers of teachers to give children individualized attention; therefore, if you want personal attention for your child, you are going to have to take charge and give it yourself. By taking time to discover your child's learning style, you can provide a foundation for your child's lifelong learning-success. With the information in this book, you will be able to nurture your child's natural gifts and natural eagerness to learn. You will learn to assess learning styles as well as valuable ways to interact with your child that encourage positive learning experiences at school and *at home.*

As a teacher, I am always looking for ways to get students more involved in the learning process, to set a fire of curiosity under them, to help them see familiar things in new ways. My greatest hope is that all my students will become self-directed, lifelong learners.

While some students seem to be naturally self-motivated, what I have discovered is that *all* children can be self-directed learners if they get the right start, and *the right start begins at home.*

Success for Every Child

Marcy stared at the paper on her desk one more time and sighed. She just couldn't figure out her homework instructions—again. Her mom, exasperated, told her to read the instructions again. This never helped and her mom, as usual, had to explain what needed to be done. Each night she struggled with her homework, and each night she ended up fighting with her mom about it.

When Marcy was brought in for a learning-styles evaluation, it was discovered that she was an auditory-verbal learner. She needed to hear her own voice in order to comprehend. She was encouraged to read the instructions out loud three or four times, and she began to understand the instructions well enough to complete most of her homework without any help. She was much more confident about approaching all of her work.

Jim could not memorize the math facts. His parents had tried flash cards, timed drills, offered rewards and had taken away privileges. Nothing worked. Jim was miserable. Every Friday, the day of the math test, he developed a horrible headache and was sick to his stomach. His grades were beginning to slip in other classes as well as math.

Jim's learning-styles assessment revealed that he had a performing personality and was talented in areas requiring body coordination. It was suggested that he practice reciting the facts while bouncing a ball or jumping on a trampoline. This met Jim's need for learning through movement, and he began remembering more and more of the math facts and slowly his scores improved.

Each person, child and adult, learns in a unique way. The idea that people are different in fundamental ways is not new. The ancient Greeks developed a system for classifying people into four types or personalities based on body chemistry, which was thought to determine temperaments, mental qualities, and abilities. Since ancient times people have been interested in finding out more about how these differences affect us. Over the years, it has become more apparent that these fundamental differences, or styles, not only influence our behaviors, but greatly affect how we learn.

More recently, the work of researchers and educators has brought the importance of individual styles to the attention of our school system. As a result, the terms temperament, modality, multi-sensory, emotional intelligence, and multiple intelligences are becoming familiar to parents and teachers across the country, and more people are talking about the crucial role of learning styles in educating our young people. For example, *Educational Leadership* magazine, a reputable journal for teachers from the Association for Supervision and Curriculum Development, frequently features the subject of learning styles—often the entire publication is devoted to this topic. Increasingly, educators realize that unique learning needs are the norm, not the exception.[1]

Researchers highly recommend working with learning styles; educators speak out about the merits of working with learning styles; teacher training programs and educational seminars across the country include workshops on learning styles. Even in the adult world, business seminars frequently feature speakers such as Brian Tracy and Dr. Tony Alessandra who talk about how to incorporate learning style information in the workplace. Yet the

> **We must start teaching the way most people learn.**
> —*Roger Perry, President, Champlain College*

way many of our schools operate on a day-to-day basis clashes severely with the notion that children's learning styles are and ought to be the keys to their education. The problem is evident as early as kindergarten, as illustrated by the following story.

THE AWARDS CEREMONY

Finally, the last day of school! It begins with all of the normal anticipation of summer vacation: visions of swimming and camping, sleeping in, playing with friends, and, most of all, no homework!

There's also the excitement of the last day itself—the sense of accomplishment in completing the year, the class party, and, of course, the awards ceremony.

Students and parents eagerly enter the auditorium where, class by class, students will be honored for their hard work, their intelligence, and their school-year accomplishments. I've heard that this school values learning styles and the individual child, and I want to get a sense of how it does this. I want to see how the students are encouraged and sent off with enthusiasm for the learning process and confidence in themselves as students. I want to observe how such an outstanding school instills an eagerness to return in September to another school year filled with positive learning experiences.

I squeeze in among the parents and teachers. The youngest students start the program. The first grade teacher eagerly takes the microphone and begins by explaining that in every classroom there are those few children who stand out from the rest—those destined to be the presidents and CEOs, the leaders—those who will accomplish great things, those who will do something worthwhile, those who will make some kind of difference. He then proceeds to honor four students in his class who apparently fit this description.

Horrors! What happened? A sick feeling wells up inside of me. Only four six- and seven-year-olds out of an entire classroom will do something of significance as adults? Can that really be true? If it is true, how can anyone possibly predict which four it will be? Based on what? But, more importantly, why only four?

I know in my heart that the parents are probably not thinking of these questions at this moment. They've just heard the authority speak—the teacher, the one who knows. They've just learned that four of the families among them are on the road to developing leaders. The parents of four future leaders are rejoicing that their children are intelligent and motivated; the other parents are probably feeling disappointed, upset, angry, resigned, not surprised or, possibly, a little scared. Even worse, they might be thinking that this scenario is perfectly acceptable.

I wish I could say that this scene took place in a dark age of education, years and years ago. I wish I could assure myself that it is a rarity in these enlightened, high-tech, politically correct times, but I attended this awards ceremony in 1996. In lapses of naiveté I fantasize that no one would utter this kind of message to students of any age (or their parents), let alone to first graders, who are just beginning their educational journeys. Yet I know only too well that this message is being delivered in our schools every single day, in many ways that are more subtle than what I saw at that awards ceremony. Furthermore, parents often accept the judgments that school authorities hand down, so, at home, children receive the same potentially discouraging messages.

Does the message conveyed by the awards ceremony apply to the "real world"? Are there really only a few smart students in every classroom who will grow up to be smart and successful adults? What about the others? Are they less intelligent? What are their chances of becoming productive and successful adults?

For the answers to these questions we need to begin by looking at how our schools usually work.

HEAVEN FORBID EVERYONE SHOULD BE SMART

In spite of teachers' best intentions, here's the interesting thing about our educational system: on the one hand, we say that we want *all* students to do their best, we want *all* test scores to improve, we want *everyone* to succeed. On the other hand, we teach and test in ways that separate the "smart" from the "not so smart." The textbook that I studied thirty years ago in an introduction to psychology course clearly states, "Intelligence tests are designed to measure the abilities that distinguish the bright from the dull."[2] That was thirty years ago, you might be thinking—ancient stuff! Educators don't think that way anymore! Don't be so sure.

Recently, I taught a technique to an elementary teacher who used it in her class. The kids loved it and really learned the material. They *all* scored high on the test and they *all* received A's! When their scores were plotted on a graph, they did not form a curve. There was no bell shape in the middle, there were no average or below average scores. *Everyone* was above average! The teacher and the kids were thrilled. A fellow teacher saw the grades and questioned their validity. How could they all get A's? Impossible—especially for the students who had a history of testing poorly! How could they suddenly test well? The first teacher defended the grades and explained that the technique she had used allowed all of the students to learn the material well. The second teacher responded, "You can't do that. We have to weed out the smart ones from the below average. We need the grades to form the *normal curve.*"

I've experienced similar reactions at the college level. One department experimented with presenting course material in a new, creative format. All of the students received high scores. This was not acceptable. The grades did not form a "bell curve" so the new format was discontinued.

What is this "bell curve" or "normal curve" that shapes the learning experiences of our students and defines who is smart and who isn't?

SEPARATING THE "BRIGHT" FROM THE "DULL"

In 1733 Abraham De Moivre discovered what we call the bell curve, or the curve of normal distribution. It seems that when you measure something in nature or in the general population and graph the results, the graph forms a bell-like shape. One of the places it shows up is on children's standardized test report forms. It is called the "normal" curve. It is the tool that is used to come up with the labels "below average," "average," and "above average."

A statistics textbook describes bell curves as follows: "A great many distributions of psychological and biological measurements are 'normally' distributed. Such diverse characteristics as sleeve lengths for adult males, intelligence test scores for schoolchildren, errors made by rats learning a maze, and achievement in statistics courses follow the 'normal distribution.'"[3]

> Excellence in education is not a matter of identifying and sorting the "good" from the "not-so-good" students. For too long we have followed a factory-model education that has been designed to sort out the so-called smart students from the slow students and then concentrate our limited resources upon the few winners who will . . . become the leaders in our country.
>
> —Dale Parnell

Notice that intelligence and achievement are mentioned above. It seems absurd to me that something as complex and important as intelligence could be interpreted in the same way as sleeve lengths and maze errors! And what does all this have to do with the subject of learning styles? We're getting to that.

The standard procedure for assessing learning in our schools is testing—intelligence testing, standardized grade-level testing, daily classroom quizzes, entrance exams, etc. When the scores from these tests are graphed, lo and behold, they form a "normal" curve. When educators first began creating formalized tests and realized that the graphs of the scores formed this curve, it was concluded that intelligence and knowledge must follow the same rules as other measurements taken in nature, such as inches of rainfall, or sleeve lengths, or errors made by rats in mazes.

In a normal curve, the majority of measurements fall near the area that forms the top of the bell. Let's say we are measuring sleeve lengths for several thousand males and find that most of them fall between 20 and 22 inches. These scores, about 68% of them, form the top of the bell and are labeled "average" for sleeve lengths. Lengths longer than 22 inches are then considered to be in the "above average" range and those below 20 inches in the "below average" range.

This is basically how we look at intelligence and school achievement. When a test is administered, about 68% of students score within that "average" range, a few score above and a few score below. People in the middle are called normal; people scoring above the middle must be brighter and smarter; people scoring below the middle must be not so bright.

It seems logical that if techniques could be found to raise everyone's scores, educators would be happy; they would continue using those techniques, so that they could reach *their* objective of bringing all test scores up. If all the students are getting good scores it means that all of them are learning, right? Wouldn't that be wonderful!

Unfortunately, in the "school world" some people wouldn't consider it wonderful, as illustrated by the above stories of the classroom teacher and the college department. The purpose of testing in many of our schools is *not* to have everyone learn the material, but to separate the "capable" and "intelligent" from the "average" and "below average" crowd. The top group is then given extra attention to encourage them to achieve. Of course, as we all know, the bottom group is labeled in various ways and also receives extra attention. However, this attention is given in the form of "help," with the attitude that these students are not as capable and need some sort of "fixing." The people in the middle group usually receive nothing extra, because they are just "average" and are neither in need of "help" nor "attention."

The injustices that result from this model affect *everyone!* People in the "average" and "below average" groups often go through life unaware of their many abilities and skills, and they limit themselves in terms of career possibilities as well as opportunities in general. The "above average" or "gifted" people often pay for their "smartness" with anxiety and distress, or the fear that they won't be able to maintain their high levels of achievement. Many people in this group feel under pressure to live up to their "potentials" and are never really satisfied with their accomplishments.

FINDING THE GENIUS IN EVERYONE

If our schools were willing to give up the bell curve, children would no longer be classified into categories that program them for the future! But, if the bell curve is so important that schools are not willing to give it up, then let's at least use it in a way that is more representative of everyone. If it is true that most things measured in nature form a bell curve, then measuring musical ability, artistic ability, or any other ability should also form bell curves. If we are so dedicated to the belief that testing and measuring are necessary for assessing what people know and can do, then why not measure all the ways that people are talented or "smart" and create many bell curves? In other words, if spelling ability were assessed, I would score in the above-average range and my husband would score in the below-average range. However, if mechanical reasoning and visual ability were assessed, my husband would score in the above-average range, and I would probably score off the bottom of the chart! With this system of assessing multiple abilities each child would be acknowledged for her particular gifts and *all* would experience being at the top of a bell curve.

> **I**f we are so dedicated to the belief that testing and measuring are necessary for assessing what people know and can do, then why not measure all the ways that people are talented or "smart" and create many bell curves?

 ## THE LEARNING STYLE MODEL

The Learning Style Model of Education looks at *all* the ways that people are talented. Each child is viewed as gifted and intelligent. The Learning Style Model also changes the way we define and assess achievement. According to Rita Dunn, who conducted a survey of research on learning styles, "No learning style is better or worse than another. Since each style has similar intelligence ranges, a student *cannot* be labeled or stigmatized by having any [one] type of style. Most children can master the same content, *how* they master it is determined by their individual styles."[4] And according to David Elkind, professor of Child Study at Tufts University and author of books on child development, "There isn't sufficient individualization in the schools. High standards are best met by in-

> " Be patient . . . with the type of mind that cuts a poor figure in examinations. It may, in the long examination which life sets us, come out in the end in better shape than the glib and ready reproducer, its passions being deeper, its purposes more worthy, its combining power less commonplace, and its total mental output consequently more important.
>
> —William James "

dividualization. Most of the printed curriculum material makes little provision for wide differences in learning styles. It's not that we shouldn't have expectations and standards, but we need to recognize that children don't all learn in the same way at the same rate."[5]

The Learning Style Model of Education presented in this book emphasizes each child's unique learning needs. Rather than applying labels—such as ADD, dyslexic, learning disabled, hyperactive, slow, average, below average, above average, gifted, unmotivated, disruptive—and attempting to "fix" or "direct" the child, this system celebrates each child's natural gifts and abilities. It encourages parents and teachers to treat each child as an individual and to find out what each child loves to do. It teaches the child how to use learning-style information to learn more efficiently in all situations.

The Learning Style Profile included in this book is designed to help you discover your child's learning style and to facilitate the Learning Style Model of Education. You will find it easier to work with your child as you become more aware of all aspects of his learning style. As you implement the suggestions in this book that are appropriate for your child's needs, "problems" will decrease and enjoyment for learning will increase (for both you and the child)! *You* will learn strategies for acknowledging and valuing your child's special attributes. *Your child* will learn strategies that will unlock potentials in academic areas and help her to become a self-directed, eager learner at school and at home.

The Learning Style Model of Education makes it possible for *every* child to experience learning-success!

In the next chapter you will be introduced to five essential concepts that help you to see yourself as the primary educator for your child and to get on your child's "learning team."

Who C.A.R.E.S.?

The Learning Style Profile in this book is based on ways of thinking about and interacting with kids that not only promote learning-success but are also considered the foundation for a successful life—a place where, as Arthur Costa puts it, "compassion and cooperation, problem solving and creativity, and communications and internal responsibility will be paramount."[1]

This chapter provides five concepts (C.A.R.E.S.) that will help you get on your child's learning team and prepare you to administer the Learning Style Profile, an assessment tool. The five concepts are:

- **C**elebrate your child's uniqueness,
- **A**ccept your role as a teacher,
- **R**espond rather than react,
- **E**xpand your view of where learning takes place, and
- **S**top blindly supporting bell curve evaluations and definitions of your child.

Each of these actions is a step toward being a full member of the team that can guide, support, and encourage your child as well as root for her learning-success. Take all the time you need to read

> **E**ach of these actions is a step toward being a full member of the team that can guide, support, and encourage your child as well as root for her learning-success.

the following material and fill out the exercises below. If some of the concepts seem foreign to you initially, try to keep an open mind and see what you think about them by the time you finish the book.

Active caring is the sign of love. The words "I love you" are empty to a child if they aren't followed up with loving actions. What are loving actions when it comes to your child's learning-success? My students and their families have taught me a great deal about actions that ensure learning-success. In a nutshell, success in learning is possible when children know that there is someone standing beside them who C.A.R.E.S.

C—Celebrate Versus Criticize

Celebrate the child you have. Don't be regretful that you didn't get a different one. Don't be discouraged because the one you have would be wonderful if only . . . Celebrate your child's skills, accomplishments, and uniqueness. If you don't celebrate them,

> **C**elebrate the child you have. Don't be regretful that you didn't get a different one.

neither will he. Infants and toddlers have different temperaments, different skills, different needs for noise, quiet, warmth, sleep, food, etc. These differences are a child's marks of distinction. As new parents we eagerly celebrate the defining traits of our children. Jesse has such a good voice; he'll probably be a singer. Madeline is so creative with her building blocks, I wouldn't be surprised if she became an architect or carpenter. Look at the way Ralph takes care of other children; he's going to be a great dad. Adults believe that these defining attributes show a child's promise. We think that they are indications of something that is *true* about the child. They are.

By the age of five or six, however, many schools have our children, regardless of background, temperament, physical differences, or other unique qualities, sitting in the same-size chairs at the same-size desks in the same-size rows. And, furthermore, attention abruptly turns from *celebrating* our children to *criticizing* them. Just yesterday, a teacher made this statement about a first grade student, "He just isn't learning to sit and pay attention, and if he doesn't learn it this year, he won't get anywhere." When children enter the schoolroom in kindergarten or first grade, their abilities to conform and perform according to preset standards are what they are judged by. Even though teachers have the best intentions to enjoy and foster individual children, many of their methodologies—praising and blaming, grading, withholding and granting privileges based on effort and/or achievement—are designed to get everyone to "toe the same mark."

> **W**hy do we stop celebrating and encouraging uniqueness, differences, preferences, and individual needs?

Why do we stop celebrating and encouraging uniqueness, differences, preferences, and individual needs? I've been told by school administrators that it isn't practical to individualize the setting, materials, and instruction. The teacher–student ratio would have to be so small that the cost would be prohibitive, and besides there is a shortage of qualified teachers. When I look around and see how many teachers have been underemployed for years and how much money we spend as a society on incarcerating criminals ($36,000 per prisoner in 1999), I wonder about our priorities. When I see the cost to children of being taught in the one-way-fits-all classroom that celebrates only *some* accomplishments, I lament our priorities.

By the time kids finish the first grade most parents have taken on the school's critical frame of mind; conformity and performance measures are what count. Memorizing facts, taking tests, and receiving grades replace investigating, wondering, discovering, playing, and asking questions. To keep the vital motivating force for learning alive in your child, celebrate her desire to wonder, play, discover, and question; celebrate his skills, interests, accomplishments, and uniqueness. Young children who are recognized for who they are don't do drugs, don't turn to violence and crime, and don't feel the need to join gangs when they are older.

Please take time to list twelve of your child's skills, accomplishments, and unique qualities. Keep them as non-school related as possible.

_____   _____

_____   _____

_____   _____

_____   _____

_____   _____

_____   _____

A—Accept Versus Avoid

Regardless of what you feel about your abilities to help your child become a more self-directed learner, it is important to accept the fact that you are the primary influence in your child's life. Far more learning about life in general takes place at home than at school. *You are a teacher.* You are, in fact, your child's primary teacher. Parents, believing that they don't have the proper training, often avoid taking an active role in educating their children. The home-school movement in this country has made a powerful statement about what "untrained" parents are actually capable of doing. Now, more than ever in history, information, materials, and inspiration are available to help *you* influence your child's education in a constructive way. Books, computer programs, workshops, classes, newsletters, educational consultants, educational supply stores, and Internet resources are available in growing numbers all across the country.

For many years I thought that schoolteachers were the primary influence for a child's learning-success. I don't think that anymore. Yes, there are cases of teachers acting as a bridge to a new way of thinking or a better way of life for a young person, and yes, teachers can provide content, exercises, and practice that promote learning. However, the truth is that no matter what kind of environment or attitude a teacher creates at school, positive or negative, your child comes home to you every day for thirteen, fourteen, or fifteen years of her life. That's a long time. You are establishing attitudes and behaviors during that time that greatly affect your child's learning-success. Enjoy the fact that time is on your side; you have many years to turn a negative school experience around or make an already good situation better.

Behavior Modeling

You are your child's first role model for how to act in the world. When your child begins school, he will practice there what he has learned from you. Research going as far back as the 1960s points out that modeling is one of the most powerful teaching/parenting tools we have to draw upon.[2] Daniel Goleman, in *Emotional Intelligence*, and Alfie Kohn, in *Beyond Discipline*, remind us of the power we have to affect the behavior of our children. Generally speaking, the old adage is true: If a parent is critical, the child learns to criticize. If a parent is tolerant, the child learns tolerance. If a parent blames others, so does the child. If a parent has a positive attitude, so will the child. If a parent instills feelings of being capable and competent, the child will take these feelings and attitudes to the classroom.

The home-school movement in this country has made a powerful statement about what "untrained" parents are actually capable of doing.

As Marsha Sinetar says in *Do What You Love and the Money Will Follow*:

We literally ingest the messages we get from our childhood, metabolizing them into words of personal strength and capability, or weakness and ineptitude. Then these ideas, strung out into repetitions reinforced by experience, form the architectural framework for all of our life experiences.[3]

What attitudes about school do you want to convey to your child?

_____   _____

_____   _____

_____   _____

What are you doing to help convey these attitudes?

_____   _____

_____   _____

R—Respond Versus React

Whether you are a *responsive* or *reactive* parent has a major impact on your child's attitudes and behaviors in the school setting. *Responsive* parents listen to and acknowledge a child's feelings, needs, and point of view. They try to follow the child's lead when appropriate. *Reactive* parents use threats, comparisons, negative labels, blame, and punishment to interact with their children. These parents let their emotions get in the way of their abilities to think and act clearly.[4]

The information that will be provided to you on the Learning Style Profile (which you will do in Part II of this book) is the result of your child's thinking about herself. In the hectic flow of daily life, there is little time to get this kind of information from a child in a discussion at the dinner table or between phone calls to friends. You say, How are you? She says, Fine. You say, What did you learn in school today? She says, Nothing. And that's that.

The amount and quality of the information that you get from the Profile puts you in a good position to talk with your child about his strengths as he sees them. The information also allows you to recognize and accept his challenges and weaknesses as he sees them. *How* you talk with your child about the Profile results will make a big difference in whether or not the information can be used effectively to encourage learning-success. The following communication basics will be invaluable as you begin to work with your child using the Learning Style Model. The communication basics are: listen, acknowledge, wait, follow.

Listen

Listening to your child's opinions and ideas engenders trust, and trust is the foundation you need to work with your child's Learning Style effectively. When your child fills out the Profile provided in this book, you are going to have new information that may not agree with the way you see him or her. You might feel frustrated and think that your child didn't fill out the Profile correctly. With the Learning Style Model, it is very important to accept her responses as they are. Your child's responses are the valuable information necessary to help renew her motivation for learning, or for advancing to a new level of engagement in the learning process. The Profile is meant to help open a discussion between you and your child about your child's

> " *Learning how to pay attention is a fantastic gift. That's what's wrong with the world: there aren't enough people who pay enough attention to other people.*
> —Clayton Barbeau *"*

strengths, learning goals, and learning needs. Your child's responses are her starting place in the discussion. Listen to them carefully and respectfully.

Parents and teachers make assumptions and judgments about kids all the time. They make plans for a child's future. They have detailed expectations for them without asking a single question about who the kids are. For the most part, it doesn't occur to us to ask what young people expect and want for themselves, or what their learning concerns and needs are as they see them. What happens to people who are always *told*, and not asked, about themselves? What is possible when adults listen to the learning needs of young people early in the child's learning experience?

Listening, and the trust it engenders, encourages children to open up and talk. A major reason young people don't talk with their parents is that they don't trust what their parents will do with the information. If they reveal too much, kids are afraid that they will get in trouble. When they know that you are genuinely interested in them and that you are tolerant of missteps and lapses in judgment, you will notice that young people have a great deal to share. Ten years of talking to kids about their Learning Style Profile, and interactions with my own son, have taught me this lesson many times over.

Acknowledge

As stated earlier, adults are accustomed to making assumptions, judgments, recommendations, and demands of young people. As a defense, many young people learn how to tune us out at early ages. This might be the position that you are in with your child as you begin the Learning Styles assessment. Listening is only the first step to improved communication. Fully acknowledging what your child tells you on the Profile, whether you agree with it or not, is the second step. To your child, your acknowledgment means that you have *heard* him. It doesn't necessarily mean you agree. Your acknowledgment can say, "I see that what you are telling me is important to you," or "I didn't realize that meant so much to you," or "I'm interested to hear what is important to you." Henry James wrote, "The deepest hunger of the human soul is to be understood." A majority of kids go to bed every night wishing that they had been *heard*. Kids who are more accustomed to lectures, suggestions, explanations, and advice than they are to acknowledgment might not know what to

> **A** majority of kids go to bed every night wishing that they had been *heard*.

say when you acknowledge them. That is when the third step to improved communication is so valuable to know and *use*.

Learn to Wait

After you have acknowledged what your child tells you, wait. Wait much longer than you think is normal, appropriate, or reasonable. In my ex-

> "What people want most is to be heard and seen for who they are.
> —Victoria Kindle Hodson"

perience, adults don't have a good sense for how long they need to be quiet in order to create the opportunity for a child to talk. When a young person realizes that you truly want to know what he has to say, that you're not just taking a pause before giving the next lecture, he will talk. I'm tempted to say I guarantee that he will talk because I haven't met a young person yet who isn't eager to talk with me at length once he knows I don't have an agenda for him. I realize that I'm not the parent of each of these kids; however, my experience with my own child tells me that it works for parents, too!

When you start listening to them, they will start listening to you. By attempting to listen to and acknowledge your child's position, you establish mutually respectful ground for interacting, and your child learns how to listen to and acknowledge you and others.

If you are used to taking the lead in your child's activities, listening and acknowledging will feel far too inactive at first. Give it a try anyway. As you practice this art of lis-

When you start listening to them, they will start listening to you.

tening, acknowledging, and waiting, you will be surprised by a new kind of joy that is experienced when you hear your child sharing more about her school experience than ever before.

Follow

Giving kids an opportunity to explore and discover for themselves is a more subtle form of listening and acknowledging. The more often you can follow their lead, the better. There are many age-appropriate opportunities in a day to follow your child's lead.

According to Thomas Armstrong:

> Children often do their best learning without adult supervision during unstructured playtime. It is often only when they make their own choices about what they wish to learn and how they want to learn it that their motivation and achievement levels go way up. Parents should realize that they can usually better help their kids by simply listening to them, respecting their lives, and allowing them the freedom to explore new ideas and subjects on their own.[5]

A story about a very young student of mine comes to mind that illustrates how this idea of following a child's lead can work.

One day, Marty, four and one-half years old, was playing with an enormous bowl, which was about one-third full of millet (hulled bird seed). In the bowl was a small glass ketchup bottle (no lid), a small metal funnel, a small measuring cup, and a plastic spoon. At first Marty had many questions for me. "What is this stuff?" "Can you eat it?" "What is this thing?" he asked as he put his index finger in the narrow end of the funnel. Then he began filling the bottle using the funnel as a scoop. By holding one finger over the small hole in the bottom of the funnel, he filled the large end full, then balanced this self-styled scoop on the narrow mouth of the ketchup bottle, deftly removed his finger from the small end of the funnel, and quickly jammed the neck of the funnel into the bottle, watching with serious pleasure as the bottle filled and the funnel emptied. He repeated the same routine many times without the slightest distraction, making small refinements in the way he placed his fingers and how fast or slowly he carried out the sequence of movements he had choreographed. What precision! I was reminded of a scientist in a laboratory. I sat there beside him wondering if and when he would discover how a funnel really works. Seeing the fun he was having, and remembering Maria Montessori's warning to refrain from spoiling the moment of discovery, I vowed not to tell him what to do.

After a while he put the funnel aside. He tried filling the bottle using the plastic spoon. This brought no satisfaction at all.

Too slow was my guess. He took up the measuring cup instead and began using it as a scoop, filling the bottle to the brim with as much grain pouring over the sides as going in. He was happy with this and kept pouring grain onto the full bottle just to see the little balls cascade and bounce. He chuckled to himself and beamed a broad grin. He told me he would like to have a whole bathtub full of millet.

As if remembering something, he became quiet and very serious again. With not one word from me, he looked over his tools for a few seconds, reached for the funnel, hesitated for another second, popped it into the mouth of the bottle and began scooping and pouring with the measuring cup. Something inside me leaped up, and I couldn't help smiling with excitement for the display of intelligence I witnessed. He filled the bottle in a new way, and he obviously liked this way best. He was completely absorbed in what he was doing. Any attempt to praise him would have broken the spell, so I kept quiet.

> **O**ne of the most important gifts we can give our children is to allow them their own learning processes, their own figuring-it-out procedures, at their own pace.

After using the funnel several more times he was finished with the bottle, the funnel, and the measuring cup and went on to other adventures with the millet.

What if I had given Marty the bottle with the funnel already in it? What if I had shown him how to use the funnel "correctly"? What if I had told him what he was "supposed to" do?

One of the most important gifts we can give our children is to allow them their own learning processes, their own figuring-it-out procedures, at their own pace.

There was very little talking while Marty was playing, but it wasn't difficult to know what to do. I simply followed his lead rather than attempting to lead him. Different children, of course, will provide different kinds of leads. Some will be more talkative. Some will be more impatient. Some will be slower to make discoveries. What is important is that you trust what your children are telling you they need to do in order to stay connected with the learning activity at hand.

The behaviors that are related to the ADD and ADHD labels might even be a reaction to too much interference or interruption in the preschool years when a child is trying to focus on an activity (see more about this in Chapter 13). In the early stages of exploration, the child's connection with an activity is like a trance. He is fixated because he is learning deeply. He is making subtle calculations that will make subsequent attempts more successful. There is great joy when a child spontaneously discovers the secrets of everyday things. Since young people are always moving into new phases of life, there are innumerable opportunities to let them take the lead and to enjoy seeing the learning process unfold.

List two things that you would like to do differently in your communications with your children to be more responsive than reactive:

1. _____

_____

_____

_____

2. _____

_____

_____

_____

E—Expand Versus Exclude

Expand your understanding of what learning is and where it happens. Learning is happening everywhere, all the waking hours of the day, every day, not just at school between the hours of 9:00 A.M. and 3:00 P.M. Your kids are learning and developing learning habits while they are at home, too. To exclude home as a learning environment is to overlook 50% or more of your child's learning opportunities and influences.

Schools are *learning-style biased*: they teach mainly to one type of learner. Because of this bias many children don't do well there. When you support your child's dispositions, talents, interests, modalities, and environmental needs (see Chapters 5 to 9) *at home*, you show your child that her ideas, best ways of learning, contributions to a group, and learning needs *are* important even though the school isn't set up to recognize them. You show your child that she can have a very vital life *in addition to* or *in spite of* school definitions and preferences. An involvement in a life *separate from school* develops confidence that will eventually affect school studies, too.

How much home-learning time does your child have each week? Include time before and after school, and weekends.

Hours each day __ × 5 = _____
Hours each weekend = _____
Total hours each week = _____

The total shows you how many hours you have to influence your child's perception of himself as a learner, his interest in learning, and his readiness to learn.

Home-learning time is not necessarily about finding more effective ways of doing homework, although it can include that. Home-learning time can be used in many ways: having discussions with your child about local and national issues, playing games, cooking, watching a movie together and talking about it afterward, doing brain-teasers or crossword puzzles, reading a favorite story, etc. You can get ideas about how to use home-learning time from your child's interests, talents, and dispositions on the Profile. You can also do things with your children that are interesting to you, which invites them to extend themselves and try something new.

> **Schools are *learning-style biased*: they teach mainly to one type of learner.**

Keep these times together interesting for everyone, positive, and short in duration, and you will not only be enjoying your kids more, but you will be using their time at home to develop valuable skills.

Remember that this time is your opportunity to give learning a new, more positive, more personal, and less formal slant. During these times your child might be practicing any number of things without the pressures of school—formulating opinions of her own, learning to take turns, learning step-by-step procedures for doing a task, following verbal instructions, supporting her point of view, reading orally, organizing things, etc. All of these skills practiced at home apply to school studies and create readiness to learn in any educational setting. Just by enjoying your child, doing things that are entertaining and/or useful in an informal setting, you can be teaching far more than you ever realized.

S—Stop Versus Support

Stop supporting bell curve definitions of your child as a learner. How did schools ever get our support for this agenda anyway?

If we do well in school, it is assumed that we will do well in life, and, conversely, if we don't do well in school, we won't do well in life. The primary expectation of most teachers and parents is for students to learn to *do school well.* Doing well for the sake of a confined system is called *institutionalization.* School is not life! School rules, expectations, lessons of conformity, dependence on others for self-definition, and working in short bursts between bells are not the skills needed for *doing life well.* All too often, schools keep young people dependent on their standards for achievement, the school's evaluations of one's progress, and the school's assessment of one's rank in the hierarchy. Many times, a school's primary mission is not to mature students into self-aware, self-motivated, self-directed, responsible people by the time they leave its hallowed halls. Competitive sorting and ranking are often the primary purposes of school. This ranking takes place in class after class, test after test, paper after paper, unremittingly, day after day, year after year. Mistakes are punished and students are compared with each other to create an atmosphere of competition. By the end of it all, thousands of kids still don't read, don't spell, and don't write. Furthermore, young people are being graduated into the "real world" thinking that they are stupid. What is the point? Where are the people shouting, "What in the world are you doing to our kids?" Where are the people saying to the kids who don't do well in a competitive atmosphere, "Of course you can do this. Let me help. I'll show you how."

According to Thomas Armstrong in *Awakening Your Child's Natural Genius* (1991):

> "Most kids spend a high percentage of their roughly 13,000 school hours from kindergarten through high school graduation focusing on tasks bearing little relationship to real-life activities . . . The schools must become centers of passion and purpose for children before the crisis in education is truly addressed."[6]

By redefining your child as a learner in terms of dispositions, talents, interests, and modalities, you can stop supporting bell-curve-determined definitions of your child. Grades and percentiles are conveniences that maintain a system; they are not the whole truth. The subtle lessons of school, as John Taylor Gatto writes, "prevent children from keeping important appointments with themselves and with their families to learn about self-motivation, perseverance, self-reliance, service to others, courage, dignity, and love."[7]

Outside-In and Inside-Out Education

Kids can be educated in two ways: 1) from the outside-in and 2) from the inside-out. Educating from the outside-in means that a child is expected to be passive most of the time. Rules, instructions, and information come from the top down, from the experts or authority figures to the students. Knowledge is dispensed and a student's role is to receive information. Shoulds, oughts, musts, commands, and demands are often the means for communicating to learners who are judged by test scores as blameworthy or praiseworthy, right or wrong, good or bad. Students are evaluated by comparing them

> " *How parents and teachers talk tells a child how they feel about him . . . . To a large extent, their language determines his destiny.*
>
> —Haim Ginott "

with each other. You are a good student, but Janice is better. Rewards and punishment are used as means for motivating learning.

Outside-in structures, including many schools, stress control and require compliance, obedience, and order above all else. Policies, programs, rules, and expectations are carefully crafted to ensure that these requirements will be met. The assumption is that kids are unruly, untrustworthy, and unable to learn self-government, self-discipline, and self-evaluation. The fear is that without an outside-in policy for maintaining control there would be chaos and nothing of value would be learned. In this School Model of Education according to Alfie Kohn, "the problem always rests with the child who doesn't do what he has been asked to do."[8] The appropriateness of standardized expectations for different learners is usually not considered.

In the words of J. F. Covaleskie, who has researched this subject extensively, "A program that teaches children that they are simply expected to obey rules, even legitimate and properly established rules, fails the children and the larger society."[9]

The second way that children can be educated is from the inside-out. In this philosophy, children are expected to be active and involved. They are seen as individual people with traits and attributes of their own. They are people to get to know, people with whom to interact. They are seen as people coming into wholeness from the inside out, on their own time schedules. Expectations and methodologies are individualized as much as possible. Parents and teachers set up appropriate conditions that encourage skill development and learning-success. Respect is the underlying principle for interaction. Since the way we view and treat a child can be a self-fulfilling prophecy, when a child's strengths are nurtured and respected, the child learns to be a confident, respectful person. Motivation for learning comes from having interests, strengths, and goals acknowledged, and from being appropriately challenged.

> " *Children are not things to be molded, but people to be unfolded.*
> —Charles F. Boyd "

The Learning Style Profile in this book encourages inside-out education. The underlying premise is that kids whose learning needs are met become trustworthy, eager to learn, and capable of self-direction.

What words does your child's teacher use to describe your child?

_____   _____

_____   _____

_____   _____

_____   _____

_____   _____

How do you think that this description affects your child's ability and motivation to learn?

_____

_____

_____

_____

How is outside-in learning taking place in your child's life?

_____

_____

_____

_____

How is inside-out learning taking place in your child's life?

_____

_____

_____

 **SUMMARY**

Taking a more active role in your child's learning process can test and also strengthen the relationship between the two of you. A new approach to interaction is the beginning of forming a learning team to guide, encourage, and cheer your child on to more and more successful learning experiences. After many years of working with parents to find new ways of interacting that include talking about and making strategies for more learning-success, I know that this is possible. The five C.A.R.E.S. actions described in this chapter were: celebrate your child as she is, accept that you are the major influence in your child's life—even for learning, respond to your child by acknowledging what she tells you, expand your idea of where education and/or teaching takes place, and stop accepting bell curve definitions of who your child is. Keep these ideas in mind as you proceed to the next section of the book.

PART 2

Do the Profile

Chapters 4 to 11 guide you through the Learning Style Profile. Chapter 4 prepares you to administer the Profile to the members of your family. Chapters 5 to 9 take you through each of the five aspects of Learning Style: Dispositions, Talents, Interests, Modality, and Environment. Chapter 10 teaches you how to put all of the information together to identify each family member's learning style. And Chapter 11 presents follow-up activities that will help the whole family to better understand and put into practice the results of the Profile.

According to Einstein, "It is nothing short of a miracle that the modern methods of instruction have not yet entirely strangled the holy curiosity of inquiry."[1] I believe that this Learning

Style Profile can be your key to cultivating curiosity and passion, and to bringing new life to your child's learning journey!

Now on to Part 2!

- **Read Chapter 4 and make copies of the assessments and forms at the back of the chapter**
- **Fill out the assessments and then transfer scores to the summary form**
- **Read Chapters 5 to 9 for information about the results**

The Learning Profile:
Getting Started

You are now ready to discover your family's learning styles. You can assess all of your children and yourselves, the parents, as well.

The Learning Style Profile, which is contained in this book, was carefully constructed to assess five aspects of Learning Style: Dispositions, Talents, Interests, Modality, and Environment. Other learning style evaluations generally assess only one or two of these aspects. Please note that no assessment can evaluate every possible combination of characteristics, and no human being can ever be completely defined by a test or questionnaire. However, the Learning Style Profile in this book is unique in putting together in one assessment so many aspects of important learning style information (see Figure 4.1).

The Profile is fun and nonthreatening. It is easy to administer and score. It is *not* a test. Rather, it is an assessment instrument devised to gather information, to increase self-awareness, to encourage discussion, and to facilitate changes in learning behaviors. Most people, even young children, really know what they are like. The Profile simply helps them sort out, define, and

Five Aspects of Learning Style

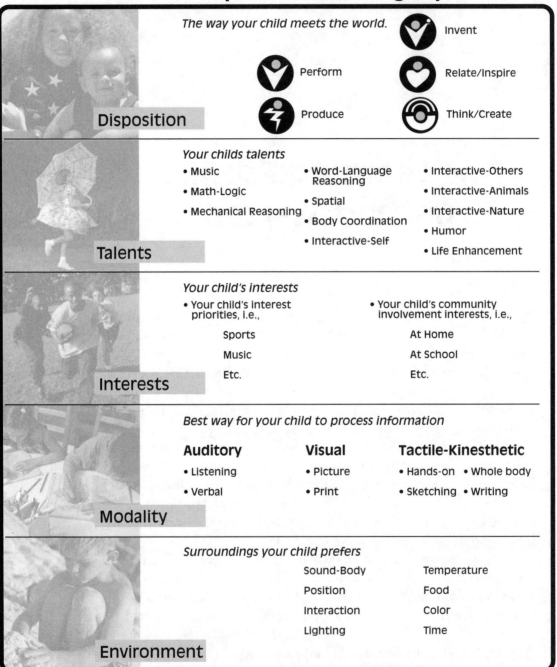

The way your child meets the world.

Invent

Perform

Relate/Inspire

Produce

Think/Create

Disposition

Your childs talents

- Music
- Math-Logic
- Mechanical Reasoning
- Word-Language Reasoning
- Spatial
- Body Coordination
- Interactive-Self
- Interactive-Others
- Interactive-Animals
- Interactive-Nature
- Humor
- Life Enhancement

Talents

Your child's interests

- Your child's interest priorities, i.e.,

    Sports

    Music

    Etc.

- Your child's community involvement interests, i.e.,

    At Home

    At School

    Etc.

Interests

Best way for your child to process information

Auditory

- Listening
- Verbal

Visual

- Picture
- Print

Tactile-Kinesthetic

- Hands-on   • Whole body
- Sketching   • Writing

Modality

Surroundings your child prefers

Sound-Body   Temperature

Position   Food

Interaction   Color

Lighting   Time

Environment

Figure 4.1 Five Aspects of Learning Style

validate what they already know about themselves. The best way to get this information is to simply ask the questions.

Please note that it is *not* the intent of this Profile to rigidly categorize people. There will be some overlap across categories, and changes in preferences sometimes occur as a child develops. The results of the Profile are *not* meant to be used as excuses for problem behaviors, to limit a child's vocational choices, or to put a ceiling on potential. The results are meant to be used to unlock potentials, increase learning efficiency, and help *all* children to become successful learners.

Some people may think that the assessments are too simplistic to provide helpful information. Ten years of use by parents, teachers, therapists, and literacy educators has shown otherwise.

I hope that you will refer to your family's Profiles often, and that they become a part of your discussions and educational planning.

HOW TO PROCEED

1. Make copies of:

☐ Learning Style Profile assessments

☐ Summary form

☐ Plan form

You will find the assessments, and the Summary and Plan forms at the end of this chapter. Make copies for each member of the family. I suggest that you create file folders and keep each person's forms in a separate folder.

2. Finish reading this chapter:

This chapter contains instructions and other valuable information to help you administer the Profile assessments.

3. Take assessments:

- ❏ Children
- ❏ Parents
- ❏ Other significant adults

Before you begin reading Chapter 5, have everyone fill out their Profile assessments: Disposition, Talents, Interests, Modality, and Environment. (Note that the preschool version has a different set-up—all the assessments are on two pages.)

4. Score:

Follow the instructions for scoring on each assessment. (Note that the preschool version has its own scoring system.)

5. Transfer results:

Transfer the results for each person to the individual Summary forms. As you read Chapters 5 through 9, you will be able to refer to the individual Summary forms, enhancing your understanding of each family member's results. (Note that the preschool version has its own Summary section—**do not transfer preschool scores to the Summary form.**)

6. Keep the Plan form handy:

In Chapter 10 you will find instructions for filling out the Plan form.

Choosing the Appropriate Version

The Learning Style Profile is for ages six to adult. If your child has difficulty reading, you can read the entire Profile to him. Accept the child's choices and resist the temptation to choose for him.

If your kindergartner or first grader can read and is able to do her own Profile, allow her to fill it out. You can also use this Profile with a kindergartner or first grader who isn't reading yet, as long as she is capable of making the choices when the material is read to her.

The preschool version of the Learning Style Profile is for children six years old and younger who are not reading yet, and who are not able to make the choices when the material is read to them. Fill it out based on your observations of the child. Have the other parent or significant adults in the child's life also fill it out, and compare results. You can use this version for three- and four-year-olds, but children who are younger than three years of age are usually too young to be assessed.

Remember to do your own Profile. When we work with or instruct others, we tend to use ourselves as the model, and we expect what works for us to work for them! Knowing your own learning style will give you valuable insights for interacting with your children—you will learn more about this in Chapter 11.

Giving Instructions to Your Child

Explain to your child that the Profile is a fun assessment, designed to determine her likes and dislikes, her strengths, and the ways she learns best. The results give ideas for activities and materials that can make it easier for her to learn, do homework, study for tests, and find out what she loves to do. Explain that there are no right or wrong answers and encourage her to make choices based on her preferences, rather than what she thinks others would want her to choose. This is her chance to focus on herself and find out what she is like.

For some children, it is difficult to do all of the Profile in one sitting. If this is the case for your child, allow him to do one assessment at a time. If necessary, you can even break up each of the five assessments and ask your child to fill out only two or three items at a sitting.

> **A**llow him to choose even if you don't agree with his choice.

Explain to your child that she can ask for help if she doesn't know a word or does not understand the meaning of an instruction. You are encouraged to give help as needed as long as you do not choose the answers for your child.

What If I Don't Agree with My Child's Responses?

Keep in mind that there are *no* incorrect responses. It is important for each child to answer the questions for himself. Again, resist the temptation to choose for the child—allow him to choose even if you don't agree with his choice.

> " *I desire that there be as many different persons in the world as possible; I would have each one be careful to find out and preserve his own way.*
>
> —Henry David Thoreau "

If your child chooses answers on the Profile that you don't think are accurate, be open and accept them. Usually, the child is right on target. Sometimes parents are surprised by the results of the child's Profile, but later they tell me that after they began paying attention they realized that the child's responses, in fact, characterized him best.

Occasionally, a child chooses items that really don't describe her style. But this occurs rarely. If it occurs with your child, simply accept the results and begin a process of discovery. This is the way your child sees herself at this time, or perhaps this is the way she thinks she *should* be. As you talk with your child and try the suggestions in this book, you'll learn together what is accurate and what works best. And your child will learn that it's okay to question and experiment.

 ## BE PREPARED FOR A SHIFT IN THINKING

As you sort out the significance of the learning style information contained in the next five chapters, you could experience a mixture of feelings. You might know deep inside that it all makes sense, yet it will sound contrary to the "rules of learning" that were passed on to you through your own school experience. In between, "Yes!—this is the way it should be," and "Why don't they know this in the schools?" you might think, "Learning is serious, it isn't supposed to be fun," and "I'm not here to indulge my child's every whim and fancy; I'm here to help him become disciplined and get his work done."

Remember the principle discussed in Chapter 3, which encourages respect for each individual child through listening and acknowledging. There is no doubt that listening, acknowledging, and valuing provide the foundation for successful learning experiences. The information in this book is an important ingredient, but your attitude and philosophy about learning are also crucial. If we truly believe as parents that each child is a unique individual, with her own set of marvelous gifts and creative abilities, then we must accept the importance of helping her grow in ways that encourage those gifts and abilities, rather than stifling them. *Respecting individual needs is not indulgent, it is intelligent.*

> *Each one of us has a gift. There is . . . the tortoise gift of the plodder, the fox gift of cunning, the dog gift of faithfulness, the song-sparrow gift of cheerfulness, the swan gift of beauty in motion.*
>
> —Hughes Mearns

What about the friend or relative who says, "The schools have always done it the same way and we all got through it fine!" Well, as you read in Chapter 1, many have not come through it "fine." Too many adults are stuck in jobs and life circumstances that cause them great stress, dissatisfaction, unhappiness, even anger. They don't realize their capabilities or how to use their gifts and their unique learning styles to function *and* to find joy and fulfillment in the "real world."

Chapters 5 through 9 discuss in detail each of the five aspects of Learning Style. If there is too much information to take in all at once, read one section at a time, implement one or two suggestions, and proceed slowly. Remember that no child's program will be perfect, and you won't be able to implement

> **T**here is no doubt that listening, acknowledging, and valuing provide the foundation for successful learning experiences. The information in this book is an important ingredient, but your attitude and philosophy about learning are also crucial.

> " *Because [children have] lived with their personal learning styles all their lives, they are usually the best ones to talk with about how they learn best.*
>
> —*Thomas Armstrong* "

every technique and strategy you learn about in this book as you strive to keep a balance with your personal needs, your family's needs, and your child's learning style needs. What counts is that you are *willing* to shift your thinking—to listen to your child, consider changes, and implement as many of the suggestions as you can.

At this time, make copies of the Profile assessments and the Summary and Plan forms that follow. You will need one of each for each member of the family who is taking the Profile. Fill out the assessments and the Summary form before reading Chapter 5. Keep these forms handy as you read the following chapters. Chapter 10 will give you instructions for filling out the Plan form.

Learning Style Profile Assessments

DISPOSITION ASSESSMENT

Allow young people to answer the questions by themselves, without prompting. Of all the sections in the Profile, this is the one that sometimes results in inaccurate information because the child's or adult's responses can be based on how they wish they were or how they think they "should" be. So encourage students to respond according to what <u>they</u> think.

Instructions:
For the following questions write one 5, one 4, and one 1.
You will have two blanks.
5 = I am like this the most!
4 = This is a lot like me.
1 = This is the least like me.

For example:
I like
 5 games.
 ___ workbooks.
 4 experiments.
 1 group projects.
 ___ wondering and thinking.

1. I...
A ___ am fun to be with.
B ___ get things done,
C ___ ask questions.
D ___ help others.
E ___ think a lot.

2. Learning is best when it...
A ___ is exciting.
B ___ happens step by step.
C ___ involves discovering things.
D ___ is done with others.
E ___ comes from my own ideas.

3. Assignments need to be...
A ___ short.
B ___ on time.
C ___ interesting.
D ___ done in groups.
E ___ important to me.

4. I like...
A ___ games.
B ___ workbooks.
C ___ experiments.
D ___ group projects.
E ___ wondering and thinking.

5. In classes or workshops, I like...
A ___ to move.
B ___ to listen quietly.
C ___ to explore alone.
D ___ to make friends.
E ___ to watch or think.

6. I like to do things...
A ___ now.
B ___ on a schedule.
C ___ for as long as I want.
D ___ when it works for everyone.
E ___ when it feels right to me.

7. Schedule...
A ___ keep me from being free.
B ___ keep order.
C ___ take time away from projects.
D ___ are OK if fair.
E ___ don't make sense to me.

8. I like to...
A ___ take things apart.
B ___ finish things I start.
C ___ figure things out.
D ___ talk to people.
E ___ use my imagination.

9. I think about...
A ___ what I'm doing now.
B ___ planning ahead.
C ___ my projects.
D ___ people
E ___ ideas.

10. I feel best when I'm...
A ___ spontaneous.
B ___ organized.
C ___ inventing new things.
D ___ helpful.
E ___ thinking or creating.

Transfer the Disposition scores to the Summary form. Total the scores horizontally by adding 4s and 5s and subtracting 1s. The highest score is the Primary Disposition. The next highest score is the Secondary Disposition.

For example:
Questions 1 and 2 - Record your responses as follows:

	1.	2.
Performing	4	0
Producing	0	1
Inventing	5	4
Relating/Inspiring	1	0
Thinking/Creating	0	5

TALENT ASSESSMENT

In the lists below, check all of the things that are easy for you. Then add up the check marks in each group, multiply by ten, and transfer these scores to the appropriate spaces on the Talent section of the Summary form.

1.

☐ playing music in my head
☐ playing an instrument
☐ whistling or humming
☐ keeping with the beat or rhythm
☐ singing
☐ learning to play new music
☐ collecting records or tapes
☐ memorizing words to songs
☐ making up songs
☐ composing music

TOTAL CHECKS ◯ ×10= ◯

3.

☐ guessing what's wrong with something
☐ fixing things
☐ taking apart/putting together
☐ inventing
☐ running machines
☐ taking care of cars
☐ building things
☐ figuring out how things work
☐ being handy with tools
☐ doing household repairs

TOTAL CHECKS ◯ ×10= ◯

2.

☐ with numbers
☐ games like chess, checkers
☐ science or math projects
☐ working with money
☐ working with computers
☐ doing experiments
☐ logic puzzles
☐ using calculators
☐ doing math problems
☐ playing with numbers in my head

TOTAL CHECKS ◯ ×10= ◯

4.

☐ spelling
☐ reading
☐ talking
☐ writing or telling stories
☐ memorizing names and facts
☐ word games like Scrabble, crossword puzzles
☐ thinking in words
☐ writing plans, outlines, lists
☐ explaining ideas
☐ getting the point when I read

TOTAL CHECKS ◯ ×10= ◯

5.

- ☐ drawing or copying pictures, designs
- ☐ thinking in pictures
- ☐ jigsaw puzzles or mazes
- ☐ remembering what I see
- ☐ reading maps or charts
- ☐ knowing where things are
- ☐ direction (finding my way)
- ☐ painting pictures
- ☐ doodling
- ☐ creating an imaginary world

TOTAL CHECKS   ×10=

8.

- ☐ making friends
- ☐ helping others
- ☐ group games or projects
- ☐ being fair
- ☐ baby-sitting
- ☐ settling arguments
- ☐ understanding people
- ☐ making others feel good
- ☐ solving people problems
- ☐ leading groups or meetings

TOTAL CHECKS   ×10=

6.

- ☐ baseball, basketball, or tennis
- ☐ dancing
- ☐ biking, skating, working out
- ☐ typing or sewing
- ☐ hiking or running
- ☐ hammering or sawing
- ☐ doing models or crafts
- ☐ skateboarding, snowboarding, skiing
- ☐ swimming or surfing
- ☐ writing neatly

TOTAL CHECKS   ×10=

9.

- ☐ raising or caring for animals
- ☐ training pets
- ☐ grooming pets
- ☐ calming down an animal
- ☐ playing with animals
- ☐ getting animals to trust me
- ☐ communicating with animals
- ☐ protecting animals
- ☐ rescuing animals
- ☐ teaching others about animals

TOTAL CHECKS   ×10=

7.

- ☐ being alone
- ☐ giving my opinion
- ☐ being independent
- ☐ looking my best
- ☐ taking care of myself
- ☐ having hobbies
- ☐ making up my own mind
- ☐ working by myself
- ☐ thinking about my life
- ☐ making plans for what I want

TOTAL CHECKS   ×10=

10.

- ☐ hiking or backpacking
- ☐ exploring nature trails
- ☐ exploring tide pools
- ☐ observing wildlife
- ☐ camping
- ☐ protecting the environment
- ☐ recycling
- ☐ watching/charting stars and planets
- ☐ climbing trees
- ☐ learning about nature

TOTAL CHECKS   ×10=

11. _____

☐ laughing
☐ doing funny things
☐ playing practical jokes
☐ making people laugh
☐ mimicking others
☐ using my imagination for fun
☐ making things fun for others
☐ telling jokes
☐ teasing
☐ being clever, tricky

TOTAL CHECKS   ×10=

12. _____

☐ cooking
☐ doing yard work, growing plants
☐ coordinating clothes and fashion
☐ cleaning
☐ decorating, painting, or wallpapering rooms
☐ organizing rooms
☐ organizing people
☐ organizing paperwork/materials
☐ budgeting or organizing money
☐ planning or organizing time

TOTAL CHECKS   ×10=

INTEREST ASSESSMENT

Interest Priority Scale   List your Interests on the priority scale: 10 = most interested, 1 = least interested. You can include favorite subjects and activities in or out of school. Transfer your choices to the appropriate columns (1–4 or 5–10) of the Interest section on the Summary form.

10. _____

9. _____

8. _____

7. _____

6. _____

5. _____

4. _____

3. _____

2. _____

1. _____

Involvement Issues   Answer the following questions, then note a few of your ideas in the Involvement Issues column of the Interest section on the Summary form.

What do you really care about?

at home:

_____

in the neighborhood:

_____

at school:

_____

in your town:

_____

in the world:

_____

How can you help take care of the things you care about?

_____

_____

_____

_____

What things do you want to do some time during your life?

_____

_____

_____

_____

MODALITY ASSESSMENT

PART I. In each set of statements, circle one choice. Then transfer the scores to the Modality Part I section on the Summary form.

1. I prefer to:
  - **(A)**   Hear a story
  - **(B)**   See a movie
  - **(C)**   Play outside

2. I prefer to:
  - **(A)**   Listen to music
  - **(B)**   Read a book
  - **(C)**   Walk or run

3. I prefer to:
  - **(A)**   Listen to the radio
  - **(B)**   Watch television
  - **(C)**   Play a game

4. The best way for me to remember is to:
  - **(A)**   "say it over and over" to myself.
  - **(B)**   "make a picture" in my head.
  - **(C)**   "just do it."

5. I understand instructions better when:
  - **(A)**   someone explains them to me.
  - **(B)**   I can read them or see pictures.
  - **(C)**   someone shows me how.

6. When I am thinking, I:
  - **(A)**   talk to myself.
  - **(B)**   see pictures in my head.
  - **(C)**   need to move around.

7. **(A)**   I remember what people say.
  - **(B)**   I notice how things look; I like colors and designs.
  - **(C)**   I often play with coins and keys in my pocket or objects on the table.

8. I am a:
  - **(A)**   listener, not a watcher or doer.
  - **(B)**   watcher, not a listener or doer.
  - **(C)**   doer, not a watcher or listener.

TOTAL ITEMS CIRCLED:

A= AUDITORY   ×10=

B= VISUAL   ×10=

C= TACTILE-KINESTHETIC   ×10=

PART II. Suppose you are learning about how the lungs work. Which of the following would be the easiest way for you to learn about this subject? Number your choices, 1, 2, and 3 for your first, second, and third choices. On the Modality Part II section of the Summary form record 1, 2, 3 next to the items that correspond to your choices.

I learn best when I:

_____ listen to someone talk (LISTENING)

_____ listen to a tape (LISTENING)

_____ talk in a group (VERBAL)

_____ talk aloud to myself (VERBAL)

_____ see pictures (PICTURE)

_____ watch movies or slides (PICTURE)

_____ look up information in reference books (PRINT)

_____ read about the lesson (PRINT)

_____ have a model to touch, take apart, or put together (HANDS-ON)

_____ act out the lesson (WHOLE BODY)

_____ draw a picture of the lesson (SKETCHING)

_____ write about the lesson (WRITING)

ENVIRONMENT ASSESSMENT

PART I. What helps you to study, do school work, or do paperwork? (Check <u>one</u> in each category.) Transfer your responses to the appropriate spaces on the Environment section of the Summary form.

SOUND

- ☐ quiet
- ☐ noise (like cars or street noise)
- ☐ music
- ☐ people talking

BODY POSITION

- ☐ sitting at a desk or table
- ☐ sitting on the floor
- ☐ lying on the bed, floor, or couch
- ☐ standing at the board or a tall table

INTERACTION

- ☐ being by myself with the door closed
- ☐ being with other people who are quiet
- ☐ being with other people who are talking or doing things
- ☐ being with a pet

LIGHTING

- ☐ bright light
- ☐ low light
- ☐ sunlight (outdoors)
- ☐ light from a window
- ☐ the kind of light doesn't matter

Parent's observations about the child's lighting needs:

_____

PART II. Check the statements that describe you the best. Then transfer your choices to the appropriate spaces on the Environment section of the Summary form.

TEMPERATURE

- ☐ I get cold easily.
- ☐ I get hot easily.
- ☐ I like the windows open.
- ☐ I like to keep the windows closed.
- ☐ I often need my sweater or sweatshirt.
- ☐ I would rather wear shorts most of the time.
- ☐ The temperature is usually fine for me.

Parent's observations about the child's temperature needs:

_____

FOOD

☐ I get hungry before lunchtime.
☐ I get hungry between lunch and dinnertime.
☐ I am usually hungry when I get home from school.

☐ I get hungry between dinner and bedtime.
☐ I get thirsty a lot.
☐ I usually don't feel hungry or thirsty.

Parent's observations about child's food needs:

_____

PART III. Fill in your answers below, then transfer them to the appropriate spaces on the Environment section of the Summary form.

Color

My favorite or best color is: _____

My least favorite or worst color is: _____

Time

My best time of day when I have a lot of energy is: _____

My worst time of day when I have no energy is: _____

Learning Style Summary

Name: _____   Date: _____

Disposition

Disposition Questions—Add 4's and 5's, Subtract 1's

		1	2	3	4	5	6	7	8	9	10	TOTALS	Activities
A	Performs												**Move:** skits, shows, demos, games, audiovisuals, sports, "real" life
B	Produces												**Organize:** schedules, outlines, workbooks, reading, writing, portfolios
C	Invents												**Discover:** projects, portfolios, debate, brainstorm, computers, "labs"
D	Relates/ Inspires												**Interact:** group projects, people stories family trees, discussion
E	Thinks/ Creates												**Create:** art, music, nature, poetry, math theory, day dreaming, philosophy, portfolios

Talents

1. _____ Music
2. _____ Math-Logic Reasoning
3. _____ Mechanical Reasoning
4. _____ Word-Lang. Reasoning
5. _____ Spatial
6. _____ Body Coordination
7. _____ Interactive-Self
8. _____ Interactive-Others
9. _____ Interactive-Animals
10. _____ Interactive-Nature
11. _____ Humor
12. _____ Life Enhancement

Interests

1-4 on the Interest Priority Scale	5-10 on the Interest Priority Scale	Involvement Issues
_____	_____	_____
_____	_____	_____
_____	_____	_____
_____	_____	_____

Modality

PART 1

PART 2

_____ **Auditory** Hear/Talk
- _____ **Listening**: Audio tapes, books-on-tape, music, rhyming, songs, stories, computers, live lectures, oral / duet reading
- _____ **Verbal**: read aloud, discuss, verbalize to self, read w/books-on-tape, interactive video / computer programs, tape reports/assignments, present orally, sing info or set to music, work with another or in a small group

_____ **Visual** See/Read
- _____ **Picture**: Videos; computers; picture time lines, cues, diagrams / charts; picture note-taking, info mapping; live performances
- _____ **Print**: reading, research, word diagrams/charts, time lines, word note-taking/info mapping, highlight printed material

_____ **Tactile-Kinesthetic** Touch/Do
- _____ **Hands-On**: touching, assembling, taking things apart, manipulating objects, textured materials, models, Legos, blocks
- _____ **Whole Body**: acting out, moving, dancing, exercising, build large things / construct, walk-on materials
- _____ **Sketching**: drawing, coloring, doodling, picture note-taking, picture information mapping
- _____ **Writing**: writing, tracing, copying, workbooks, research, outlines, word notetaking / information mapping

Environment

Sound _____   Lighting _____   Color _____

Body Position _____   Temp _____   Time _____

Interaction _____   Food _____

Preschool Assessment Page 1   Name: _____ Date: _____

Section A: Disposition

Read through each section and check the items that best describe the child most of the time. Count the total number of checks in each section and record the totals. Circle the 2 highest scores and record their Disposition names in the Summary Section.

Performing

__ Active

__ Moves from thing to thing

__ Likes to be the center of attention

__ Likes to be "fun"

__ "Charges" into a group

__ "Entertainer"

__ Likes games/competition

__ Takes things apart for fun

__ Likes to laugh and joke

__ Takes risks/puts on a show

Total _____

Producing

__ Organized

__ Plays quietly for a long time

__ Likes to be a helper, wants to get things done

__ Likes to do things "right"

__ Observes a group to be able to fit in

__ "Rule Keeper"

__ Likes to color & look at books

__ Puts things away, is neat and orderly

__ Likes schedules and routines

__ Careful, purposeful, sometimes bossy

Total _____

Inventing

__ Focused

__ Engages in "experiments"

__ Likes to be with others who like to "invent"/"explore"

__ Likes to ask questions

__ Shies away from groups

__ "Little Scientist"

__ Likes to collect/tinker

__ Takes things apart to discover

__ Gets lost in projects

__ Prefers to be alone or with adults

Total _____

Relating/Inspiring

__ Sensitive to others' feelings

__ Thrives on group interaction

__ Likes to be friends

__ Likes to talk and be social

__ Looks for "warm" frienships

__ "Diplomat"/"Mediator"

__ Likes cooperative projects

__ Shares activities & belongings

__ Likes to be read to/cuddle

__ Expresses feelings and is hurt easily

Total _____

Thinking/Creating

__ Pensive/Reflective

__ Watches others play/work

__ Likes to be quiet and alone

__ Likes to daydream/create

__ Warms slowly to a group, or stays on the edge

__ "Creator"/"Dreamer"

__ Likes to observe, imagine, wonder

__ Gets involved in arts, crafts, music, or dancing

__ Notices beauty in nature

__ Often seen as witdrawn or shy

Total _____

Section B: Modality
Total the check marks in each column. Note the highest score and record Modality name in Summary Section.

Visual
__ Likes picture books, puzzles
__ Is drawn to colors, shapes, patterns
__ Likes to color and draw
__ Remembers what has been "seen"
__ "Watches" to learn things
__ Keeps things neat and clean
__ Prefers table games to outside play

Totals _____

Auditory
__ Likes tapes and music
__ Tunes in to sounds and noises
__ Likes to be read to
__ Remembers what has been "heard"
__ "Listens" to learn
__ Talks to self when playing
__ Prefers talk to motor activity

Totals _____

Tactile/Kinesthetic
__ Likes running, climbing, jumping
__ Touches everything
__ Likes to play with sand
__ Remembers what has been "done"
__ "Mimics" to learn
__ Doesn't mind getting dirty
__ Prefers outside play to table games

Totals

Section C: Environment
In Summary Section, record items checked.

When doing chores or at play (s)he likes:
__ quiet
__ noise
__ music
__ having others around
__ being alone

Section D: Interests
Record in Summary Section.

Favorite Toys:

Favorite Colors:

Favorite Pastimes:

Section E: Talents
In Summary Section record Items checked.

Check talent areas:
__ Language/Verbal
__ Artistic/Visual
__ Music
__ Numbers
__ Mechanical
__ Logic/Reasoning
__ Coordination
__ Social
__ Humor
__ Life Skills

Section F: Inner Clock
Record times in Summary Section.
Time of day when most:

Active: _____   Cooperative: _____
Productive: _____   Tired: _____

Comments: _____
_____
_____

Summary

Section A. Disposition
1. _____
2. _____

Section B. Modality

Section C. Environment

Section D. Interests

Section E. Talents

Section F. Inner Clock
Active _____
("play time")

Cooperative _____
("teaching/task time")

Productive _____
("teaching/task time")

Tired _____
("rest/break time")

PLAN

Disposition

Talents

Interests

Modality

Environment

Areas for Growth	Life Goals

Dispositions: The Way the World Sees Us

The terms disposition, personality, and temperament all attempt to define the same part of a person. A disposition or combination of dispositions is an aspect of us that is more inborn than developed—hardwired into us, so to speak. Disposition, therefore, is difficult to change. Our dispositions are what we show the world. In daily life we interact with another person's disposition, not a particular talent, modality, or interest. In a way, *all the other aspects of learning style are expressed through our dispositions.*

Dispositions basically determine the ways people work, communicate, and learn. The Learning Style Profile identifies five distinct Dispositions: Performing, Producing, Inventing, Relating/Inspiring, and Thinking/Creating. Detailed explanations of each of these dispositions are provided in Chapters 5a–e that follow. Verbs are used to name the categories rather than nouns (such as Performer, Producer, Inventor) because it is important to describe people by their actions instead of assigning career-like labels to them. (See Figure 5.1.)

A person's disposition affects behavior as well as learning. I often see parents and teachers nagging at children, arguing with

Disposition Traits

Performs
Center of attention
Likes spontaneity
Likes challenges
Fun oriented
Entertaining
Competitive
"Hands-on"
Humorous
Jokester
Playful
Active
Fun

Produces
Likes plans & schedules
Often does well on tests
Likes routines & rules
Memorizes facts well
Efficiency oriented
Wants continuity
Traditional
Organized
Focused
Diligent
Orderly
Prompt

*How does
your child
meet
the World?*

Thinks • Creates
Creates mental images
Thinks in abstractions
Enjoys being alone
Open to new ideas
Idea oriented
Preoccupied
Imaginative
Daydreams
Questions
Wonders
Doodles

Relates • Inspires
Cares about feelings of others
Can "get into another's shoes"
Creates/enjoys team effort
Works best with others
Sacrifices for others
Wants harmony
People oriented
Cooperative
Inspiring
Friendly
Caring
Fair

Invents
Considered to be "smart"
Asks a lot of questions
Articulate with hands
Enjoys being alone
Invention oriented
Concrete thinker
Experiments
"Hands-on"
Technical
Discovers
Focused

Figure 5.1 Disposition Traits

them, and punishing them for the same misbehaviors over and over again. How much of the problem is the fact that two people with two different dispositions are seeing things in very different ways? Although each thinks he or she is right, fighting, as you already know, won't get you anywhere in the long term. Think of all the heated disagreements that result from the fact that you are a morning person and your child, husband, or wife is a night person.

> **K**nowing about disposition differences can have the welcome effect of turning an argument into a problem-solving session.

What about the different concepts people have about time? If you say to one person, I'll meet you in ten minutes, he'll be there in exactly ten minutes. Another person with a different disposition will be there in a half hour. It isn't that this person is necessarily irresponsible but rather that she tends to get lost in projects, ideas, or plans and forgets the time. This behavior is hardwired into her disposition. Yelling or punishing does no good, and punitive actions are likely to harm the relationship over time. It isn't as if this person can't or shouldn't learn anything new about how to be on time; it's just much better to use problem-solving methods to help her be on time. (See Chapter 12 for more information on solution-focused problem solving.)

If you are arguing with a child daily over such simple matters, you may well be faced with disposition differences. If you continue to argue about these matters, you might as well be pushing a wall. Wall pushing is counterproductive no matter how hard, how creatively, or how often you push. Knowing about disposition differences can have the welcome effect of turning an argument into a problem-solving session.

THE PRICE OF NOT ACCEPTING YOUR CHILD'S DISPOSITION

If we don't learn to accept and work with a child's disposition— the aspect of his learning style that is most apparent to others—

he doesn't get the acknowledgment and acceptance that is a basic human need. When we aren't accepted for who we are, we don't feel safe in our environment, and relationships and learning often suffer. And we don't just pay a price as a child—many people pay a price for their entire lives.

Safety First

One thing many brain researchers agree on is that "Learning environments must feel *emotionally safe* for learning to take place. When a child feels intimidated, rejected, or at risk, an overproduction of noradrenalin [stress hormone] causes that child to focus attention on self-protection rather than on learning."[1] Safety is a basic human need that is a prerequisite to academic learning. Safety means more than the absence of violent abuses. Put-downs, intimidation, negative labeling, and overemphasis on a child's mistakes and shortcomings create feelings of incompetence and cause stress hormones to be secreted throughout the child's body that prepare him to defend himself. Instead of paying attention and staying on task, kids who feel under attack can spend a great deal of time in heightened emotional states, inwardly or outwardly protecting themselves.

> **I**nstead of paying attention and staying on task, kids who feel under attack can spend a great deal of time in heightened emotional states inwardly or outwardly protecting themselves.

When parents and teachers know what a child's disposition is, and when they are willing to work with it rather than get angry, punish, or argue with her, they will get much better learning results because the child's basic need for safety is being met.

Our Deepest Need

I'm sure you've met adults who are insatiable in their need to be noticed, to control things, to instruct, to entertain, to take care of others, to psychologize, philosophize, or to tell you about their latest new project. These people are *still* trying to be acknowledged for who they are—Producing, Performing, Relating/Inspiring, Thinking/Creating, or Inventing people. Perhaps this need to be recognized for ourselves is the deepest need of all.

Until this need is met, we are like broken records playing the same old song over and over again.

In the chapters that follow, you will be given ideas for how to acknowledge and interact with each of the dispositions to facilitate successful learning. As you read the information, remember that acknowledging

> " *In general, only a child who feels safe dares to grow forward healthily. His safety needs must be gratified. He can't be pushed ahead, because the ungratified safety needs will remain forever underground, always calling for satisfaction.*
> —Abraham Maslow "

an idea does not necessarily mean that you agree with a person. Two points of view can exist in the same place at the same time. As Victoria Kindle Hodson writes, "Just because two people disagree, it doesn't mean one is right."[2]

PRIMARY AND SECONDARY DISPOSITIONS

Each of us has some attributes from all five of the dispositions identified in the Profile; however, two, or sometimes, three dispositions usually dominate.

The disposition that gets the highest score is the primary disposition. Taken alone, this doesn't mean as much as it does in relationship to the second highest score, called the secondary disposition.

Please note:

- If the gap between the primary and secondary dispositions is ten or more points, the characteristics of the primary disposition are likely to dominate.
- The smaller the gap is between the primary and secondary dispositions, the more the two interact and share dominance.

■ Sometimes a person has three scores that are within four or five points of each other. In this case, the characteristics of three dispositions interact and share dominance.

Each person's combination of scores is unique to that person and tells something about how the different dispositions interact for that person. For example, a person who has a score of 42 in one disposition and scores ranging from 3 to 10 in the others will have a very different pattern than someone who scores about 30 on three dispositions. Remember that there is no "better" or "worse" combination of scores. Each disposition is equally valuable and the scores simply give an idea of how strong or weak a particular disposition is for a person.

If a person scores low in a disposition, it doesn't necessarily mean that he has no skills in that area. For example, scoring –5 in Relating/Inspiring does not mean that this person dislikes people or is hostile toward them. It simply means that *by nature* Relating/Inspiring considerations won't have highest priority when it comes to learning and working. After administering the Profile to the staff of a community organization for young people, the director told me that she thought the results were wrong because they didn't reflect her concern for others. As we talked, it became clear that she did have a strong desire to treat others fairly. However, it was based on a belief that treating others well is the right thing to do, not because she spontaneously enjoys being with people and helping them feel comfortable and appreciated. In fact, during the talk with her I learned that she was really a very private person who didn't enjoy groups at all. Similarly, a low score in Producing doesn't mean that this person never gets anything done. Many people get mountains of work done because they have learned Producing skills, not because they genuinely enjoy organizing, planning, scheduling, and turning out yet an-

> **T**he complexity you find in the Learning Profile is evidence of each person's uniqueness.

other finished product. The low scores help us to better under-stand why we might have difficulty in a particular area or why we have to work extra hard to learn skills in that area.

Wow! This is getting complex, you might be thinking. The complexity you find in the Learning Profile is evidence of each person's uniqueness. This is what the Profile celebrates in every child. Keeping the complexity in is what makes these Profiles be-lievable to the kids.

 ## DO DISPOSITIONS CHANGE?

For the most part, primary and secondary dispositions keep their dominant positions over time. In some cases, the primary may drop to secondary and the secondary may rise to primary posi-tion. These are rather insignificant changes.

Sometimes overall scores even-out with time. Very high highs come down a little, and very low lows come up a little. When these scores are graphed (see Chapter 11), the peaks are not as high, and the valleys are not as deep.

Once in a while a complete switch in scores may occur. Two predictable factors influence such changes. A dramatic event such as the death of someone close to you or some other kind of emotional shock has been known to affect disposition scores. The other way that the disposition scores can change radically occurs when people fill out the Profile assessments the way they think they "should" be. False scores like this result, for example, when a seven- or eight-year-old who takes the Profile is very aware of predominant "Producing" require-ments of the school, society, and perhaps the home, and thinks she "should" have these characteristics. The first time she takes the disposition assessment, her primary disposition turns out to be Producing because she is trying so hard to please the people around her that she chooses items that fit this style. When she takes the Profile in her early teens, it often turns out that she has found another voice to speak from, one that is more her own, and thus Producing is no longer her primary disposition.

Reassessment every two or three years is a great way to check in with ever-changing needs, preferences, and goals. Some people reassess every year when they put together plans for each successive school year.

 ## SUMMARY

Knowing the characteristics of your child's various learning dispositions and discovering how to work with them will help you turn arguments about school and studies into productive problem-solving sessions.

The chapters that follow give important information for understanding each disposition including: Learning Characteristics, Preferred Setting, Contributions to a Group, Areas for Growth, Relationship Conflicts, Ideal Curriculum, Homework Helps, and Motivators.

These chapters are a quick resource to help readers understand their children's dominant dispositions. To make your task easier, we have purposely simplified the presentation. Please keep in mind that every child's disposition is much more complex than can be represented in this reference-like format. Remember that each of us has some characteristics from each of the dispositions and that usually two, sometimes three, of them dominate.

> *When you learn how to learn in your preferred style—the way that best suits **your** brain—it's like writing with your preferred hand. The result is much better, easier, and quicker.*
>
> *—Colin Rose*

Some combinations of dispositions can be confusing. For example, you might have a child whose dominant dispositions are Performing and Inventing. A person with a Performing Disposition usually enjoys being the center of attention, and a person with an Inventing Disposition usually enjoys working alone. Learning to balance two conflicting forces is the primary skill this person needs to develop. She needs to learn when to redirect her energy from outward activities to quieter, less public pursuits.

One of my students has this combination of Performing and Inventing Dispositions. He uses his Performing Disposition in class to make jokes and distract other students from their work. He uses the Inventing side of his Disposition to create exotic recipes and meals as well as to design, build, and maintain a hydroponic gardening system to grow herbs and vegetables for his cooking projects. When he figures out how to use both aspects of his disposition in coordination with each other, it is difficult to say what he will do. Perhaps he will be a well-known chef like Julia Child or Graham Kerr, the Galloping Gourmet. My job is to support his efforts to integrate the various aspects of himself.

> *We are all so different largely because we all have different combinations of intelligences. If we recognize this, I think we will have at least a better chance of dealing appropriately with the many problems that we face in the world.*
> —Howard Gardner

As you continue to read you will gain insight into how to work with and balance your child's dispositions, as well as how to integrate them with their talents, interests, and modalities. See Greg's and Ann's stories in Chapter 10 for more on this subject.

The Performing Disposition: Move

To get along best with Performing people, it is important to acknowledge their needs for spontaneity and playfulness.

People with Performing Dispositions are among the most sought after, seen, and wealthy people in our society. They are high-profile stars in the movie and music industries. They are entertainers. It is often not until after they finish high school that their gift for entertaining blossoms because in a family or classroom they can be disruptive. Ironically, kids with strong Performing Dispositions are often sitting outside the vice-principal's office waiting to receive yet another reprimand for smart-mouthing a teacher who has run out of warnings and patience. An audience is what Performing people enjoy most, and they have no hesitation about creating one whenever they can. A classroom of captive, often bored students provides an ideal audience for their antics and shenanigans.

Bold and unrelenting in their efforts to get a laugh, they stir up arguments or otherwise attract attention to themselves and are often known for being the class clown. Performing students are often labeled hyperactive or ADHD. In my experience teaching in alternative educational programs, kids with

Performing Dispositions are bright, witty, and outspoken. These kids often enjoy challenging authority, rules, and traditions. Of all the Dispositions this is the one that schools have the most difficulty containing.

In a family, this is the child who drives siblings crazy with taunting and teasing. Parents lose patience with Performing kids because they don't seem to take agreements, rules, and expectations seriously. Wherever they go, they find themselves "in trouble," which can result in discouragement and withdrawal or rebelliousness.

The father of one of my students has a Performing Disposition. He was told hundreds of times by his teachers to stop making funny voices and sounds, which he did spontaneously and incessantly. He was in trouble a great deal of the time. He is now the voice of one of Disney's most loved animated characters.

> **The father of one of my students is a Performing Disposition. He was told hundreds of times by his teachers to stop making funny voices and sounds, which he did spontaneously and incessantly. He was in trouble a great deal of the time. He is now the voice of one of Disney's most loved animated characters.**

A similar story has been reported about Jay Leno. Robin Williams' or Lucille Ball's or Whoopi Goldberg's teachers must have some interesting things to tell about these highly gifted comedians as children.

Although most actors, singers, and musicians have a Performing Disposition, not all people with this disposition become entertainers. Many athletes, trial lawyers, and politicians are Performing people, as well as those who are never really "on stage" but are the life of the party at home and at gatherings.

The Performing Disposition is best described by the word "move." The underlying objective of this style is to be spontaneous.

One of Bill Cosby's teachers complained that he seemed to think it was his job to entertain people inside and outside of the classroom. He had potential but . . . ! Bill's mom preserved his sixth-grade report card on which his teacher noted that he was a "disruptive force" in class.

 ## LEARNING CHARACTERISTICS

Performing people prefer subjects and activities that are entertaining by nature, have immediate relevance, offer variety and challenge, provide hands-on experiences, and give plenty of opportunity to move, act, and do. They learn best when the teaching materials and techniques used are short and to the point, allow movement, and involve games, manipulatives, and audiovisuals.

 ## PREFERRED SETTING

Performing people need flexible spaces that provide lots of room to move around. They thrive in atmospheres that are fun and challenging and allow for unscheduled free time. They love field trips and "real-life" learning situations.

 ## CONTRIBUTIONS

Performing people bring fun, laughter, adventure, and a sense of excitement to a situation. They can be playful, dramatic, flexible, clever, and witty. They contribute a sense of energy, outspokenness, and a willingness to take risks.

AREAS FOR GROWTH

Performing people usually have little interest in keeping a schedule, planning ahead, keeping things in order, or reserving time for quiet thinking. They have a hard time setting appointments and are known to impulsively change plans in an instant, without regard for other people's plans or feelings. They can have difficulty with problem solving (because it takes too long) and are not great about following through on commitments (because they're on to bigger and better things). Some of these behaviors might be listed under Areas for Growth on the Plan form. Then you can talk to your child about how to channel his energy in appropriate ways, such as fiddling with Silly Putty, Legos, or squeeze balls. He can choose something to keep in his pocket for occasions when he needs to be quiet.

> *Hide not your talents,*
> *They for use were made.*
> *What's a sundial*
> *In the shade?*
>
> —Ben Franklin

RELATIONSHIP CONFLICTS

The most valuable personal characteristic for Performing people is spontaneity. People with the Performing Disposition are often discounted for their desire to be "center stage" and they believe that their intentions to bring fun and laughter to a situation are often misunderstood. Sometimes they are seen as shallow, rowdy, irresponsible, or inconsiderate. When this disposition is not acknowledged, the "problem" behaviors increase. Children who grow up with negative reactions to their desires for fun and adventure become the adults who are never on time, miss appointments, tell inappropriate jokes, and so on. Parents who teach their children to use the Performing Disposition appropriately in various situations help them become adults who are able to meet their own needs while respecting the needs of others.

IDEAL CURRICULUM

Filmmaking, learning to play a sport, and building a rocket are examples of subjects that are entertaining by nature and give plenty of opportunity to move, act, and do. Applying math principles to designing and constructing a skate-board ramp or working with maps to plan a vacation trip are examples of activities that provide immediate relevance and hands-on experience. Playing basketball to learn math facts or a board

> *Because there can be no Recreation without Delight which depends not always on Reason, but oftener on Fancy, it must be permitted Children not only to divert themselves, but to do it after their own fashion.*
>
> —*John Locke*

game to develop reading skills are also examples of activities that allow movement and offer variety and challenge.

These students enjoy activities that allow them to change things, compose, construct, design, formulate, generate, originate, pretend, reconstruct, reorganize, revise, suggest, and visualize.

 ## HOMEWORK HELPS

- Encourage movement breaks every fifteen to twenty minutes when doing paper-and-pencil assignments.
- Encourage study techniques that involve movement— e.g., to memorize math facts, spread flash cards on the ground, bounce a ball on a card, then shoot a basket while reciting the fact. Any activity involving hopping, jumping, skipping, running, or dancing is great.
- Play board games or computer games to teach or reinforce any subject matter, including history, geography, science, math, or a foreign language. Or make up your own game!
- Help the student to put on a skit or demonstration to show understanding of the material when studying for a test; suggest the student act like a reporter and tape the

lesson, then play it back; have the student set the information to a familiar song and sing it.
- Relate the lesson to a "real-life" situation when possible; for example, the math equation $3 \times 5 =$ _____ is like knowing five people and having to get each of them three presents, so how many total presents do you have to buy?
- Ask the teacher to allow skits or demonstrations in place of written reports.

 MOTIVATORS

Performing people are motivated when they are acknowledged for being fun, witty, clever, and bringing enjoyment to others. They are also highly motivated by the chance to have free time, by the opportunity to choose their activities, and by being allowed to entertain.

QUICK REFERENCE CHART—PERFORMING DISPOSITION

Note: Sources for the resources listed below can be found in Appendix II.

PROGRAM EMPHASIS: MOVE

PREFERRED ACTIVITIES: skits, shows, demos, games, audiovisuals, sports, "real-life" experiences

HELPFUL MATERIALS

Math
- Can Do Videotapes (exercise with math facts) (5 yrs. to 11 or 12 yrs.)
- Wonder Number Game (5 yrs. to adult)
- S'Math (5 yrs. to adult)
- Math Trivial Pursuit (Primary: Grades 1 to 3; Intermediate: Grades 4 to 6)
- On Cloud Nine (5 yrs. to adult)
- Touch Math (5 yrs. to 12 or 13 yrs.)
- Large walk-on number mats or clocks (store-bought or homemade, 5 yrs. to 9 or 10 yrs.)
- Math computer games (all ages)

Read/Spell
- Sing/Spell/Read/Write (5 yrs. to 8 or 9 yrs.)
- Phonics Tutor (computer program, 5 yrs. to adult)
- Play N Talk (5 yrs. to adult)
- AVKO (5 yrs. to adult)
- Wilson Reading Program (5 yrs. to adult)
- Computer games (all ages)
- Star Trek Series, The Great Series (sixth grade up)

Write
- What to Do When They Don't Get It (information mapping, all ages)
- Computer games (all ages)

Other Subjects
- Large walk-on maps (store-bought or homemade, 5 yrs. to adult)
- Presidential Card Game, Geography Rummy (at educational supply stores)
- GeoSafari (for many subjects, 8 yrs. and up)
- Science Trivial Pursuit (primary, intermediate, junior high)
- Lyrical Life Science (9 yrs. to 15 yrs.)
- Board games, card games, computer games (all ages)

(continues)

(continued)

TEACHING TECHNIQUES

- Bouncing ball on flash cards, then shooting baskets or running bases, or adaptations of other sports
- Rhythmic activities such as hopping, jumping, and skipping while reciting/memorizing
- Jokes, rhymes, riddles
- Movie script, play script, music video
- Poster, scale model, totem pole
- Videotaping, audio-taping, slide show, puppet show
- Singing, dancing, song lyrics
- Timeline, chart, scrapbook
- Acting out, pantomime

The Producing Disposition: Organize

To get along best with Producing people, it is important to acknowledge their needs for order and efficiency.

People with Producing Dispositions fill the ranks of business, from secretaries to accountants to management. They strive to keep society organized and efficient. They get things done on schedule and on budget. Often, the more expectations they are trying to meet and fulfill, the greater the challenge and the more fun.

The traditional school system rewards children with Producing Dispositions. Classrooms, for the most part, are arranged for children who are well-practiced or naturally gifted in the Producing skills. Because their lessons are turned in on time, neatly written, with the proper headings and margins, and they don't mind sitting in one place for long periods of time, children with Producing Dispositions are a joy for teachers to have in class. From the information I've gathered by using the Learning Style Profile with students for the last ten years, I have found that children with the Producing Disposition comprise between 8% and 16% of a regular classroom—or roughly, three to six students out of thirty-five. These kids thrive on planning, organizing, and scheduling. These are the children many parents wish they had! Of course, many other children cooperate in the classroom, get work in on time, and strive to meet the standards of the teacher; however, students with Producing Dispositions seem to have an internal need to complete tasks once they've been assigned. In fact, in many cases the joy is not in the subject, but in finishing the work and crossing it off the "list."

> **They get things done on schedule and on budget.**

Children who demonstrate a Producing Disposition at school may not do so at home. A secondary Disposition may take over at home—before and after school. Those children who continue Producing behaviors at home as well as at school are often a delight to parents.

Producing is perhaps the most valued, most necessary disposition in our society. Producing skills are required to carry any project through to completion; therefore, most of us develop some Producing skills whether we want to or not. In fact, some adults who are *not* Producing people by nature score high in Producing Disposition. For these people, the Producing skills are so deeply ingrained in them by the time they are adults, that they automatically make Producing Disposition responses on the Profile. In this case, it is important to look very carefully at the secondary disposition—the second highest score—for deeper insight into disposition. Some people believe so strongly that they "should" be excellent in Producing skills, that they also score a false high in this category. These people need to pay attention to their secondary score as well. Occasionally a child will score a false high in Producing Disposition, because she is surrounded by people who value these skills and she wants to please them.

> " *At the end of each week, take your calendar and plan the following week. I plan out the next week and month in advance at the same sitting.*
>
> —*Patricia Fripp* "

The Producing Disposition is best described by the word "organize." The underlying objective of this style is to have order and to be efficient.

 ## LEARNING CHARACTERISTICS

Producing people prefer subjects and activities that are structured by nature; have sequential, ordered components; offer routine and drill; and give opportunity to take notes and be organized. They learn best when the teaching materials and techniques used are logical and sequential, allow the use of workbooks, and involve planning, scheduling, and due dates.

 ## PREFERRED SETTING

Producing people need quiet spaces that offer routine and orderliness. They thrive in atmospheres that are consistent, secure, and predictable. They love schedules, lists, and planning ahead.

 ## CONTRIBUTIONS

Producing people bring routine, order, and procedures to a situation. They can be focused, thorough, diligent, and very responsible. They contribute a sense of structure, tradition, continuity, and the importance of customs and following the rules. Avoiding waste in all forms is also an important aspect of this disposition.

> **Producing is perhaps the most valued, most necessary disposition in our society.**

 ## AREAS FOR GROWTH

You might be thinking that you don't know any kids who are like this! That's because there are only about 3 out of 35 in a typical classroom. But they definitely exist and I have met many. In fact, parents and teachers who don't themselves have the Producing Disposition often report that these kids "drive them crazy" with their needs for order and keeping to a schedule.

Producing people usually have little interest in "wasting time" meditating on nature, experimenting and exploring, or talking things out. They have a hard time breaking their routine or changing plans just to have fun or help someone out. They feel a strong need to be on time, honor commitments, and be responsible, often choosing the "rules" or the schedule over "people" issues. Becoming more flexible or taking time to relax might be listed under Areas for Growth on the Plan form. For example, a child who spends hours on homework with no break can learn to take short stretch breaks or a five-minute walk because this is a healthy behavior to encourage.

 The enlightened time manager allots time for every aspect of his life. He even allots time for drifting, by scheduling time to do nothing.

—Jim Rohn

RELATIONSHIP CONFLICTS

People with a Producing Disposition are often discounted for their desire to organize and keep things running smoothly. Whereas other dispositions may see them as rigid and controlling, they believe that their intentions to keep order are misunderstood. Often, these children have an unusual problem: Their organizing skills are held up as the standard to siblings and classmates, making them targets of resentment or jealousy. It is important to help these children learn how to be flexible in various situations without giving up their need for Producing behaviors.

IDEAL CURRICULUM

Classifying living things, diagramming sentences, and learning to alphabetize are examples of subjects that are structured by nature and have sequential, ordered components. Workbooks and worksheets are examples of materials that offer routine and drill. Developing timelines and outlines are examples of activities that involve logical arrangement and organization. Multiple-choice tests and fill-in-the-blank questions are examples of techniques that provide opportunities for note-taking and memorizing. Some of the traditional methods used in classrooms such as book reports and research papers work well because they involve due dates, planning, and scheduling of time.

> *" I remember as a little girl making daily schedules for summer vacation. Of course, my brother would never follow them and I was quite distraught—how could anyone not see the value of keeping to an efficient schedule? I didn't learn this from my parents—it was something I started doing intuitively as soon as I began to write at age 5.*
>
> *—Mariaemma Pelullo-Willis* "

These students enjoy activities that allow them to define, identify, label, list, locate, name, recall, spell, tell, underline, fill in the blank, describe, interpret, put in order, paraphrase, summarize, apply, analyze, categorize, classify, compare, determine the factors, diagram, differentiate, dissect, distinguish, choose, decide, prioritize, and rank.

HOMEWORK HELPS

- Provide a quiet space away from disorder or chaos.
- Allow the student to have a consistent routine for homework, including a scheduled time.
- Praise the student for being organized, neat, and punctual.
- Help the student memorize by being available to practice with flash cards or listen to the student recite.
- Remind the student to highlight information in textbooks (if allowed to mark the books) or to outline or use information mapping (discussed in Chapter 7) when studying for tests.
- An open-classroom type of setting might be too chaotic for this student. Ask the teacher to allow the student

to have a routine, or place the student in a more structured classroom setting.

- Many of the materials listed in the Reference Charts for other Dispositions will work fine for this learner, as long as private, "work alone with my books" time is also provided.

- It is easy to take this learner for granted and provide only workbook-type activities. As long as a lesson is organized and sequential, adding some fun can enhance learning for this child.

- Involve this learner in methods and materials that add a creative dimension and broaden the learning experience. This learner needs a break from the routine and rote assignments, just as much as the other learners.

MOTIVATORS

Producing people are motivated when they are acknowledged for being organized, neat, productive, efficient, and punctual. They are also highly motivated by the chance to set goals, by personal approval, and by "good job" comments, stickers on papers, and grades.

QUICK REFERENCE CHART—PRODUCING DISPOSITION

Note: Sources for the resources listed below can be found in Appendix II.

PROGRAM EMPHASIS: ORGANIZE

PREFERRED ACTIVITIES: schedules, outlines, workbooks, reading, writing, portfolios

HELPFUL MATERIALS
Math
- Any organized, sequential program
- Workbooks
- Key Curriculum (10 or 11 yrs. to adult, fractions to geometry)
- Mastering Mathematics (by topic not grade level)

Reading/Spelling
- Sing/Spell/Read/Write, Play N Talk, Phonics In Song

Write
- Workbooks
- Daily Grams (8 yrs. to 12 or 13 yrs.)
- What to Do When They Don't Get It (information mapping, all ages)

Other Subjects
- Super Workbooks (all age levels)
- Portfolio Assessments (all ages)
- Historical TimeLine (all ages)
- Computer programs that are organized and sequential

TEACHING TECHNIQUES
- Keeping calendars, schedules, due dates
- Portfolios, scrapbooks, photo albums
- Flowcharts, family trees, timelines
- Contracts, petitions, statement of rights
- Rules of order, etiquette, etc.
- Research paper, graph, outline
- Resume, brochure, recipe

The Inventing Disposition: Discover

To get along best with Inventing people, it is important to ac-knowledge their needs for intellectual stimulation, competence, and a chance to make a practical contribution.

Who are the famous inventors you know? I think of Johann Gutenberg, Thomas Edison, Wilbur and Orville Wright, Madam Curie, Henry Ford, Richard Feynman, and, more re-cently, Bill Gates. What is it that all inventors have in common? Their focus is on their inventions. Nothing matters to them as much as the project they're working on. Meals don't matter. Doing chores doesn't matter. Getting to soccer practice on time doesn't matter.

People with an Inventing Disposition prefer subjects or ac-tivities that allow experimentation. To a person with an Inventing Disposition, nothing is quite so compelling as a mechanical prob-lem that could be solved in a creative way. Getting the job done quickly is not important. Getting the job done efficiently is not important. Above all, the aesthetics of the device, structure, or creation are not important. It doesn't have to look good. What is important is that it works in a unique way. People with Inventing

Dispositions will spend long periods of time reading or surfing the Internet for ideas and theories that shed light on practical problems that interest them. Even if these people don't enjoy reading, the desire to know more and to find a solution is often stronger than their aversion to books in general.

 Thomas Edison's teachers said he was too stupid to learn anything.

Not all Inventing people become famous or create marketable innovations. Most Inventing people apply the skills of this disposition to everyday life situations—figuring out how to get the window to stay propped up, transforming an old recipe into a new dish, running the computer wire so that it doesn't show, setting up the dog dishes for continuous feeding, and so on. Inventing people love to have unlimited time to do whatever it is they need to get their ideas to work. Because they get so focused and involved in their projects, they often lose track of time and are late for or completely miss appointments.

As a rule, Inventing people enjoy brainstorming and debating, if they can do it with "sharp" people who are knowledgeable about the topic being discussed. However, once they are absorbed in their exploration or project, they often are not inclined to interact and view talking as a waste of time. They often prefer working independently rather than in groups.

> **B**ecause they get so focused and involved in their projects, they often lose track of time and are late for or completely miss appointments.

Inventing people sometimes view writing as a waste of time. They just can't understand why someone would take the time to write a report on something that has already been written. If you need information about satellites, for instance, you go find books about satellites, look up what you need, and apply it in a practical way to what you are working on. From their point of view there is no need to write the old information all over again—they could be spending that time doing something more worthwhile, like creating something new or finding the solution to a problem.

 Orville Wright was expelled from the sixth grade for bad behavior.

As children, these people are very inquisitive and the adults around them are often annoyed at the number of questions that they ask. This is the child who is told in class to stop asking so many questions and just listen. Sometimes this child seems to ask questions that have nothing to do with the lesson, which makes matters worse, because the teacher thinks that he is not paying attention. In reality, the child *was* paying attention, which is what stimulated the questions in the first place, triggering new ideas and, perhaps, earning him the label of ADD. In other cases, adults become exasperated because they don't know the answers to the questions, and classmates are irritated because they view this child as a nerd or a know-it-all.

The Inventing Disposition is best described by the word "discover." The underlying objective of this style is to be smart and competent.

 ## LEARNING CHARACTERISTICS

Inventing people prefer subjects and activities that are experimental by nature, that provide inspiration and new solutions, and that give opportunities to question, design, and discover. They learn best when the teaching materials and techniques used are direct and offer "intellectual" ideas, theories, models, and time for exploration.

 ## PREFERRED SETTING

Inventing people need flexible spaces that provide room for labs, experiments, and models. They thrive in atmospheres that encourage questioning, exploring, debating, and unscheduled time to work independently.

 ## CONTRIBUTIONS

Inventing people bring innovation, enthusiasm for learning, and a sense of discovery to a situation. They have the ability to be independent and can speak directly and to the point. They contribute an interest in the sciences, technical know-how, and problem-solving skills.

 ## AREAS FOR GROWTH

Inventing people can have little interest in being playful or in spending time talking or "relating." They easily forget appointments and often spoil other people's plans, because they get lost in projects and lose their sense of time (much like the absent-minded professor in the movie of that name, more recently remade as *Flubber*). They can be quite serious and focused, yet lack skill in organizing and planning. Being on time or spending time with a sibling might be listed under Areas for Growth on the Plan form. For example, a child could learn to set a timer to remind her to stop building with the Legos and get ready for the 4-H meeting.

 ## RELATIONSHIP CONFLICTS

People with a strong Inventing Disposition are often discounted for their technical know-how and problem-solving skill. They believe that their intentions to discover and "make things better" are misunderstood. Other dispositions can see them as too serious, unfeeling, disorganized, and possibly workaholic. When this disposition is not acknowledged for its positive contributions, these children doubt their intelligence and feel discouraged. They seek validation in their discoveries and could become lon-

Benjamin Franklin only went to school from age eight to age ten.

ers, growing up to become adults who have trouble relating to others. It is important that these children learn interaction and organizational skills, so that they can integrate their Inventing Dispositions into their daily lives.

 ## IDEAL CURRICULUM

Engineering, electronics, architectural designing, and the sciences are subjects that are experimental by nature and give plenty of opportunity to question, design, and discover. Doing experiments or constructing theoretical models are examples of techniques that inspire exploration and new approaches to old problems. Independent projects and "intellectual" debates are examples of activities that tap these students' problem-solving skills.

As students these people are likely to enjoy activities that allow them to apply, compute, conclude, construct, demonstrate, determine, draw out, give examples, illustrate, make, operate, show, solve, state a rule or principle, analyze, categorize, classify, compare, contrast, debate, diagnose, diagram, differentiate, dissect, distinguish, examine, specify, change, compose, create, design, find an unusual way, formulate, generate, invent, originate, plan, predict, pretend, produce, reconstruct, reorganize, revise, suggest, support, visualize, write, juxtapose, combine, and analogize.

 ## HOMEWORK HELPS

- Engage the student in a debate on the subject being studied.
- Encourage study techniques that involve drawing or constructing a model—this could be as simple as information mapping (see Chapter 7).

- Provide computer programs to teach or reinforce a subject.
- Have brainstorming sessions; "collect" and "classify" the information.
- Provide hands-on models or visual representations (videos, CD-ROMs) whenever possible for the subjects being studied.
- Ask the teacher to allow projects in place of written reports.

MOTIVATORS

Inventing people are motivated when they are acknowledged for being clever and smart, for making discoveries, and for solving problems. It is also highly motivating for them when people actually put to use their contributions, inventions, and technical know-how.

QUICK REFERENCE CHART—INVENTING DISPOSITION

Note: Sources for the resources listed below can be found in Appendix II.

PROGRAM EMPHASIS: Discover

PREFERRED ACTIVITIES: projects, portfolios, debates, brainstorming, computers, "labs"

HELPFUL MATERIALS
Math
  - Abacus Math (4 yrs. to 10 or 11 yrs.)
  - Math Shop or Math Strategies computer programs (all ages)
  - About Teaching Math, Family Math (all ages)
  - Computer programs (all ages)

Reading/Spelling
  - Wilson Reading Program (5 yrs. to adult)
  - AVKO (5 yrs. to adult)
  - Star Trek Series, The Great Series (sixth grade up)

Write
  - What to Do When They Don't Get It (information mapping, all ages)

Other Subjects
  - Portfolio Assessment (all ages)
  - Backyard Scientist (4 yrs. to 14 yrs.)
  - Historical TimeLine (all ages)
  - Switch On Electronic Circuit Kit (8 yrs. to 13 or 14 yrs.)
  - Science Trivial Pursuit (primary, intermediate, junior high)
  - Janice Van Cleave's Spectacular Science Projects (8 yrs. to 12 yrs.)
  - Science by Mail (grades 4 to 9)
  - What About Series (grades 1 to 4)
  - Dorling Kindersley and Usborne materials (all ages)
  - Computer programs for any subject (all ages)

TEACHING TECHNIQUES
  - Home or classroom "museum"
  - Museum exhibit
  - Relief map, diorama, terrarium
  - Survey, current-events report
  - Time capsule, portfolios
  - Scientific instruments, experiments
  - Computer programming
  - Electronics repair, auto mechanics
  - Blueprints, schematic diagrams, drafting

The Relating/Inspiring Disposition: Interact

To get along best with Relating/Inspiring people, it is important to acknowledge their need to contribute to the well-being of others.

Mahatma Gandhi, Martin Luther King, and Mother Teresa all had Relating/Inspiring Dispositions. The foundational desire of a person with a Relating/Inspiring Disposition is to create the greatest good for the most people. In their unrelenting need to see that others are treated fairly, they can become an inspiration to schools, communities, and nations. In addition to the world-famous people listed above, Relating/Inspiring people often choose to work as benefactors, sponsors, nurses, teachers, and counselors. Known for having "heart," many of these people are not happy unless they are creating opportunities for others or creating harmony where there has previously been discord. Relating/Inspiring people sometimes neglect their own families and friends because they are so busy taking care of others.

Children with strong Relating/Inspiring Dispositions are chatty. They often know the latest news and/or gossip. In class, they pass notes and talk when they're supposed to be working. At home, they spend lots of time on the telephone, and sometimes,

99

with their need to keep in contact with their friends, stress a household so much that they are given their own phone. Emotions run high among these young people. They are perceptive and sensitive to the feelings of others and readily offer compassion. They are also sensitive to their own feelings, and their spirits can be easily dashed by friends who want to play with somebody else for a while. From a parent's perspective it often seems that friends are too important to these kids. But without friends these Relating/Inspiring kids lose their sense of purpose and meaning.

> **K**nown for having "heart," many of these people are not happy unless they are creating opportunities for others or creating harmony where there has previously been discord.

A Relating/Inspiring person can very easily neglect his own needs. Because this person values teamwork, "class spirit," and emotionally supportive environments, he can easily be taken advantage of and can find himself saying "yes" to helping out on numerous committees and projects. Sometimes, this disposition becomes too dependent upon others for support. This person can have hurt feelings and become discouraged if he is not recognized for his kindness and goodwill.

The Relating/Inspiring Disposition is best described by the word "interact." The underlying objective of this style is to be caring, to treat others as special and to be treated as special in return.

LEARNING CHARACTERISTICS

Relating/Inspiring people prefer subjects and activities that are social by nature, involve human-behavior issues, incorporate personal feelings, and give plenty of opportunity to interact. They learn best when the teaching materials and techniques used offer individualization, involve small groups, and allow cooperative interaction.

PREFERRED SETTING

Relating/Inspiring people need small group spaces that provide room to talk and discuss. They thrive in atmospheres that are interactive, cooperative, and fair. They love personal attention and focus on fairness, values, and team spirit.

 CONTRIBUTIONS

Relating/Inspiring people bring harmony, cooperation, and sensitivity to a situation. They can be kind, fair, and thoughtful. They contribute a sense of teamwork and emotional support.

 AREAS FOR GROWTH

Relating/Inspiring people usually have little interest in working independently, in "wasting" time on relaxing quietly, or in subjects that lack a human connection—such as math and most sciences. They are attracted to people who are in trouble or need to discuss a problem. They can easily become sidetracked by someone who needs help, and can end up disappointing family and friends who are counting on them. They are sometimes late for appointments because something more important inevitably comes up that requires their attention. Learning to work independently for short periods of time might be listed under Areas for Growth on the Plan form. For example, a child could learn to set a timer and challenge himself to finish a certain amount of work during that period.

> *What I want in my life is compassion, a flow between myself and others based on a mutual giving from the heart.*
> —*Marshall B. Rosenberg*

RELATIONSHIP CONFLICTS

Relating/Inspiring people are often discounted as being overly sensitive for their desire to be helpful to others or the world. Because some are active in causes they strongly believe in, they are often attacked politically. They believe that their intentions to foster cooperation and harmony are misunderstood. Sometimes they are viewed as too talkative, too focused on causes, and too sensitive. When this disposition is not acknowledged for its strengths, these children become less likely to learn independent skills and more likely to rely on someone else's approval or a "pat on the back." It is important that these children learn how to find value in themselves independently from others, without giving up their need for Relating/Inspiring behaviors.

> *. . . it is our nature to enjoy giving and receiving in a compassionate manner.*
> —Marshall B. Rosenberg

IDEAL CURRICULUM

Journalism, psychology, counseling, and speech are examples of subjects that are social by nature and give plenty of opportunity to talk and discuss. Learning history through stories about people, conducting interviews for research, and corresponding with pen pals to develop writing skills are examples of techniques that look at human behavior issues and provide a personal touch. Working on cooperative projects and having group discussions are examples of activities that allow time to relate and offer the chance to develop team spirit.

> *The best minute I spend is the one I invest in people.*
> —Kenneth Blanchard, Ph.D., and Spencer Johnson, M.D.

These people enjoy many kinds of activities as long as they can be done with others. They are likely to enjoy activities that give examples, compare, debate, diagnose, differentiate, distinguish, suggest, support, defend, justify, select, give opinions, reorganize, visualize.

HOMEWORK HELPS

- Recognize the student's need to discuss and talk through the lesson.
- Encourage study techniques that involve relating, studying with another person, alternating reading aloud to each other, discussing the meaning of the lesson.
- Pretend the student is involved in the subject being studied—if she were Madame Curie why would she have become a scientist, if she had been a Pilgrim how would she have felt in the New World?
- Encourage the student to do oral presentations to an imaginary audience when studying for a test—it is his job to convince the audience of the importance of the information.
- Relate lessons to social events—e.g. if the child is doing addition problems, pretend the numbers relate to giving a party: Three people said they were coming to the party, then two more came, how many came altogether?
- Ask the teacher to allow small-group interaction, working with a partner on cooperative projects or writing assignments, more discussion time, and taped "interviews" or oral presentations in place of written reports.

> **Relating/Inspiring people are motivated when they are acknowledged for noticing others and for being kind, fair, thoughtful, and considerate.**

 ## MOTIVATORS

Relating/Inspiring people are motivated when they are acknowledged for noticing others and for being kind, fair, thoughtful, and considerate. They are also highly motivated by the chance to talk, getting a personal note or pat on the back, and receiving personal attention.

QUICK REFERENCE CHART— RELATING/INSPIRING DISPOSITION

Note: Sources for the resources listed below can be found in Appendix II.

PROGRAM EMPHASIS: INTERACT

PREFERRED ACTIVITIES: group projects, people stories, family trees, discussion

HELPFUL MATERIALS

Math
- Can Do Videotapes (5 yrs. to 12 or 13 yrs.)
- Family Math (all ages)
- Real Life Math Mysteries (grades 3 to 12)

Reading/Spelling
- Sing/Spell/Read/Write (5 yrs. to 8 or 9 yrs.)
- The Great Series (sixth grade up, high-interest, easy reading)
- Pen Pal Newsletter (elementary)

Write
- What to Do When They Don't Get It (information mapping, all ages)
- Studentreasures™ ("publish" own book, grades 3 to 8)

Other Subjects
- Historical TimeLine Figures (all ages)
- Family History Project (11 yrs. to adult)
- What Do You Think? (kids' guide to daily dilemmas, elementary to junior high)

TEACHING TECHNIQUES
- biography, autobiography
- editorial, proposal, petition, statement of rights
- oral history, family tree
- journal, memoir, timeline
- photo album, scrapbook
- eulogy, last will and testament
- news story, children's book
- current events report, time capsule
- story, fable, parable, survey

The Thinking/Creating Disposition: Create

To get along best with Thinking/Creating people, it is important to acknowledge their need to contribute new ideas.

Thinking/Creating people have some characteristics in common with Inventing people; however, practical application of their work for concrete, realistic uses is not generally important to them. Thinking/Creating people want to contribute at another level—one that uses real-life issues and concerns as the basis for their inspirational or thought-provoking works. Some may want to inspire, some may want to instruct, and some may want to describe. They can spend a great deal of time in deep thought and contemplating abstract ideas such as space, time, meaning, or purpose, and the relationships among people and/or things. Theirs is a world of ideas and the expression of those ideas through formulas, solutions to philosophical problems, and works of art—paintings, drawings, sculpture, poetry, essays, music, plays, and dance.

Thinking/Creating people who find expression in philosophy, mathematics, and sciences tend to function best in the realm of pure philosophy, math, or science. They thrive on abstraction. Their products are formulas and theories. People with an Inventing bent often take on the task of applying the Thinking/Creating person's work to find solutions to actual ecological, social, educational, political, or biological problems and goals.

> **T**he Thinking/Creating child is often quiet in the classroom. Absorbed in thought, she may be jolted back to classroom activity when the teacher calls on her to answer a question.

Albert Einstein, Pablo Picasso, Diego Rivera, Stephen Hawking, Alvin Ailey, Emily Dickinson, Ralph Waldo Emerson, Henry David Thoreau, and Maya Angelou are examples of Thinking/Creating people.

The Thinking/Creating child is often quiet in the classroom. Absorbed in thought, she may be jolted back to classroom activity when the teacher calls on her to answer a question. She might doodle or look out the window with a glazed stare while the teacher is talking. The customary accusation is "You aren't paying attention." These children usually don't make waves in the classroom. They are able to entertain themselves for long periods of time and give the impression that they are appropriately busy often enough to be left alone. Some are seen as withdrawn or shy. Others enjoy the stimulation of trying out their ideas on the teacher and arguing their point.

 The sculptor Rodin's father said his son was an idiot, and his uncle called him uneducable.

Parents sometimes worry about Thinking/Creating children. The question I hear most is "Is it normal for a child to spend so much time playing alone?" Some of these children have an intricately developed fantasy life that seems excessive to a parent. "Is it good for a child to spend so much time disconnected from reality?" is another question that comes up frequently. Deep interests, long attention span for specific things, and a rich fantasy life are normal characteristics of Thinking/Creating children. Because of this they are often labeled ADD. (See Chapter 13 for more information on this.)

The Thinking/Creating Disposition is best described by the word "create." The underlying objective of this style is to contribute new ideas or to help others see things in a new way.

 ## LEARNING CHARACTERISTICS

Thinking/Creating people prefer subjects and activities that are creative by nature, have artistic or philosophical aspects, offer beauty and aesthetics, provide artistic expression, and give plenty of opportunity to wonder, think, and dream. They learn best when the teaching materials and techniques used allow for time alone and involve arts and/or the creative process.

 ## PREFERRED SETTING

Thinking/Creating people need spaces that allow them to "escape"—to design, create, compose, formulate, or think. They thrive in atmospheres that encourage openness and wonderment and allow for unscheduled time to doodle or daydream. Some appreciate opportunities to enjoy art, have an intellectual discussion, or read literature.

 ## CONTRIBUTIONS

Thinking/Creating people bring creativity and a sense of beauty and openness to a situation. They can be imaginative, observant, and philosophical. They contribute an appreciation for wondering, imagining, composing, formulating, and for aesthetics and the arts.

 ## AREAS FOR GROWTH

Thinking/Creating people usually have little interest in strict schedules, interacting in groups, or completing projects. They may forget appointments if they are involved in a creative project. They can get lost in daydreaming or become so focused on their work

Beethoven's teacher said he was hopeless as a composer.

that they ignore the people around them. Relationships suffer when their actions are interpreted as moody or inconsiderate of others' plans and feelings. Learning to keep a schedule or plan ahead could be listed under Areas for Growth on the Plan form. Making picture charts and discussing the value of tasks are ways of making things more meaningful for this child.

RELATIONSHIP CONFLICTS

People with the Thinking/Creating Disposition are often discounted for their desire to be imaginative or philosophical. They believe that their intentions to contribute new ideas are misunderstood because others view them as illogical, aloof, spacy, and irresponsible. When this Disposition is not acknowledged for its positive contributions, these children can become depressed and become reclusive. They have a tendency to create their own world and can shun interactions with others. As adults, unless they have a strong secondary Relating/Inspiring or Performing Disposition, these people might keep to themselves to avoid risking rejection. It is important that these children learn interaction skills so that they are able to integrate their Thinking/Creating Disposition into their daily lives.

IDEAL CURRICULUM

Literature, poetry, art, and drama are examples of subjects that are creative by nature and give plenty of opportunity to wonder, think, and express oneself imaginatively. Drawing pictures to understand a math concept or writing a poem to remember history facts are examples of techniques that allow creative expression. Listening to music while reading, doodling while listening to a presentation, or doing assignments in a quiet spot surrounded by nature are examples of activities that support the need for aesthetics and beauty.

These people are likely to enjoy activities that require them to compose, construct, design, find an unusual way, formulate, generate, invent, originate, visualize, write creatively/imaginatively, juxtapose, combine, analogize, diverge, create.

HOMEWORK HELPS

- Encourage drawing and doodling during study times.
- Experiment with different types of music in the background when studying for tests—Baroque is especially good for helping some children focus.
- Provide time and space for quiet, alone time.
- Encourage the student to draw pictures or write a poem to understand a concept or summarize a lesson or book; suggest writing a song or setting the information to a familiar melody.
- Encourage information mapping with pictures (see Chapter 7) when studying for tests or to make information more understandable and manageable when reading chapters on any subject.
- Ask the teacher to allow posters, collages, poems, or other artistic presentations in place of written reports.

MOTIVATORS

Thinking/Creating people are motivated when they are acknowledged for being creative, artistic, open, and observant. They are also highly motivated by the chance to work on creative projects, the opportunity to have alone time, and having their work displayed or recognized in some way.

QUICK REFERENCE CHART— THINKING/CREATING DISPOSITION

Note: Sources for the resources listed below can be found in Appendix II.

PROGRAM EMPHASIS: CREATE

PREFERRED ACTIVITIES: art, music, composing, imagining, wondering, thinking

HELPFUL MATERIALS

Math
- Abacus Math (4 yrs. to 10 or 11 yrs.)
- It's Alive and Kicking (grades 3 to 9)

Reading/Spelling
- Drawing with Letters and Numbers (elementary grades)
- Draw Write Now (6 yrs. to 8 yrs.)
- Sing/Spell/Read/Write (5 yrs. to 8 or 9 yrs.)
- AVKO (5 yrs. to adult)

Write
- What to Do When They Don't Get It (information mapping, all ages)
- Studentreasures™ (publish own book, grades 3 to 8)

Other Subjects
- History Through Art (CD ROM program, all ages)
- Art with Children (elementary grades)
- Color the Classics (composers, 8 yrs. to 10 or 11 yrs.)
- Build a Doodle (5 yrs. to 9 or 10 yrs.)
- New Each Day or Audio Memory cassettes (songs about grammar, geography, etc; elementary grades)
- Portfolio Assessment (all ages)
- Coloring Book series: anatomy, zoology, biology, botany, etc. (high school and college)
- books and programs on art, nature, poetry, music

TEACHING TECHNIQUES
- essay, fable, parable, poetry
- myth, biography, autobiography
- collage, mural, mosaic
- diorama, shadow box
- musical instrument, songs
- painting, drawing, sculpture
- journal, memoir, timeline
- puzzle, brainteaser, riddle
- research paper, survey
- scale model, scientific instruments

Talents:
Our Natural Gifts

Talents are often taken for granted. Each of us has a specific combination of them. It is never more obvious just how varied these talents are from person to person than when your spouse, who loves to dance, wants to take ballroom-dancing lessons, and you are "rhythmically challenged" and don't enjoy dancing at all, or when a group you belong to votes to have a sing-a-long, and you never could carry a tune. At school our children face a daily round of similar challenges as they move from subject to subject or class to class with varying degrees of support from their talents. English class might be a chance for your child to shine, but math causes heart palpitations and sweaty palms. Although talents are largely inherited, they can also be developed through consistent training. You may have heard the saying, "Success is 10% inspiration and 90% perspiration." For example, some incredibly gifted people have no interest in developing their talent for music to a recognizable level of success, and then there are other incredibly hardworking people with little music talent who become very successful.

Talents show up as skill and ease in learning a subject, or even disinterest and boredom when a subject is too easy. Some

> " *One of the greatest gifts is the ability to encourage others and help them develop their talent. Teachers we remember with gratitude have this wonderful quality.*
> —Christopher News Notes "

disinterested, bored kids are labeled "gifted" and thrive in classes that are especially designed to be challenging for them. Other bored young people who don't fit the "gifted" label drop out of school and steer by their own wits. Many of these kids are gifted for art, humor, performance, or other abilities that are more difficult to provide for in classrooms.

Talents, as much as we appreciate them, are often misunderstood and mishandled by well-meaning adults. Parents can block the growth of talents in two ways: 1) by *forcing* children to pursue talents that the parents observe or 2) by *failing to encourage* a talent that a child is interested in developing.

 ## WHOSE TALENT IS IT ANYWAY?

Parents often encourage the development of a child's talents with unusual zeal and personal self-sacrifice. Even when a child has lost interest in soccer, or ballet, or piano, a parent will insist that the child attend lessons and continue to practice. You might be one of those moms, like several I know, who spends twenty or more hours a week hauling kids from one activity to another. If the kids are doing things they truly enjoy, I can see the point. However, what is the purpose of cajoling children to pursue talents they aren't interested in? Parents tell me that when the child is an adult he will be grateful for the consistent urging they provided. This reminds me of "two-wrongs-make-a-right" reasoning. It doesn't make sense. Years of pain and nagging will possibly have a pleasant outcome in a nonspecific, remote future?

Nagging and preaching to your child about fulfilling a talent she is not interested in falls on deaf ears most of the time;

young people are primarily interest-driven, not talent-driven. (Interests will be talked about at length in the next chapter.)

"What if my child has been studying clarinet for two years and wants to discontinue the lessons?" you might be wondering. "Won't it be a great loss to stop now, just when he could really start to learn something?" More harm than good will be done in the long run if you decide to enforce your will on your child, and you can be sure that you are asking for a daily power struggle in the short run. Are you sure that you want to do this to yourself or to your child? No wonder parents feel overburdened and burned out. If you are in this situation, ask yourself why *you* want this for your child.

YOU WANT TO BE WHAT?

Not giving encouragement to a child's desire to pursue a talent is a problem of a different kind. It is, however, as much of a mistake not to encourage talents as it is to encourage them for your own reasons.

What if you have a child, like one of my students, who is incredibly gifted in skiing and wants to prepare for the Olympics? If your expectation as parent is that your daughter *should* do all her homework, get excellent grades, and have a "normal" social life, at the same time that she is preparing for the Olympics, you may be creating a roadblock for something that is important for your child to do. In a case like this, it might be more realistic to adjust your expectations to include your child's love for skiing.

> **It is, however, as much of a mistake not to encourage talents as it is to encourage them for your own reasons.**

Getting all A's may not be as important to your child as it is to you, and if you can be flexible, you may see your child blossom in unexpected ways.

Furthermore, children who are gifted in athletics and are in training usually don't have time to have a large group of friends; that can be *normal* for them. You will be greatly disappointed and frustrated if you hold fast to a desire for this Olympic hopeful to have a "normal" social life if your definition includes attending proms, football and basketball games, and going to movies with her friends. If homework takes up time that your daughter needs to be working out, you might want to make a plan that allows your child to do less homework. Consult with your child's teacher about this. Do you think that B's and C's are acceptable grades if a child is enthusiastically pursuing her talents? As stated earlier, "Don't let the bell curve define who your child is!"

If you find that you have difficulty changing your expectations to support your child's talents, hopes, dreams, and expectations for herself, it is important for you to look at the reason you need your child to behave in a particular way. Watch out for your "shoulds" and your ideas about the "right" ways to do things. If you find yourself using these words to your child or in your own self-talk, stop and sort out your thoughts. There is a gold mine here if you are willing to look carefully at why certain expectations are so important to you. Maybe some voices from your past are whispering in your ear that you "should" have done things differently, and now that you have a child you are trying to make certain that she does things the "right way."

 TWELVE TALENTS

Talents meet the following criteria: 1) they are done with ease, as if natural to the person; 2) without previous instruction, they put a child immediately "ahead" of others in a specific area of learning; 3) they remain dormant if not developed, but they are not lost if they aren't used; and 4) whether consciously developed and used or not, they have an underlying effect (for example, a talent for music gives a person's dancing a more rhythmic quality). Talents can be active or dormant. They can be known or unknown. In fact other people are often more aware of our talents than we are. Talents work closely with two other aspects of learning style: interests (see Chapter 7) and dispositions (see Chapter 5).

Many human attributes could be called talents. The Learning Style Profile includes twelve Talent areas. These are informal categories, observable to varying degrees in most people. The twelve talents identified for the purpose of this Profile are: Music, Math-Logic Reasoning, Mechanical Reasoning, Word-Language Reasoning, Spatial, Body Coordination, Interactive-Self, Interactive-Others, Interactive-Animals, Interactive-Nature, Humor, and Life Enhancement. You might be surprised at some of these categories. Perhaps you haven't thought of them as talents before. People are talented in many and varied ways and it is important to identify as many of these ways as possible. There are, no doubt, other talents that have not been included in this Profile. You are encouraged to notice your child's many unique gifts and to think of them as talents.

What is most surprising about talents is that we can be very gifted in a particular area and not have the least interest in it. The daughter of a good friend tests in the ninety-ninth percentile for math on standardized tests, and she hasn't any desire to study math. It isn't challenging enough to hold her interest. She prefers acting and dance, and that's what she's studying. Her parents have accepted her decision to study the "less practical" subjects and find that, as a result, not only is their daughter more content, but their relationship with her is closer.

Sometimes, a child is interested in and very happy developing a talent. In this case, the child's talent could lead to a particular life direction. If our schools were set up dif-

> **If our schools were set up differently, children would be allowed to begin their school lives guided by their talents.**

ferently, children would be allowed to begin their school lives guided by their talents. In other words, each child would be absorbed in developing the particular talent areas that he is *interested in*, and the other subjects would be integrated around these talent areas!

I am reminded of an eleven-year-old student who has a talent for baseball. All he wants to do is to watch, play, and think about baseball. He isn't interested in reading, writing, math, or history. Using an idea of Pastor Gregg Harris, a program was developed for him that builds skills in all of these areas by integrating educational goals with his talent for baseball. At first, biographies of famous players were read aloud to him. Later, he read them himself. He retold the stories to friends and relatives. He wrote letters to some of the living baseball heroes. He made a timeline of his favorite player's life and related it to national and world events. Using his collection of baseball cards he made a chart of statistics on various plays and compared and contrasted them—learning to figure averages, percentages, and ratios. As he followed his favorite team around the United States and the world, he learned about geography by putting pins in a large map of the world that had been put on the wall of his bedroom. The various kinds of pitches and their velocities brought physics to the foreground, and he made graphs and charts to explain these concepts.

> " A major premise of talent-oriented education is that all students deserve instruction and learning opportunities at a level and pace that are appropriate for their current development and talents.
>
> —John F. Feldhusen "

Without once referring to reading comprehension, arithmetic, science, history, or geography, as the above example shows, a child can sleuth for information energetically, share her surprise at what she finds, make inferences, draw conclusions, and find additional springboards for collecting even more information. Many of my homeschool students proceed through the school year in this manner—with great enthusiasm and commitment to the direction that their talents lead them.

Another approach to talents in the classroom is to use talent-based study stations. Two years ago I helped a kindergarten teacher set up such a curriculum for her class. The first month, students cycled through study stations for six of the twelve talents listed in this chapter. The second month, the six remaining talents were used as study stations. Content for the stations was changed weekly. One girl chose to stay in the Spatial Talent station most of the time. A boy was continually drawn back to the Music Talent station. Yet another boy was fascinated by the exercises at the Interactive-Self station and spent as much time as he could in it.

Many years ago I visited a model classroom for sixth graders in Washington state. It was set up with one work station for each of Howard Gardner's multiple intelligences, which are loosely similar to the talents listed in this book. The students cycled through each of the work stations on a regular basis. They were required to finish the work in each of them; however, they had ample time to tarry and pursue their own leads when they were so inclined. The teacher told me that he often received students who were discipline problems or below average in their performance. He also told me that after a few weeks in his class, it was impossible to identify the students with learning or social difficulties.

Talent-based learning stations guarantee that children will be exposed to a range of talents, and that they will learn new skills and can study in-depth when they are ready. In these situations it is impossible to determine who is smarter than whom, and disruptive behavior is minimized because children are allowed to move about, talk to each other, and work together. All students participate in their own learning process, at their own pace, and in their own way.

> **A talent could be the starting point toward helping a child to feel competent and confident.**

Besides pointing to possible career choices, talents can also be utilized to help your child experience learning-success at school. As you look at each of the twelve talents individually, you will learn ways of using your child's talents to help with schoolwork. But keep in mind that these talents are your child's special gifts. When a child is interested in a talent, remember to also acknowledge and encourage that talent for itself, apart from the school situation. A talent could be the starting point toward helping a child to feel competent and confident. Let's take the example of the eleven-year-old boy who has a talent for baseball again. Imagine that he is your son and that he doesn't like school, that he doesn't feel competent or confident there. If you are willing to support his talent and build upon it by using it as the basis for many different kinds of reading, writing, math, geography, and history activities, this child will begin to feel competent in an area of his life. With competence, his confidence is apt to grow, and the new skills and feelings of achievement are likely to transfer to school participation and performance.

The more aware you are of your child's talents, the easier it will be to think of ways of incorporating them to facilitate learning-success at school. The more you acknowledge and support the talents your child is interested in, the more open he will be to participating in activities which do not come naturally to him (at home or at school) when it is necessary to do so.

Music Talent

Music Talent shows itself as skill in playing instruments, singing, humming, whistling, listening to music, tapping out a rhythm, or memorizing songs. It can also show itself as having an ear for different types of music, different instruments, harmonies, and so on. In the teenage years, an ear for music can surface as an interest in collecting and listening to CDs and tapes.

To the detriment of our children, music is one of the subjects that has been cut from primary and elementary school curricula in many parts of the country. In Canada some school districts have passed a new law requiring all children to create an original composition in music in order to graduate from elementary school. In the United States, however, if music isn't part of the home, many children don't get a chance to uncover their Music Talent at all.

Composers, musicians, vocalists, conductors, arrangers, and lyricists all possess this talent.

Applications to Learning-Success

Musically Talented children can use music for learning in various ways. In general, people can memorize large quantities of information quickly and easily by setting it to song and singing it (this is how we all learned the alphabet, and some adults still need to sing it in order to recite it in correct order!). Preschools and kindergartens make frequent use of this technique. It has also been discovered that comprehension and retention can be greatly increased by reading material to the rhythm of a musical piece playing in the background. According to Chris Brewer and Don Campbell, authors of the book *Rhythms of Learning*, classical music seems to be the best and, in particular, Baroque music, because it has a pulse similar to the rhythm of the human heartbeat.[1]

While these methods seem to enhance learning for most people, they can become crucial for the musically talented child. At home, experiment with singing and reading to music. Ask your child's teacher to consider alternatives to written assignments, which might include composing a song to report on a topic, or doing a singing presentation of information to be memorized (for example, states and capitals, parts of speech, vocabulary word definitions, etc.). More ways of using music as a learning tool are discussed in Chapter 9.

Math-Logic Reasoning Talent

A person with a Math-Logic Reasoning Talent for *numbers* can do well in traditional educational settings. This child catches on quickly to mathematical patterns, easily memorizes facts and formulas, and is able to crank out worksheets and timed quizzes.

Some students, however, have a type of Math-Logic Reasoning Talent that allows them to troubleshoot computer problems, do logic puzzles, understand electrical circuitry, or understand the mathematical concepts of acceleration, angle, and thrust involved in passing a football or skateboarding. Many of these students don't do well with rote learning; they resist repetitive worksheets, have trouble memorizing math facts, and are inaccurate when working with numbers. A friend's husband, for example, can make incredible decimal calculations in his head, but he is not allowed to touch the checkbook because, inevitably, he makes a mistake when adding or subtracting. Unfortunately, the adults who work with these students incorrectly conclude that they are not "good at math," even though they are probably more competent in math than the kids scoring A's on the worksheets. These kids could be exploring complex math concepts if given the chance to work through their learning styles.

Scientists and mathematicians are among those who have a Math-Logic Reasoning Talent. Two people who come to mind are George Washington Carver and Albert Einstein. Math-logic reasoning is also involved in such skills as working with money, devising experiments, playing chess or checkers, and drafting-designing-building.

Applications to Learning-Success

The child who has a talent in math-logic reasoning, but who is not good with numbers, does better with "real-life" math problems than rote worksheets. To help this child with the mechanics of math (computation), use a program like *Touch Math* (information on this and other resources mentioned below can be found in Appendix II) and allow a calculator at home. Support your child's talent by doing fun math activities such as those found in the books *Family Math* and *About Teaching Math*. If your child enjoys working on the computer, purchase programs such as *Gizmos and Gadgets*, *How Things Work*, and *Sim City*, all of which explore geometry principles and other math concepts. Ask the teacher to consider allowing alternatives to the standard drill worksheet or workbook assignments, which permit the child to work on math by using his talent. For example, the teacher might accept work completed in *Touch Math*, printouts that document progress on computer programs, or evidence of a math project from *Family Math*.

Mechanical Reasoning Talent

Is there someone in your house who loves to fix things? Or maybe just loves taking them apart and putting them back together? Many of us wish for just this sort of person when the lawn mower won't start or the paper jams in the printer. A gift for mechanical reasoning is the driving force behind some people's mania for inventing, building things, and figuring out exactly how things work. Some people show their talent for mechanical reasoning by maintaining cars, computers, or appliances. Others can run every imaginable kind of machine as if they had been operating them for years.

David Macaulay, who wrote the children's book *The Way Things Work*, has a Mechanical Reasoning Talent and so do plumbers, electricians, builders, and machinery operators.

Applications to Learning-Success

Children who have a Mechanical Reasoning Talent are very rarely recognized and acknowledged as "smart" in the classroom. These kids are usually very hands-on and are strongest in the Tactile-Kinesthetic Modality (Modality is discussed in detail in Chapter 8). It is important that we praise this talent and allow a child to use it as often as possible. For example, suppose the topic in history is ancient civilizations. This is the child who would easily understand why the aqueducts worked the way they did and could do a demonstration project which she presents to the class. Through this project she would learn other details about the time period that she probably would not process from simply reading the textbook or hearing a lecture. She would feel competent and acknowledged by her teacher and peers. If it is not possible for this talent to be incorporated into your child's school program, celebrate it at home by recognizing it frequently. Also look for ways to incorporate it when the child is doing homework and is having trouble mastering a concept.

Word–Language Reasoning Talent

Word–Language Reasoning Talent has two parts: a proficiency with words and a strong reasoning ability with language. It is possible for a person to have ability in only one area of this talent or in both.

The Word aspect of the talent shows up as skill in playing Scrabble or other word games. It can show up as interest and proficiency in using the dictionary or in doing crossword puzzles. Have you ever met a person who collects books on the history of words? Such a person has a Word Talent. Notice that the talent is for using words in isolation. Word Talent can show itself as skill in spelling, reading aloud, talking, telling jokes and stories, memorizing names and facts, or learning vocabulary words and foreign languages.

The Language Reasoning aspect of this talent shows up as an ability to explain ideas; talk things out; discuss options; produce plans, outlines, and lists; and write essays, stories, and even poetry. These skills seem to come naturally to those with a Language Reasoning Talent. Any project or activity that requires working with language comes easily to this person. He always gets the joke, gets the drift, or gets the point. This person understands puns, irony, personification, metaphor, simile, and symbols quickly and easily. People with this talent are apt to do well in traditional school settings; however, when their facility is developed far beyond the level of peers, material that is appropriate for their classmates is not challenging to them. Especially if they are extroverted, these children can be stigmatized as "know-it-alls," "too smart for their own good," or just plain "weird."

Poets, writers, and diplomats take for granted their talent for Language Reasoning.

Applications to Learning-Success

Students who have a talent for words or language reasoning usually think in words. They understand language, grammar, and parts of speech; diagramming sentences makes sense to them. Since schools emphasize these skills, there are generally plenty of activities in the classroom that utilize this talent. Most assignments, including homework, involve working with word-language reasoning. As a rule, students who have this talent are recognized and praised frequently.

Spatial Talent

Drawing or copying pictures or designs, painting, thinking in pictures, remembering what is seen, and knowing where things are (including oneself) are characteristics of people with a Spatial Talent. These are the doodlers in class. Sometimes the margins of their homework are covered with small drawings. People with

Spatial Talent are good at jigsaw puzzles or mazes and instinctively know how to find their way in new territory. These people are likely to know where north, south, east, or west is no matter where they are. But in case instinct fails, they are also good at reading maps and charts. Kids with this talent are able to see images in their minds and rotate the images so that they can see all sides of them.

Architects, drafters, contractors, visual artists—including house painters and home decorators—have this talent.

Applications to Learning-Success

Students who have a Spatial Talent are often also strong in Visual Modality (see Chapter 8 for more on the Picture Learner). These students need to see diagrams, charts, graphs, and pictures in order to understand concepts and retain information. If the school curriculum does not incorporate visual formats, supplement at home with models, videos, CD-ROMs, and other visual material, which will help them learn the subjects they are studying. If drawing comes easily, suggest that they take picture notes in class (talk to the teacher about this so that he won't conclude that the student isn't paying attention). Also, encourage doodling and "drawing things out" to increase comprehension and retention. This can be applied to math word problems, English literature, history, science experiments, or any topic being studied. Ask the teacher to accept alternative assignments such as presentation boards, collages, drawings, and even homemade videos.

Body Coordination Talent

At the level of large motor skills, people who enjoy and/or excel at hiking, bicycling, skating, skateboarding, skiing, swimming, dancing, or sports of any kind have a Body Coordination Talent. These people demonstrate an ability to do complicated physics calculations that result in perfect football passes, skateboard jumps, and other athletic feats. This talent can also show up as skill in typing, sewing, hammering, sawing, or doing models, which are examples of activities that involve small motor skills.

In the classroom, students with this talent are often fidgety; they are the students who balance their chairs on the two back legs or tap a pencil on the desk or turn around to nudge their neighbor. Sitting still is a major challenge for children with a Body Coordination Talent. Children with this talent and a Tactile-Kinesthetic Learning Modality are among the most difficult for teachers to handle in a traditional classroom setting. (See Chapter 8 for an explanation of Modality.)

Athletes, dancers, builders, craftspeople, seamstresses, and tailors are examples of people who have this talent.

Applications to Learning-Success

Students who have this talent can use it in various ways to help with their learning and schoolwork. Often they comprehend or memorize information better when they are moving! Moving keeps them focused on what they are doing. This student could play basketball, hopscotch, or jump rope while studying. For example, put math facts or other information on individual cards, spread them on the ground, bounce a ball on a card, say the fact, and shoot the basket! How about jogging or hiking while listening to a book-on-tape or a chapter from a textbook that the student has recorded? Making models, doing sewing projects, or building something could be suggested to the teacher as alternative assignments when studying a particular subject. A child learning to tell time could sew or craft a large clock. A student learning about the planets could construct a model showing their relationships to each other. For geography, a child who loves to saw and hammer could "build" the states or countries being studied. Even learning math concepts and formulas can be facilitated through sewing and craft projects or large motor activities. By providing as much opportunity as possible for such activities at home, you will be helping your child acquire skills and learn material required by the school in a way that works for him.

Interactive-Self Talent

People with an Interactive-Self Talent often enjoy being alone. In fact, because of the high priority they place on being independent, they might even be reclusive. They think about themselves a great deal and often understand their motives and desires very well. These introspective people are clear about their own opinions and many of them are quite happy to share them. However, they can give the impression of being preoccupied and often they are. These people are often good at taking care of their own needs.

Some of the people who have this talent are interested in introspective activities including religious studies, meditation, and self-development.

Applications to Learning-Success

The student with this talent usually works well by herself. She is able to work from a list of assignments, figure out a routine that works best for her, and complete the tasks. Often, this is the student who shrinks away from group activities or class projects. She would rather do it herself in her own way. A child who is very tuned-in to her needs might also question the schedule or the rules when they interfere with what she has planned. For instance, if she feels that she needs more time to finish an assignment and this is interrupted by P.E., she will probably have a tough time participating wholeheartedly in P.E. because she will still be thinking about the assignment.

Interactive-Others Talent

The focus for people with an Interactive-Others Talent is being social, making friends, understanding people, and to varying degrees, making others feel good about themselves. These people are most comfortable in groups—some are more comfortable in small groups, some in large groups. The Interactive-Others Talent gives these people an uncanny ability to welcome others, settle arguments, and to be fair in all interactions.

In the classroom, a child with this talent is likely to pass notes and whisper to neighbors. For some young people with this talent, associating with friends is their primary motivation for being in school.

People with an Interactive-Others Talent are interested in group activities, helping others, and, sometimes, joining social causes.

Applications to Learning-Success

Students with this talent often learn best when they can work in groups or at least with another person. Some teachers set up their classrooms so that students have the option of working in pairs or small groups. At home, it is important to recognize that homework and studying are facilitated when the child can interact with someone. If this child has a friend with the same talent, consider having them do homework and study together after school.

Interactive-Animals Talent

Unless you have met someone with a talent for interacting with animals, you may not believe that it exists. My son is one of these people, so I know that there are such people. I sometimes call it the Dr. Doolittle Talent. These people have a rapport with animals that verges on magic. They can train them, calm them when they are upset, and generally communicate with them far beyond telling a dog to sit or roll over. The talent that they possess generates trust in the animal that results in what appears to be a bonding process.

These people make wonderful veterinarians, animal trainers, rescuers, and keepers. Horse whisperers and some jockeys have this kind of talent with horses.

Applications to Learning-Success

If your child has this talent, allow him to study with his pets around him. Whenever possible, use animal examples to help him understand a math problem or some other concept. Books about animals might encourage him to read more. He could also learn a lot about science, history, and social studies by studying animal topics. Some great CD-ROMs do virtual dissection and teach a lot about the anatomy and biology of animals. Developing a budget for a pet's care and doing the shopping can increase math skills, and keeping track of vet visits, vaccinations, and other pertinent information can help a child acquire organization and planning skills.

Interactive-Nature Talent

Children with this talent have difficulty being indoors. You will find them outside in a tree, a mud puddle, a patch of dirt or grass investigating some natural phenomenon—light, air, water, or creatures in nature—insects, frogs, butterflies, spiders, snakes, or other small creatures. This person's talent often translates into feeling confined indoors and a need to be outdoors, no matter what the weather. Some people with this talent are concerned with taking care of nature as well as enjoying it. They tend to get involved in recycling, protecting the environment, and conservation.

This talent might lead adults to becoming forest rangers, tour guides for a national park, tree care specialists, lifeguards, or enjoying other jobs having to do with ecology or the environment.

Applications to Learning-Success

The child with this talent needs as much time in nature as possible. Experiment with allowing her to study in the backyard, at the park, beach, or in the woods (assuming these areas are close by!). Whenever possible, use examples from nature to help her to understand a math problem or some other concept. Books about nature might encourage reading. She could also learn a lot about science, history, and social studies by studying nature topics. These students often think up great projects that have to do with ecology and the environment, such as recycling, planting trees, developing community gardens, etc. These projects can be the stimulus for math and writing activities, verbal presentations, and the development of organizational and planning skills.

Humor Talent

Many people don't think of a sense of humor as a talent. The fact is, many careers depend upon a special gift for turning an ordinary situation into one that will make people laugh. People with this talent are not embarrassed to display out-of-the-ordinary behavior in front of others. They are willing to be laughed at, and they are willing to laugh at others in a playful way. These people can be tricksters who make the most of April Fool's Day, Halloween, and any other occasion that encourages them to play practical jokes. People with a talent for humor are often great mimics, and they can make otherwise dull activities fun.

 Charles Schulz failed many subjects in high school and his cartoons were rejected by the yearbook staff. He was also turned down by the Walt Disney Studios when he applied for a cartoonist job.

Comics, clowns, humorists, and cartoonists are among those who possess this talent to make others laugh.

Applications to Learning-Success

Students with this talent have a really tough time with the usual seriousness of the classroom and schoolwork in general. But their need for fun and humor can be incorporated into study time, especially at home. The movie *Mrs. Doubtfire* comes to mind; when Robin Williams returns to his children as the nanny, he makes sure they complete their chores and homework, but they all have fun doing it. They take frequent breaks to do funny things, and sometimes they incorporate the fun into the required task. Your child could show his cleverness by making silly sentences from his vocabulary words. He could think up humorous rhymes to memorize facts, names, and dates. He might create an amusing skit or dance to demonstrate his knowledge of a topic or to study for a test. If he likes cartoons, these could be used to increase reading skills. If he likes to make up his own cartoons, ask the teacher if he could do some of the assigned reports in a cartoon format.

Enhancing Daily Life Talent

Talent in Enhancing Daily Life goes unacknowledged for the most part. People who cook wonderfully well or who create lovely, livable, cozy, or inspiring places have a talent for enhancing daily life. Some people display this talent in the way that they coordinate their wardrobes. Others, who love to clean and organize spaces, are among the least acknowledged of those who possess the talent. It is obvious from their often tireless work that these people are expressing a desire to add aesthetic value to the ordinary, every day routine.

 Julia Child didn't discover that she could cook until she attended her first cooking school when she was thirty-four years old.

Stay-at-home moms and dads, interior decorators, landscape architects, chefs, clothing designers, gardeners, maids, plasterers, housepainters, floral designers, and people who like to arrange spaces and cook meals all possess a talent for enhancing daily life.

Applications to Learning-Success

The child who loves to cook, clean, decorate, garden, or organize can learn a great deal from these activities. Cooking presents an opportunity to work with math, especially fractions and measurement conversions. It can also involve budgeting, shopping, and working with money. Gardening can involve the geometry side of math, as well as some of the same aspects as cooking. Cooking and gardening can offer lessons in science, history, and world cultures. Decorating and organizing can involve design, math, and office skills. Books about cooking, decorating, or gardening might encourage reading for this child.

CAREERS: THE RELATIONSHIP BETWEEN DISPOSITIONS AND TALENTS

Any one of the twelve talents listed in this chapter can be expressed through any one of the five dispositions (see Figure 6.1 on page 132). The ways that talents manifest through dispositions can be indicators of likely careers.

Parents are, of course, concerned about what their children are going to do to earn a livelihood as adults. For the most part, I think that the number of careers or job options acknowledged by our society is limited. Sometimes when I'm traveling and I meet new people in distant places, I'm fascinated by the ways they are meeting their livelihood needs. The local professional women's network that I belong to has also expanded my view of the number of creative things there are to do in life.

The Careers Chart (see Figure 6.1 on page 132) is a tool that encourages you to expand your thinking about the number of ways it is possible for talents to manifest as livelihood or careers. When you see the number of career possibilities there are, I hope you realize that your child will be able to find a place within the larger scheme of things. The Careers Chart shows how the twelve talents interact with the five dispositions to produce sixty career categories. Each career category has individual careers listed in it. As you can see, it is a work in progress. It will probably never be complete, since career possibilities are limited only by the imagination.

Here is an example of how the Careers Chart works. A person with a Music Talent who has a Performing Disposition might be a concert pianist, a singer, a conductor, or a member of an orchestra. This is the usual relationship between a talent and a career that we think of when we say, "Allison is so talented in music, I think that she will be a violinist." The conclusion is that a Music Talent is meant to be performed. What is interesting is that not all people with a talent in music have the disposition to be a performer. Some people with Music Talent have a Producing Disposition. These people might sponsor concerts, manage ticket sales, or do administrative work for a choir, orchestra, or opera group. Still others with a Music Talent and a Relating

Disposition might teach music. Some with an Inventing Disposition and a Music Talent might make musical instruments. A person with a Thinks/Creates Disposition might compose original scores.

Although the Learning Profile can be used as a tool to facilitate career choices, it is not meant to be a job-search tool. The chart is most helpful for talking in general terms about the range of possibilities there are and the kinds of skills, talents, and interests that certain careers require. It increases awareness of the many options available for our young people to explore.

Parents often say that it isn't practical or fair to lead children to believe that they can pursue their interests, talents, goals, and passions because not all of us can have jobs that are sustaining at those levels. In the Learning Style Model of Education, people are encouraged to develop the things they love to do and practice them with great enthusiasm *in their free time* if not in their work. The richness of after-hours activities can even contribute to feelings of well-being during the working hours. Who knows what the world would be like if we all kept our interests, talents, goals, and dreams alive.

When you understand the numerous ways a talent can be expressed in various dispositions, the wide range of livelihood, career, and free-time occupations becomes clearer. The hope is that you will feel more confident that your child will find a way of expressing his uniqueness in the real world.

> **The richness of after-hours activities can even contribute to feelings of well-being during the working hours.**

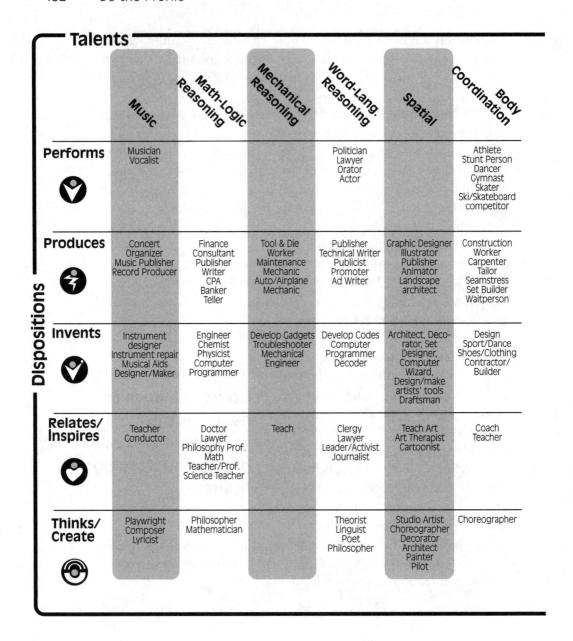

Talents

Dispositions

	Music	Math-Logic Reasoning	Mechanical Reasoning	Word-Lang. Reasoning	Spatial	Body Coordination
Performs	Musician Vocalist			Politician Lawyer Orator Actor		Athlete Stunt Person Dancer Gymnast Skater Ski/Skateboard competitor
Produces	Concert Organizer Music Publisher Record Producer	Finance Consultant Publisher Writer CPA Banker Teller	Tool & Die Worker Maintenance Mechanic Auto/Airplane Mechanic	Publisher Technical Writer Publicist Promoter Ad Writer	Graphic Designer Illustrator Publisher Animator Landscape architect	Construction Worker Carpenter Tailor Seamstress Set Builder Waitperson
Invents	Instrument designer Instrument repair Musical Aids Designer/Maker	Engineer Chemist Physicist Computer Programmer	Develop Gadgets Troubleshooter Mechanical Engineer	Develop Codes Computer Programmer Decoder	Architect, Decorator, Set Designer, Computer Wizard, Design/make artists' tools Draftsman	Design Sport/Dance Shoes/Clothing Contractor/ Builder
Relates/ Inspires	Teacher Conductor	Doctor Lawyer Philosophy Prof. Math Teacher/Prof. Science Teacher	Teach	Clergy Lawyer Leader/Activist Journalist	Teach Art Art Therapist Cartoonist	Coach Teacher
Thinks/ Create	Playwright Composer Lyricist	Philosopher Mathematician		Theorist Linguist Poet Philosopher	Studio Artist Choreographer Decorator Architect Painter Pilot	Choreographer

Figure 6.1 Careers that Combine Dispositions and Talents

	Interactive Self	Interactive Others	Interactive Animals	Interactive Nature	Humor	Life Enhancement	
	Actor	Actor		Sky Diver	Clown Comic Mime		**Performs**
	Publish Write self help books/articles	Publish Write	Forest Ranger Publisher	Editor of nature magazine Forest Ranger	Publisher Writer	House Husband House Cleaner House Wife Gardener Publisher, Chef House Painter	**Produces**
	Design Relaxation devices/equipment	Design Communication Devices/systems	Oceanographer Botanist Biologist Zoologist Design Outdoor gear/equipment	Design outdoor equipment Botanist Biologist Oceanographer	Develop Gags, Tricks, Magic	Develop Recipes, Tools/Gadgets	**Invents**
	Clergy Teacher	Priest/Minister Philanthropist Anthropologist Nurse/Therapist Teacher/Activist Doctor	Guide Teacher Activist EPA Agent Zoo Worker Trainer	Guide Teacher	Teacher Clown	Teach Cooking, Home Ec., Budgeting, Decorating	**Relates/ Inspires**
	Writer Playwright Clergy Choreographer		Nature Artist Writer Photographer	Photographer Painter Pilot	Mime	Interior Designer	**Thinks/ Create**

Figure 6.1 continued

7

Interests:
So Easy to Overlook

Some parents are surprised at their children's responses on the talent and interest assessments because they reveal new information. Other parents might feel that they haven't learned anything from these two assessments because talents and interests are usually the most obvious and easily observed characteristics of learning style. If you are in the latter group, be patient. As you work through the other chapters of the book, you will learn many techniques that will make a difference for your child's learning, and you will also discover new ways to think about the talents and interests that your child has. In addition, you are communicating to your child that you value his opinions regarding his talents and interests, because you are *asking* about them rather than *assuming that you already know!*

Interests are your easiest access to, and the most observable aspect of a child's learning style because they are in the forefront of your child's mind. They are what children often nag us about. You might think that by transporting kids to soccer games, ballet classes, swimming meets, or any number of other activities you are involved daily in your child's interests. It depends on whose choice the activity is. Most of us have interests and talents mixed up in a strange way that keeps kids busy yet doesn't always satisfy

> " *We are meant to work in ways that suit us . . . This work, when we find it and do it—if only as a hobby at first—is a key to our true happiness and self-expression.*
>
> —Marsha Sinetar "

their need to pursue *their* interests. We want them to develop the talents that are so obvious to us, and they want to pursue their interests. When interests are viewed separately from talents and seen as valid expressions of your child's learning style, they provide important information. If you get some clarity about this subject, you might even be able to cut down on the time you spend chauffeuring your kids around. When kids are pursuing interests, they are focused, energetic, and enthusiastic. It's not hard to understand why many of these same kids slump at their desks when it comes time to do their uninteresting homework.

Pursuing interests provides a counterbalance to daily stress-creating activities. Most of the schoolday children are meeting external standards and following rules set down for them. Participating in free-time activities that they choose can be restorative and crucial to mental and physical health.

In spite of the obvious benefits of developing interests, many adults don't know what their own interests are. Or they know but don't make time for them. Pursuing interests is a vital part of healthy living.

INTERESTS ARE NOT TALENTS

Interests are *not* talents, and unfortunately, without some attention to the difference between the two, parents often tell children what they "should" be interested in based on a quick assessment of their talents. Have you heard yourself telling your child that she "should live up to her potential" or that he "should" be a singer or a writer, etc.? Interest-driven creatures that they are, children usually

Pursuing interests provides a counter-balance to daily stress-creating activities.

have no idea what you are talking about. In spite of your best intentions to give guidance that will develop their talents, you have the best chance of nurturing talents through the back door—by listening seriously to your child's interests. Sometimes a child's interests support his talents and sometimes they don't. Making assumptions about what your child *should* be interested in will plant seeds for resistance and maybe even a full-blown power struggle. Your best bet is to set aside *your* desire to develop the talents that are so obvious to you, and support your child's interests. Actually, your participation in your child's interests depends upon how much time, money, and energy you are willing to contribute.

PRIORITIZING INTERESTS

Short-Term Interests

Children try on ideas the way we try on clothes or shoes when we're shopping. For young people, ideas translate into interests quickly; therefore, short-term interests come and go. In fact, you could meet yourself coming and going as you try to keep up with some of your child's latest great ideas. Short-term interests often show up between 1 and 4 on the Interest Priority Scale in the Profile. Even though they have lower priority they need to be dealt with, if only because they made the list. Talk over these short-term interests with your child and get more information. Ask what he needs from you to support his interest. Based on what you find out you can make some decisions of your own about how you want to participate, or if you're going to participate at all. Too much time spent on your child's short-term interests might burn you out for making a commitment to those interests that have long-term potential.

> **C**hildren try on ideas the way we try on clothes or shoes when we're shopping.

Long-Term Interests

Long-term interests usually show up between 5 and 10 on the Interest Priority Scale. Whether they actually become long-term is not the point. The point is that your child feels an urgency for them, which is why their numbers are higher. Take them seriously and find out how you can help. It is tempting to take over and start telling a child what she needs to do; after all, what does a child know? However, by letting your child take the lead when there is little chance of harm, she will learn invaluable lessons about herself, her decision-making process, her ability to get information, and her willingness to make commitments and stay with them.

It is through long-term interests (six months to a year or more) that you may see talent being developed. You can be sure that if your child pursues an interest for more than six months, he is developing a new facility, if not an inborn talent. A child who practices kicking the soccer ball every week for six months is learning something. It might be how to function as a team member rather than how to dribble the ball. It might be how to stick with something that is difficult rather than how to score. We don't always know the reasons why a child chooses a certain interest to pursue. Parents provide the most valuable support when they stay in the background, watch, listen, and learn about their child.

> **P**arents provide the most support when they stay in the background, watch, listen, and learn about their child.

If you are accustomed to being in charge, it might seem strange to you to have your child committed to an interest that is completely his own. Helping children pursue interests is not about pushing them to be the best in the dance class or making sure they "stick to it" and keep attending soccer practice whether they hate it or not; it is about being supportive.

INVOLVEMENT ISSUES

The idea for identifying a child's Involvement Issues has come from listening for years to kids talk with great passion about all kinds of issues, from "save the whales" to "planting trees." Some kids want to be involved in real-life issues, and why not? Involvement Issues are an aspect of interests that pertain to participating in the larger community to support things that the child really cares about. Finding out about your child's Involvement Issues is a way of talking about and encouraging respect—a way of giving back to the community and the world. Not all children will show interests here, so don't be concerned if your child doesn't.

> **W**hen a child is acting on behalf of something that she loves or respects, she feels purposeful. And to have a purpose is the surest way I can think of to feel connected to life and worthwhile as a person.

You will notice that the Involvement Issues section of the interest assessment asks your child to list things that he really cares about: at home, in the neighborhood, at school, in your town, in the world. These things can be living or non-living. This list becomes the foundation for learning more about these issues and getting involved in helping to take care of them. A high school student who loves animals is a trainer at a children's zoo in Santa Barbara; another is a natural-born horse whisperer and travels to study with the masters while practicing her skill locally. Two students who were concerned about the negative treatment of local police officers planned a celebration for the community to honor them. Many students are working in small groups to bring attention to ecological concerns and world peace.

Involvement Issues simultaneously develop the child and contribute to the well-being of something that has meaning and value for that child. When a child is acting on behalf of something that she loves or respects, she feels purposeful. And to have a purpose is the surest way I can think of to feel connected to life and worthwhile as a person.

INCORPORATING INTERESTS INTO THE SCHOOL PROGRAM

Besides providing an outlet for your child's enthusiasm and helping to build confidence and self-direction, interests can be used to help with schoolwork, much like talents. For example, if your child is crazy about dolphins, he could choose a book about dolphins for an assigned book report (often teachers leave it up to the students to choose a topic). If she is involved as a coach in a Special Olympics program, this could be the topic for an oral presentation. If he is helping to raise funds for a cause, there is plenty of opportunity for math lessons. If she is involved in Scouts, she is learning about science, history, math, and many other subjects and skills. In fact, I find the requirements for earning Scout badges and other merits quite amazing. It is remarkable what these young people achieve. For a child who is serious about Scouting or 4-H activities, it is almost like attending a second school!

> "
> *One never learns to understand truly anything but what one loves.*
>
> —*Goethe* "

DELIGHT— THE NUMBER ONE MOTIVATOR

Greg Harris, a pastor, tells of doing very poorly in school, no matter what his parents or teachers did to get him to change. Then he discovered turtles and for one summer became a budding herpetologist, reading, studying, and actively learning everything he could about turtles. When summer came to an end he went back to school to the same routine of poor grades and unused potential. Years later, in preparing for the ministry, Harris became interested in the question: What makes people learn? He came to realize that

> *You should be doing what you love.*
> —Barbara Sher

people (that includes children), study the things that "delight" them . . . Without coercion, without tests to study for, without school. The key I discovered was delight. It is the spark and motivation for all true study. Where there is no delight, there is no sustained effort to understand . . . All children are studying! Their interests may not seem important to us, but children are always applying themselves to learn what delights them.[1]

Becky Rupp, author and mother of three, has chosen to homeschool her children. She writes:

Children, given the freedom to pursue their own interests, do. The writers write; the scientists spend whole days in the basement where they've set up a chemistry lab. This means that not all academic subjects get equal enthusiasm, equal dedication, and equal time. My husband and I provide the fundamentals of a basic education, but the boys, inevitably, pick and choose. We lay it out; they take what they need. Each according to his own gifts.[2]

Not all of us have the opportunity to homeschool; however, comments such as Rupp's and Harris's give a sense of how important interests are in the learning style picture. I hope that you are inspired to be aware of and to encourage the things that delight your child. After all, the more you acknowledge and support your child's interests and follow his delight, the more tolerance he will have for activities that aren't as interesting to him.

> . . . the more you acknowledge and support your child's interests and follow his delight, the more tolerance he will have for activities that aren't as interesting to him.

8

Modality:
More Than Auditory,
Visual, or Kinesthetic

Perhaps the most familiar aspect of learning style to both parents and teachers is modality. When presenting workshops I often ask the audience what is meant by learning style. The most common answer is, "Oh, you mean whether a student is auditory, visual, or kinesthetic." Comments such as, "She's an auditory learner," or "He learns best with tactile activities," refer to sensory modalities, and most people have come to think of modality as synonymous with learning style.

There are three things to remember about modality:

1. Modality is only *one* aspect of learning style.

2. Modality refers to the modes or senses through which people *take in* and *process* information.

3. There is more to modality than simply labeling a person auditory, visual, or kinesthetic.

 THE BIG PICTURE

The concept of learning modalities sounds simple enough— "visual people" need to learn visually, "auditory people" need to learn auditorily, and so on. The reality is much more complex because we receive different kinds of visual, auditory, and tactile-kinesthetic input.

The Learning Style Profile looks at the differences *within* the modalities as well as *between* the modalities. For example, "touch," "draw," "write about" are different types of tactile-kinesthetic activities. Music, conversation, and audio tapes of a lecture offer different kinds of auditory input. It is important to make these distinctions. Because there are different ways to express each modality, you might have different kinds of kinesthetic learners: one who learns better with drawing, another who needs to take things apart, and a third who chooses a combination of these. Each person's set of modality strengths is unique, and may even differ with the situation or learning activity.

> **T**here is more to modality than simply labeling a person auditory, visual, or kinesthetic.

As we take a closer look at each of the modalities, the possible combinations will become evident.

The Auditory Modality

Auditory material includes noise, music, songs, lectures, verbal explanations, taped information, stories told aloud, conversations, and the sound of one's own voice.

Listening Learners

An Auditory Learner *usually* comprehends and processes information better when it is presented verbally. Yet other aspects of this modality are often overlooked. For example, music can greatly enhance the ability to learn and some people need background noise in order to concentrate (see Chapter 9 on Environment). Some students do better when they can listen to a tape rather than a live lecture, and others seem to grasp and remember concepts better if they are taught through stories.

Some people are so proficient at learning through the Auditory Mode, that incoming information which is not auditory might actually interfere with their learning. For example, if a speaker is referring to charts and graphic illustrations, this learner might need to ignore that part of the presentation (even closing his eyes!) in order to focus on the auditory information. For Auditory Learners, sounds can be the source of ideas.

It is important to identify for each learner what works best in different situations. Noise might be helpful when working on math problems but not when reading history. Use of rhyming songs might be the only way for a particular type of Auditory Learner to memorize math facts. Books-on-tape could be helpful for someone who has trouble comprehending when reading silently.

Verbal Learners

A special type of Auditory Learner needs to talk and discuss: the Verbal Learner. For this child, talking is necessary for processing information. The act of verbalizing what he knows helps him to process and remember the information. He needs to actually *say* the words, not simply hear someone else say them. Reading instructions aloud to one's self has worked wonders for many Verbal Learners who have trouble understanding written directions.

Knowing about the Verbal Learner helps us to understand a common scenario that is experienced by parents and teachers: A child has trouble with directions in a text or workbook. She tells the adult that she doesn't understand and needs help. Usually what happens next is that the adult says something like, "What do you mean you don't understand? Read what it says." When this child reads the instructions out loud, she says, "Oh, I get it now," and is able to complete the task. The adult is annoyed because it seems that this child understood all along and simply wanted some attention. The adult becomes more annoyed if this scene occurs frequently.

Actually, these children aren't looking for attention; they really don't understand the instructions until they are read aloud. Not realizing that the magic ingredients are the oral reading and auditory feedback, and *not* the adult attention, these children continue to call for help each time. Simply teaching these students to verbalize instructions eliminates frustration for everyone. But can verbalizing be acceptable in the classroom?

Traditionally, any kind of verbalization has been discouraged in the classroom, and reading aloud to oneself has even been considered a "special needs" behavior—that is, something that is done by students who are not capable of doing it the "right" way.

Verbalizing *is* the right way for the Verbal Learner and it is no more a "special need" than any other child's learning need. All learners have their own unique needs, and one need is not any better or more important than another. Encourage your children to verbalize when they need to and be available to talk through lessons and assignments as the need arises.

> **T**raditionally, any kind of verbalization has been discouraged in the classroom, and reading aloud to oneself has even been considered a "special needs" behavior—that is, something that is done by students who are not capable of doing it the "right" way.

Some Verbal Learners do best when they can work with someone else. Try to provide someone to work at least part of the time with your child on homework, studying, etc. Homeschoolers can arrange for their children to work in pairs or small groups as needed. Many classroom teachers have organized their rooms so that students have the option of working together or alone. If time with an adult is important for your child, even a short period of one-on-one time with a parent or teacher can be effective.

Verbal Learners benefit from talking out loud in many situations—following a recipe when cooking, working out directions on a map, reading the instructions for assembling a desk, memorizing the names of the continents, understanding the concept of gravity, figuring out what to wear to the prom, making a difficult decision, and so on. Other options for children who need to express themselves verbally include reading along with books-on-tape or working with interactive video/computer programs. Verbal Learners do their best on assignments that involve verbalizing. Teachers could encourage these students to make an audio or video report, prepare oral presentations, participate in a discussion, tell a story, even set information to a melody and sing it. When the goal is for a child to demonstrate understanding of a body of knowledge, it pays to discover the many alternatives to the written report.

The Visual Modality

There are two types of Visual Learners—Picture and Print. Although very different types of learners, they are usually lumped into one category. The result is that Picture Learners are often mistakenly given printed-language techniques instead of pictures to help them learn. For example, Picture Learners often have difficulty with reading and spelling because whole-word or sight-word methods of teaching are believed to be best for Visual Learners. This would work if our language symbols represented words or concepts the way Chinese or hieroglyphics do; but since our letters represent sounds, the whole-word method doesn't make sense to Picture Learners.

> **. . . Picture Learners are often mistakenly given printed-language techniques instead of pictures to help them learn.**

Picture Learners

Visual material for Picture Learners includes charts, graphs, designs, forms, layouts, maps, objects, drawings, movies, and dramatic performances. Temple Grandin's *Thinking in Pictures* and Ronald Davis's *The Gift of Dyslexia* do a great job of describing the Picture Learner. This person translates all types of incoming information into pictures before processing, memorizing, or acting on anything. Some people think entirely in pictures, which is very difficult to understand for a person who thinks in words! Strategies and techniques that transform verbal and printed language into picture formats are very helpful for this type of Visual Learner.

Picture Learners learn best from various forms of graphic presentations. These include pictorial charts or graphs, sequential drawings, and time lines with pictures. Picture note-taking can work like magic to help these learners organize information, comprehend written or auditory material, or write a report. Another excellent tool is information mapping, a method of taking information that is read, heard, or experienced, and plotting it out on paper with words, phrases, and/or pictures. It provides a "visual" representation or format of the material to be learned or written about. (Other authors refer to it as Mind Mapping, clustering, and graphic organizing.)[1–3] Many learners benefit from "moving" pictures, such as movies, CD-ROMs, or live presentations. Videos and computers are excellent tools for some Picture Learners. For reading and spelling, the AVKO and Wilson programs are among the few that are suited for Picture Learners.

Print Learners

Print Learners think in words. That is, they see *words* in their minds when they are listening, memorizing, recalling, and thinking. While Picture Learners are busy trying to convert language into pictures, Print Learners are converting pictures into words. Simply highlighting printed material in different colors is a great strategy for many of these learners. Children who visualize printed language are usually natural readers and spellers and are able to use this highlighting technique to process and memorize more efficiently. Some Print Learners are confused by diagrams and illustrations. For example, if this learner is reading a how-to manual, he might need to ignore the pictures and concentrate on the written information.

The Print Learner needs to read and write in order to process information efficiently. This is probably the "dream" student for many teachers—give this child a book to read, a workbook to complete, a topic to research, or an outline to develop, and this student is happy. In fact, many Print Learners would rather be left alone in a corner to read and study quietly by themselves. They want to be as far away as possible from the Verbal Learners who need to discuss everything!

Print Learners benefit from marking the material as they read it (such as underlining or using a highlighter), taking notes in word-mapping (information mapping using words and no pictures) or outline formats, writing down incoming auditory information, and translating visual information into words.

The Tactile-Kinesthetic Modality

Tactile refers to touch and Kinesthetic refers to movement. Touch and movement keep Tactile-Kinesthetic children most alert in the learning situation.

For those who are not Tactile-Kinesthetic Learners, this is probably the most difficult modality to understand. It is also the one that can get children in the most trouble in school, since movement in a learning situation is usually interpreted as disruptive rather than intelligent. The student who is tapping his foot or doodling while the teacher is presenting a lesson, or the child who is touching the new computer before the parent has finished giving instructions, is more apt to get into trouble than to be spurred on. These children receive information more efficiently when they are able to touch things and move around. Many parents and teachers have had an experience with a child who was jumping around or coloring or fiddling with something—seemingly "not paying attention"—who, when asked, could repeat word for word what the adult had said.

> . . . movement in a learning situation is usually interpreted as disruptive rather than intelligent.

Tactile-Kinesthetic kids have a great deal of pent-up energy when they are confined to classrooms for hours each day, with few movement activities being incorporated into their schedules. We can label them hyperactive, or we can choose to respond to their legitimate learning needs. At the very least, we can legitimize some of their ways of keeping busy, so that they are not seen as disruptive when they are supposed to be sitting quietly and listening. For example, doodling, coloring, squeezing clay, and sewing are all acceptable ways of quietly keeping the hands moving while the parent or teacher is presenting a lesson or during a group discussion.

Have you ever attended a meeting where one or two women crocheted or knitted the entire time? I have never seen anyone question that, or feel insulted because the women were "not paying attention." If anything, we admired their efficiency for being able to do two things at once. In contrast, I can't tell you how many times a parent has grabbed an object from a child who is quietly twirling it in his hands while having an intelligent conversation with me, and angrily commanded, "Stop that and pay attention to her!" This child had chosen a most appropriate way of meeting his movement needs while remaining respectful to the other people in the room, and now he was being punished for it. We can help Tactile-Kinesthetic kids by encouraging them to come up with socially acceptable ways of moving that allow them to stay in control of themselves, and follow the rules.

> **. . . doodling, coloring, squeezing clay, and sewing are all acceptable ways of quietly keeping the hands moving while the parent or teacher is presenting a lesson or during a group discussion.**

Other perplexing "rules" that Tactile-Kinesthetic kids run into include: "Don't point with your finger when reading" and "Don't use your fingers to add." Both of these activities are great strategies for these learners! *Encourage* your Tactile-Kinesthetic child to use her fingers to add, subtract, multiply, or do any math (fingers can be as efficient as an abacus or a calculator!), and please allow your child to track with his finger when he reads. Using the fingers adds the needed tactile and kinesthetic components.

Whenever possible, incorporate movement into learning. Tactile-Kinesthetic Learners need to draw or make a model of a pyramid rather than read about it. They need to plant a real garden rather than hear a teacher talk about one. They need to touch and examine the structure of leaves, work with models of the planets, use an abacus and other manipulatives for math, act out the story of the Pilgrims, memorize facts while exercising or playing basketball, learn how to print by tracing textured letters. They can involve their whole bodies when learning to tell time with giant clocks, or walk through a country by using large floor maps. Also teach them to take frequent breaks, to stretch, jump, run, or simply walk around the room—this will help them be more focused when doing paper and pencil tasks.

> *Kinesthetic learners are less verbal, less expressive, less likely to be the first to raise their hand in class because they need to go "internal" to check out their answers before offering them.*
> —Eric Jensen

You might be thinking, Oh, these kids just want to have fun and we don't have time for that. Well, first of all, there is nothing wrong with having fun; in fact, fun enhances the learning experience. Both the quality and quantity of learning increase when a student is enjoying the process. Even beyond this, it's important to understand that Tactile-Kinesthetic Learners *need* the types of activities described above in order to learn. Their brains process best when information is coming through touch or through movement, or through a combination of touch and movement. When they are literally reaching out to touch something, it is because they are responding to the demands of the Tactile-Kinesthetic Modality.

Both the quality and quantity of learning increase when a student is enjoying the process.

Below are descriptions of the basic types of Tactile-Kinesthetic Learners. The first three describe the typical Tactile-Kinesthetic child who needs to move and do. Some children are a combination of these three. The fourth type describes children who learn by writing; they usually do not require the touch and movement that the other types do.

Hands-on Learners

The Hands-on Tactile-Kinesthetic Learners process best through hands-on activities such as constructing, assembling, taking things apart, working with textured materials, and manipulating objects.

Whole-Body Learners

The Whole-Body Tactile-Kinesthetic Learners need to act out, walk around, play, exercise, build, give live demonstrations, and use whole-body movements.

Sketching Learners

The Sketching Tactile-Kinesthetic Learners learn through drawing, coloring, and doodling.

Writing Learners

For some children, writing is the Kinesthetic activity that helps them learn. That is, they need to write things out, in manuscript or cursive, in order to process, understand, and remember information. These children usually do not need the touch and movement required by true Tactile-Kinesthetic people and more closely resemble the Print Learners described above. In fact, for many Print Learners, it is writing that translates information into the visual format that they need.

MORE EFFICIENT PROCESSING FOR EVERYONE

One of our jobs as parents and teachers is to help individual children discover and use their modality strengths in order to learn more efficiently. Is there a basic modality rule that might help us increase learning in general? A study done by Specific Diagnostic Studies showed that on average 29% of elementary and high school students learn best through the visual mode (pictures), 34% through the auditory mode (sound or music), and 37% through the tactile-kinesthetic mode (moving, touching, doing).[4] Immediately it becomes obvious that the traditional classroom, which is set up to teach mostly to the auditory mode, is serving only about 34% of its students!

We've probably all heard the general principle that states we learn 10% of what we read, 15% of what we hear, 40% of what we see, and 80% of what we experience. When we attend workshops or seminars as adults, this principle is often quoted so that we will be more open to the hands-on activities and learning games that have become so common in workplace presentations and personal development courses.

> **T**he traditional classroom, which is set up to teach mostly to the auditory mode, is serving only about 34% of its students!

In *The Learning Revolution*, by Gordon Dryden and Jeannette Vos, we read that:

> The best learning systems are simple. Better still, they are fun. Generally they have this in common: they encourage you to . . . learn much faster: through music, rhythm, rhyme, pictures, feelings, emotions and action. Overwhelmingly the best learning methods are similar to those we used as infants.[5]

And Peter Kline tells us:

> You were born to learn with your whole body and all your senses. You were not born to sit in a chair eight hours a day and listen to someone talk, or to pore over books year in and year out . . . Until recently (only minutes on the evolutionary scale) there were no books, no classrooms and no lecturers . . . If we pay attention to the learning of babies and young children, we can see how similar it is to the way our ancestors learned throughout their lives.[6]

The basic rule, then, seems to be the same for everyone; that is, the more we can teach through doing experiential techniques, the better. Generally, this principle *is* applied to the teaching of toddlers and adults. Yet in the classrooms that our children inhabit every day, the reverse is practiced: They are taught primarily through lecture (teachers talk, kids listen) and reading (assignments are given to read the book in class or for homework). Even more distressing is that the need for hands-on learning is considered by some educators to be a sign of lower intelligence and a predictor of inferior career potential—in other words, those who learn best through the Tactile-Kinesthetic mode are considered incapable of higher-level thinking or higher-level jobs.[7]

> **. . . higher-level reasoning skills are achieved precisely when we allow a person to learn through his strongest modality, whatever it may be.**

It takes a shift in thinking to realize that higher-level reasoning skills are achieved precisely when we allow a person to learn through his strongest modality, whatever it may be. Einstein and Edison are among our famous inventors and scientists who were Tactile-Kinesthetic Learners. And what would we do without engineers, mechanics, electricians, landscape architects, computer programmers, and so many others, whose expertise and incredible skills are rooted in hands-on intelligence?

The traditional school model not only shortchanges Tactile-Kinesthetic Learners, it also shortchanges all the other learners, because lessons that incorporate moving and doing are helpful for everyone. So after you begin applying the information about your child's unique modality needs, remember to bring some action into the picture even for the Auditory and Visual Learners, because experience is still the best teacher!

SUMMARY

At this point you might be thinking, How will I ever be able to provide for the modality needs of each of my children? And how could a teacher possibly provide for the needs of each child in the classroom?

Relax. It's not as difficult as it might appear at first. Here are some helpful hints:

1. Look at the results of the modality assessment for each of your children.

2. Choose one or two activities from the Modality Quick Reference Charts below and experiment.

3. Teach your children about their modality strengths so they will know how to meet their own learning needs.

Chapter 10 will go into more detail about combining the information from all of the Profile sections. For now, here is a way to put together the modality information. The Modality Quick Reference Charts at the end of the chapter will also help.

Suppose that in Part I of the modality assessment your child scored highest in Visual and second highest in Tactile-Kinesthetic, and in Part II chose Picture, Hands-on, and Whole-Body Learner. Now you are wondering which activities to choose from the list for these modalities. Many things that you know about your child will provide clues.

The traditional school model not only short-changes Tactile-Kines-thetic Learners, it also shortchanges all the other learners, because lessons that incorporate moving and doing are helpful for everyone!

For example, if you know your child dislikes working on the computer and does not like to dance, you would not choose these activities. If your child loves to assemble models, watch National Geographic programs, and is dramatic, start with videos, building, and acting.

Now, when your child is studying about Egypt and having trouble understanding or retaining the information, you could provide a video about Egypt. You could encourage him to act like a reporter gathering information for a newscast, and have some-one videotape him. If a report is required for school, you could find out if the teacher would accept a model of an Egyptian city

> *Research on learning teaches us that learners of all ages use combinations of these modalities, and may vary the recipe according to the situation.*
>
> —*Priscilla Vail*

and a show-and-tell presentation with little or no writing involved.

Also think about your child's other strengths. For instance, she might like to sing (even though the Auditory Modality is not her dominant one). If that's the case, she can learn to easily memorize information for a test by setting it to a melody and singing it. (Try singing the Declaration of Independence to the melody of "Twinkle, Twinkle Little Star!")

These are examples of how modality information is put to best use when the strategies chosen form a bridge between the student's most developed processing mode and the skill or concept that he is trying to learn.

Remember that your child will appreciate all your attempts to acknowledge and meet her modality needs. As you work together to find what works best, the whole process will become easier and more fun!

QUICK REFERENCE CHART—AUDITORY MODALITY

Note: Sources for the resources listed below can be found in Appendix II.

PROGRAM EMPHASIS: hear/talk

Listening:

HELPFUL MATERIALS

Math
- Can Do Videotapes, Arithme-toons, Math Mystery Theater, Audio Memory cassettes

Reading/Spelling
- Sing/Spell/Read/Write, Play N Talk, Phonics In Song

Other Subjects
- *Boomerang* (magazine on cassette), New Each Day cassettes, Audio Memory Cassettes, Lyrical Life Science

TEACHING TECHNIQUES

- audio tapes, books-on-tape, music, rhyming, songs, stories, computers, live lectures, oral or duet reading

Verbal:

HELPFUL MATERIALS

Math
- Bornstein Memorizer cards, Rhyme Tymes, TNT™ Fact Kit

Reading/Spelling
- Sing/Spell/Read/Write, Play N Talk, Phonics In Song

Other Subjects
- Lyrical Life Science, New Each Day and Audio Memory cassettes, Stories and Plays Without Endings

TEACHING TECHNIQUES

- reading aloud, discussing, verbalizing to oneself, reading along with books-on-tape, interactive video/computer programs, taping reports and assignments, oral presentations, setting information to music and singing it, working with another person or in a small group

(continues)

QUICK REFERENCE CHART—VISUAL MODALITY

Note: Sources for the resources listed below can be found in Appendix II.

PROGRAM EMPHASIS: see/read

Picture:

HELPFUL MATERIALS

Math
- On Cloud Nine, Abacus Math, Touch Math, Multiplication Rock Video, Mathematics (high-school video/computer program)

Reading/Spelling
- AVKO, Wilson Reading Program

Other Subjects
- Graphic Organizers, National Geographic videos
- Cartoon Guide series: American history, economics, physics, genetics, etc.
- Coloring Book series: anatomy, zoology, botany, geography, etc.

TEACHING TECHNIQUES

- videos, computers, picture cues, picture diagrams or charts, picture time-lines, picture note-taking and information mapping, live performances

Print:

HELPFUL MATERIALS

Math
- Mastering Mathematics, Video Tutor

Reading/Spelling
- Phonics Tutor, Ultimate Phonics

Other Subjects
- Graphic Organizers, Stories and Plays Without Endings

TEACHING TECHNIQUES

- reading, research, word diagrams or charts, timelines, word note-taking and information mapping, highlighting written material, workbooks

QUICK REFERENCE CHART—
TACTILE-KINESTHETIC MODALITY

Note: Sources for the resources listed below can be found in Appendix II.

PROGRAM EMPHASIS: touch/do

Hands-on:

HELPFUL MATERIALS

Math
- On Cloud Nine, Abacus Math, Touch Math

Reading/Spelling
- Sing/Spell/Read/Write, Wilson Reading Program

TEACHING TECHNIQUES

- touching, constructing, assembling, taking things apart, manipulating objects, textured materials, models, blocks, Legos

Whole Body:

HELPFUL MATERIALS

Math
- Can Do Videotapes, Number Mat (see *What to Do When They Don't Get It* in Appendix II)

Reading/Spelling
- Sing/Spell/Read/Write, Play N Talk

Other Subjects
- Stories and Plays Without Endings

TEACHING TECHNIQUES

- acting out, moving, dancing, exercising, building, walk-on materials

Sketching:

HELPFUL MATERIALS

Math
- Touch Math

(continues)

(continued)

Reading/Spelling
- Wilson Reading Program, Draw Write Now, Drawing with Letters and Numbers

Other Subjects
- Graphic Organizers, Stories and Plays Without Endings
- Cartoon Guide series: American history, economics, physics, genetics, etc.
- Coloring Book series: anatomy, zoology, botany, geography, etc.

TEACHING TECHNIQUES

- drawing, coloring, doodling, picture note-taking and information mapping

Writing:

HELPFUL MATERIALS

Math
- Touch Math

Reading/Spelling
- AVKO, Wilson Reading Program, Studentreasures™

Other Subjects
- Graphic Organizers, Stories and Plays Without Endings

TEACHING TECHNIQUES

- writing, tracing, copying, workbooks, research, outlines, word note-taking and information mapping

Environment: Beyond a Desk and Four Walls

Most of us would agree that our environment, or surroundings, can greatly affect our ability to think, learn, and work. We realize that if we are too hot or too cold, or very hungry or thirsty, our concentration will be affected. We also know how hard it is to give our complete attention to work or study when the wind is blowing or spring is in the air or the first snow is starting to fall. We realize that the noise level might be annoying, the light too dim or too bright, the seating uncomfortable, or the layout of the room too distracting for us to process information efficiently. Some of us know that we won't get anything done unless we are alone, while others can't function if they *are* alone. Still others are very sensitive to elements of beauty and harmony and have a difficult time being productive in unattractive surroundings.

Yet we tend to greatly underestimate the role of environment for learning and the necessity for taking it into account in the classroom. Instead, we tell our children that they need to learn to ignore the surroundings—to concentrate no matter what else is going on. Even when other students are distracting them, they are to stay completely focused, somewhat like the guards at

Buckingham Palace. Those who don't, won't, or can't stay focused are labeled ADD, ADHD, distractible, undisciplined, or problematic.

> **W**e tend to greatly underestimate the role of environment for learning and the necessity for taking it into account in the classroom.

The traditional setting for "efficient" study insisted upon by teachers and parents is this: The student should be alone, in a quiet place, sitting at a desk or table, with plain surroundings, preferably in the morning when the student is "fresh." This is recommended for homework and studying for tests. It is interesting that this notion continues to be passed on, even though many people have realized as adults that this is not *their* ideal setting for learning or working. I hope by the end of this chapter you will understand how essential it is to change outdated ideas about a child's study environment.

STUDIES

Abraham Maslow's now famous system, called the Hierarchy of Basic Human Needs, helps to explain why a person cannot pay attention to academic learning if the need for nourishment is not

> " *We may accidentally reduce motivation and learning by keeping a traditional seating pattern.*
> —Eric Jensen "

met and if the environment is not safe and secure. Only when these basic needs have been taken care of are we free to concentrate on more intellectual pursuits. For the most part, we go along with this thinking, and we understand that children who are in situations of poverty, neglect, fear, or trauma of some sort do not have environments that are conducive to learning.

What about the rest of our children, those who live in "normal" circumstances? Can their environments really affect their learning?

Rita Dunn, who has researched the subject of learning styles for at least thirty years, has demonstrated that many aspects of the environment affect learning, including sound, lighting, temperature, seating design, food availability, time of day, opportunity for movement, and number of participants. Adapting to the needs of individual children in each of these areas results in greater concentration and improved learning for all students.[1]

Oh, sure, you're thinking, my child's teacher is going to allow food and drink in class, arrange the furniture differently, dim the lights, and encourage a radio with headphones, just because these are my child's environmental needs! Well, it is possible. Across the country, with greater frequency, teachers are rearranging

> **A**cross the country, with greater frequency, teachers are rearranging their classrooms to better fit the needs of individuals within the group.

their classrooms to better fit the needs of individuals within the group.[2] This topic is also coming to the attention of architects and others involved in developing architectural design ideas for schools.

FUTURE SCHOOLS

American School & University asked the nation's leading educational architecture firms for input on building schools for the future.[3] The magazine was looking for ideas on designing school environments that are more conducive to learning—facilities that provide flexible spaces that can be arranged to satisfy a variety of teaching and learning styles. One firm commented that "With the 21st century almost here, it is sobering to realize that architects and educators have yet to generate a concept for the classroom of the future that looks much different from the classroom as we have known it for the previous 100 years." It went on to say:

> A fundamental change in curriculum delivery . . . easily can be accomplished with no increase in room size. Instead, it simply needs a

fresh approach to classroom furniture and layout. Those who doubt the vital relevance of furniture to pedagogy would do well to consider the impact of the Harkness table at Phillips Exeter and other leading private secondary schools, where all classroom instruction takes place around large oval tables that can accommodate 12 students and one instructor. These tables have encouraged and supported the notion of the teacher as the facilitator for the past 70 years . . . The problem, of course, is that no public school system can afford the 12:1 student-teacher ratio . . . However, with the coming of . . . computer networks, the Internet, distance learning . . . it should be possible for students in public schools to begin to experience the kind of classroom facilitation that, until now, only has been available to students in elite private schools.

Participating architectural firms submitted ideas centered around the concept of flexible learning spaces, or learning centers, designed to provide user-friendly environments for learning by accommodating various modes of instruction—teams, pairs, independent, small group, and large group. Most included provisions for natural lighting, various seating arrangements, integrated learning, and interactive learning. I am encouraged by the vision of these architects and the forward-looking educators who are engaging in this type of dialogue. I am also reminded of Maria Montessori and the careful attention her schools give to the learning environment.

> **. . . our preferences or needs might vary with the task or combination of factors involved.**

 ## ELEMENTS OF ENVIRONMENT

The Learning Style Profile in this book looks at the following aspects of environment: sound, body position, interaction, lighting, temperature, food, color, and time. It is important to keep in mind that these elements can become more or less significant depending on the situation and what we are being asked to do. In other words, our preferences or needs might vary with the task or combination of factors involved. If we are working where the sound and seating suit our needs and the task does not require intense concentration, then the time of day might not affect us. It is also important to remember that for some students each of these elements or combination of elements can be more crucial than for other students.

In this chapter you will take a look at each of the environmental elements and how they might be varied for different types of learners. If you feel like you are getting too much information all at once, slow down and take it section by section. Remember that you are getting the complete picture about environment so that you will be aware of its many aspects. In most cases, it is not possible to satisfy *every* aspect for each child, but knowing about all of them will give you more opportunities to choose as many as you can for *your* child. As you work with your child you will probably find that even one or two environmental changes can make a great deal of difference.

Sound

This element of environment includes two possibilities: the need for quiet and the need for noise.

Need for Quiet

Some people need total quiet when they are thinking, studying, or working on a project. If there is any sound at all, they are distracted and unable to work. "Noise" could mean people talking, music playing; a radio or TV on; or back-ground noises such as street sounds, rain, or wind. Even noise coming from a distance, such as construction sounds, bells chiming, or sirens can interrupt thought and concentration. Children who are very sensitive to all sound have a tough time in the classroom where there is usually a great deal going on.

> **C**hildren who are very sensitive to all sound have a tough time in the classroom where there is usually a great deal going on.

who are very sensitive to all sound have a tough time in the classroom where there is usually a great deal going on. At home, also, it could be too noisy for them to do homework and study effectively.

Options for the child who needs quiet include:

- Provide a room that is quiet where the child can go to study alone.
- Provide earplugs for the child if a separate room is not available.
- Have a family discussion about the importance of respecting this child's need for quiet and uninterrupted study time.
- Ask the teacher if the child can wear earplugs when working alone on certain tasks.

Need for Noise

Some people cannot function if it is too quiet! In order to focus they *need* background noise—people talking, music playing, radio or TV on. Noisy classrooms suit the needs of children who need sound. However, these children do not do well at home if they are required to work or study alone in a quiet room. All through my own school years, I did most of my homework and studying either lounging on the couch with the TV on, or lying on the bed with the radio on. Since my grade point average was always between 3.8 and 4.0 my parents never questioned my routine!

> **A**s you work with your child you will probably find that even one or two environmental changes can make a great deal of difference.

This was my way of providing some auditory relief for the endless hours I spent by myself doing homework.

Options for the child who needs noise include:

- Allow the child to work in a room where normal activities are going on.
- If the home is a quiet one, allow experimentation with radio or TV on as background noise. (Of course if TV is

not acceptable in your household, do not offer this as an option!)

■ Experiment with music of the child's choosing (within reason—do not offer as an option music that you feel is not conducive to learning, for example very loud music or inappropriate rap music). Also try classical, and, in particular, baroque music, which is reported to stimulate brain areas that facilitate learning. Many children balk at this type of music at first, but later they decide they like it and ask for it!

■ Distinguish between music and other sound. Some children are distracted by conversation or even general background noise, but not by music. In some cases, having music on helps to block out the other distracting sounds.

> " *Science is now corroborating age-old intuition. We know that music using certain types of rhythm does bring about a state of relaxed alertness and physical calm.*
>
> —Colin Rose "

■ Talk to your child's teacher about playing soft music in class. Studies have shown that music can enhance learning and productivity in the classroom; in fact, most students are positively affected.[4]

■ Some teachers will allow students who need music to use a tape player with earphones.

Body Position

While some children need to sit up at a table or desk to do their best work or thinking, just as many do better in other positions. Reclining or sitting on a bed, couch, bean bag chair, or the floor are alternatives. Still others need to be standing up, perhaps working at an easel, a board on the wall, or a tall drafting table. Being able to get up frequently and walk around might be desirable. Some people do their best thinking when they are moving!

At home, you and your child can experiment with different arrangements. At school, the teacher might allow carpet mats for those who do better on the floor. Some teachers encourage students to change postures as needed. Having guidelines for using mats or moving about the room without disrupting the class helps to make free movement possible. A tall counter or table could accommodate those who need standing up time.

Options for body position include:

> **B**eing able to get up frequently and walk around might be desirable. Some people do their best thinking when they are moving!

- Sitting: desk, table, floor
- Reclining: bed, couch, floor
- Standing: easel, board, drafting table, counter
- Teacher allowing students to work on carpet mats or at the board

Interaction

People have different interaction needs when they are learning. The child who needs to work alone is usually the most easily accommodated, since this is still thought to be the best study method both at home and at school. Yet, for the children who really do need to be alone, the crowded classroom is less than ideal, and the home setting can also be a problem if an empty room is not available. Every effort should be made to provide a private space. Sometimes this can be done easily with inexpensive curtains, screens, or room dividers. When none of these is an option, an open space or corner separated with chalk, tape, paint markings, pillows, or furniture can give the illusion of a private space. In one classroom, a student took his work to the floor space underneath a table, where he was able to work independently and quietly.

The child who needs other people around is often banished to his room to study alone, because that is the traditional study setting. For this child, the classroom easily provides the other people. At home, this child needs to work in spaces where other family members are present. Those children who need quiet do best when the other people are also working quietly; those who need background noise do better with activity (refer to the above section on sound regarding conversation versus "working" noise).

When other people are not available during study time, pets can be as (or more) effective in filling the need to have other living beings around.

> **W**hen other people are not available during study time, pets can be as (or more) effective in filling the need to have other living beings around.

Some children need to interact with another person or in a small group. Verbal learners often fit this category. As discussed in Chapter 8, it is a good idea to have someone available at least part of the time when this child is doing schoolwork. You can also allow studying with a buddy or two.

Options for interaction include:

- Alone: separate room, private space created with room dividers, small space created with markings or furniture
- With others: in the same room with people working quietly, in the same room with people busy with conversation or other activities, or with pets
- With interaction: with a buddy or parent, with a small group of students
- Ask the teacher if it is possible to create some small private spaces in the classroom to accommodate children who need to work alone
- Ask the teacher if it is possible to provide a classroom space to work with a buddy or in a small group

Lighting

People are affected differently by various lighting situations.[5,6] Is the lighting bright or low, natural or artificial? If artificial, is it incandescent, fluorescent, or full-spectrum?

Fluorescent lighting in particular has been shown to negatively affect children and adults. It can cause headaches, difficulty reading, eyestrain, irritability, and hyperactive behavior.

Plants will not survive under fluorescent lighting although we expect people to! Full-spectrum lighting, commonly used to grow plants indoors, more closely resembles the full spectrum of light present in nature. Plants thrive under full-spectrum lighting and positive effects have been documented in the classroom as well. At home, if you have fluorescent lights, try switching to full-spectrum. Several brands are available at nurseries, building supply stores, and in home improvement catalogs. It could make a big difference in attitude and productivity for the whole family!

Some schools have switched to full-spectrum lighting after realizing the benefits. In an experiment reported by Eric Jensen, students in classrooms with full-spectrum lighting missed significantly fewer school days than those in the other classrooms. Furthermore, ordinary fluorescent light has been shown to raise the cortisol level in the blood, which is likely to suppress the immune system.[7]

> **P**lants will not survive under fluorescent lighting although we expect people to!

If you have mostly incandescent lighting in your home, this should be fine, as long as the brightness is adjusted for individual needs. Jensen also reports that many students who are fidgety and restless where the lights are bright, relax and perform better in low-to-moderate light situations. Dimmer lighting seems to have a calming effect, especially at younger ages, and the ideal lighting seems to be indirect natural sunlight. When it is not possible to switch to full-spectrum lights or to dim the lights, have your child try wearing sunglasses or a visor to cut down on the brightness.

Note your child's choices on the Profile, then add your observations about how your child is affected by various types of lighting.

Temperature

Is it too hot or too cold? As we all know, hot and cold are relative. My husband and I never agree on the temperature— one of us is always either too hot or too cold! We can usually solve the problem with clothing changes.

However, there are instances when a room is simply too warm or too cool for everyone. Again, as with the other aspects of environment, some children are more affected by uncomfortable temperatures than others. But classrooms that do not have adequate heating or cooling systems might be affecting the learning efficiency of a majority of the students. Space heaters or fans might be enough to do the trick at school and at home. For those students who are unusually warm or cool when the majority seem to be comfortable, experiment with changing clothing, sitting next to a window, or using a small personal heater or fan, as the situation warrants.

Note your child's choices on the Profile, then add your observations about how your child is affected by room temperatures.

Food

Availability of food and drink can also affect learning efficiency. Some students do better when they can snack throughout the day. If this is the case with your child, provide healthful food and drink such as fruits, vegetables, whole-grain cereal bars, nuts, rice cakes, yogurt, unsweetened fruit juices, vegetable juices, and water. More and more teachers are recognizing that the need for frequent food intake is legitimate for many children and are allowing students to have snacks and water bottles in class.

Note your child's choices on the Profile, then add your observations about your child's nourishment needs.

Color

The effect of color on mood and activity has been studied for years, especially by media marketers. Color plays a big part in advertising, and marketers know which colors will get us to buy, to stay longer, to spend more, etc. We know that some colors depress and others energize, some are soothing and others make us feel rattled. Some colors slow us down, and some make us feel hyper.

Besides the general color principles that seem to apply to everyone, a person's favorite colors can also dramatically affect mood and activity.

When we are surrounded by our favorite colors we tend to think more positively and feel more motivated. When surrounded by colors we don't like, the opposite happens, and we can actually feel restless, upset, distracted, unhappy, even angry. Just as with any of the other elements of environment, different people are more or less sensitive to color.

> " . . . *When architects changed schoolroom walls from orange and white to blue, students' blood pressure dropped and their behavior and learning comprehension soared.*
> —*Dr. Morton Walker* "

At home, parents can help their children decide on how to incorporate favorite colors in designated areas. For the classroom, children can learn to buy school supplies in favorite colors. Will having your favorite color around guarantee passing the test or getting an A on a paper? No, but color can substantially change mood and outlook, and it's one more piece of the puzzle that can contribute to a more positive learning experience. Talking to your child about color is also another way of letting him know that you are listening and that his needs and preferences matter.

Children (and adults) can learn to:

- Add favorite colors (to the extent possible) to a personal room, study space, desktop, or office in the form of paint, art, rugs, plants, furniture, pillows, or other accessories.
- Use pens and notebooks in favorite colors when taking tests or doing other paperwork.
- Wear favorite colors to an important interview or other appointment.
- Stay away from disliked colors.

Time of Day

Like adults, children operate differently at different times of the day. Taking this element seriously means being flexible about the time of day that children are asked to do schoolwork. According to Rita Dunn's extensive research, "*Most* students are *not* morning-alert . . . Only about one-third of more than a million students we have tested prefer learning in the early morning, and the majority prefer late morning or afternoon . . . Many do not begin to be capable of concentrating on difficult material until after 10:00 A.M. and many are at their best in the early afternoon."[8] A recent article in the L.A. Times stated that teenagers were the subject of a bill being presented to California's 106th Congress by Rep. Zoe Lofgren (D-San Jose). The bill, called the "Zzzs to A's Act," would encourage high schools to start classes after 9 A.M. "so that teens are in school during their most alert hours and can achieve their full academic potential."[9]

This is probably the most difficult element of environment to apply. Those who homeschool are in a better position to arrange a schedule that takes advantage of each child's best time of day. In the regular elementary classroom, a child is not able to make choices about his schedule. Furthermore, math and reading, which are considered the most important subjects, are often taught first thing in the morning. In high school, the student sometimes has a little control over the schedule and can choose a physical education class or study hall for first and second periods. College students have even more leeway and are often able to arrange class schedules to better meet their learning needs.

What about the old saying, "The early bird catches the worm"? Isn't it generally true that disciplining yourself to get up early gives you a good start on the day and forms good habits? Actually, yes, it is true. I am not suggesting that children sleep until noon, or get up whenever they feel like it, or just lounge around until they are bored enough to do some work. However, I am asking us to question the *order* of activities that we require a child to engage in throughout the day.

The study mentioned above tells us that, for most children, academic learning is probably done best in the late morning or

> **I am asking us to question the order of activities that we require a child to engage in throughout the day.**

early afternoon. If this is true, are there other things they could do early in the morning?

On the farm, children rose early and did all kinds of chores before heading off to school. This is a big clue. Children were getting up and doing physical activities. They were feeding animals, cleaning barns, milking cows, tending the garden, and cooking breakfast. They were spending their first hours outdoors, engaged in valuable work, interacting with people and animals, and eating a full meal. My guess is that by the time they started off to school (walking and thus getting even more exercise), their minds were clear and alert and ready to start higher level thinking. It should also be mentioned that these children (and their parents) had early bedtimes.

> **F**or most children, academic learning is probably done best in the late morning or early afternoon.

Our typical present-day child drags himself out of bed, throws some clothes on, maybe munches on a donut, and rushes out the door, arriving at a classroom where the first thing he will do is sit and listen to a lesson or write in a workbook. What if he at least got to do some stretching or warm-up activities before starting on academics?

Many years ago, when I was the director of a private school, all of the students began their day with an exercise program. In some private religious schools students begin the day with a church service. Some schools serve breakfast to make sure the kids have the nourishment that their brains require. Some of the homeschool families that I work with start their school day with a family meeting, at which they discuss how each person feels that morning, what each person's goals are for the day, what each person is happiest about, the most excited about, the most grateful for. All of these activities give kids a chance to warm up and get their brains in gear! Your child's teacher might be open to experimenting with stretching, simple exercises, and/or warm-up discussions in the morning. Reading and discussing a positive, inspiring story, such as those in *Chicken Soup for the Kid's Soul* and *Chicken Soup for the Teenage Soul* by Jack Canfield and

Mark Victor Hansen, is another great way to start the day. In religious schools, the morning activities could include prayer, Bible stories, or other religious readings.

If the teacher is not able to provide a warm-up time, think about doing something at home before leaving for school. I know that in many households the morning is a very hectic time, as the whole family is struggling to get to where they need to be. Bedtimes can also make a difference for the dynamics of what occurs in the mornings. A late bedtime usually means it is more difficult to get up in the morning. Think about your family situation, you might be surprised at what you can come up with. It could be as simple as two minutes

> **A**ll of these activities give kids a chance to warm up and get their brains in gear!

of jumping jacks or a quick walk around the block. If you are a family that rises early, there might be time for some stretching and exercise routines. If your kids end up watching cartoons while you are preparing breakfast, you can put on a math video instead, which will have them doing exercises *and* practicing math facts (see Appendix II for *Can Do Videotapes*). How about putting on energizing music and jogging in place to the rhythm? Even though you can't change the time that your kids actually start schoolwork, you can at least give them some waking up activities that will make them better prepared for the classroom.

Parents can experiment with:

- Movement activities: stretches, exercises, rhythmic movement, dancing, aerobics
- Discussion activities: family meetings, problem solving, goal setting, planning the day
- Story activities: read inspiring, motivating stories and let kids discuss
- Fun activities: puzzles, brainteasers, coloring, drawing, crafts
- Asking the teacher to consider starting the day with movement, discussion, story activities, or brainteasers

THE TEACHER WON'T CHANGE ANYTHING!

Yes, it's true—you can share all the information in this chapter with the teacher, and he won't change a thing! Then what?

To begin with, acknowledge your child's needs, thus validating her feelings. Then seek solutions. For example, if your child complains that she just can't think about math first thing in the morning, instead of saying, "Well, there's nothing you can do about it. All the other kids seem to be able to do it. Math is at 9:00, you're just going to have to put up with it. Pay attention and don't get distracted!" try this, "I am so sorry math is early. I know that's your least favorite time of day, and you have to deal with an important subject like math. Let's brainstorm—I bet we can come up with great ideas to make it easier for you." Then review the section on Time of Day for ideas and see what you can figure out together. (See more about solution-focused problem solving in Chapter 12.)

> **W**e cannot always control what happens in certain places, such as the classroom, but we can use our brains to come up with solutions that will help us to do better.

Discuss the various aspects of environment with your children and talk about changes that can be made at home. Explain that we cannot always control what happens in certain places, such as the classroom, but that we can use our brains to come up with solutions that will help us to do better. You can ask for your child's ideas on how she might get along in class when she wishes it was warmer, or she could snack, or that the light wasn't so bright, or she could turn on the radio, and so on. She might learn to think of it as a daily challenge or game— What can I do today to turn the negative into something positive and fun?—a skill that will prove to be useful many times in her life!

You might be surprised at the ideas your child comes up with. Sometimes, simply having this conversation, showing that you understand and are willing to make some changes at home, really listening to your child's concerns, and encouraging creative problem solving—sometimes, this is enough to help your child do better in the classroom, even when the teacher changes nothing.

As mentioned earlier, you will not be able to make *all* the changes required for every aspect of your child's learning style. Remember that balance is the key. Consider family priorities, your own needs, *and* your child's needs, as you learn to work together.

 ## ONE LAST THING

For those who still aren't quite sure, or who still need permission—yes, it's okay to allow your child to work on his book report spread out on the floor, with the cat curled next to him, and the CD player on. If this is what he needs, it's more than okay, it's essential!

10

Putting It All Together

You've just finished taking an in-depth look at the five aspects of learning style. You are now probably thinking, Where do I go from here? How can I put all of this information together? If you are feeling a little overwhelmed, relax! This chapter will help you put it all together by taking it one step at a time. Then, in Chapter 11, you will learn more about how to use this information with the whole family.

 FILL OUT THE FORMS

If you have not already done so, make copies of the assessments found in Chapter 4 and have each member of the family fill them out. Also make copies of the Summary form and the Plan form for each child. Follow the instructions for scoring each of the assessments and transfer the scores and responses to the Summary form as directed.

The Summary

This form brings together all of the information about your child for each of the five aspects of learning style. After you have transferred the scores and responses to this form, go back through it *with your child* and note the following:

Disposition Section

Circle or highlight the two dispositions that received the highest totals. If a third disposition score is very close to the top two, highlight this disposition as well. Note that negative scores are possible, for example, −4. This simply means that this person is very low in the characteristics of this disposition and does not indicate a "problem." Remember that there are no "right" or "wrong" answers, or "better" or "worse" scores on this Profile.

Talents Section

Scores of 60 or above indicate talent areas. Occasionally, a child will choose almost everything on the page or hardly anything. If either of these happens, it could indicate that the child does not have confidence in his own abilities. Accept the responses for now and plan to readminister this part at a later date, perhaps after you have been working with the Learning Style Model for awhile and the child's confidence has increased.

Most children, however, are aware of their talent areas and do not have difficulty choosing the items that reflect these talents. Circle or highlight the talents that have a score of 60 or above.

Interests Section

Note all of the chosen Interests. In particular, be aware of those listed under Involvement Issues and rated 5 to 10 on the Interest Priority Scale.

Modality Section

Part I scores indicate overall modality strengths. Circle or highlight the highest scores. Part II scores indicate specific ways of learning within each modality. Circle or highlight the three items chosen.

Environment Section

Note the choices in each element of environment.

The Plan Form

On this form record the "ideal" learning activities for your child—what you would do if anything were possible. Work on this form *with your child*. Younger children can participate to the degree that it is appropriate.

If you don't feel ready to fill out this form, finish reading this chapter and then come back to it. The stories about real families that come later in this chapter will help you be more confident about completing this form.

Step 1

Go back through the Profile chapters (5 to 9), use the charts, and note in each section of the Plan which materials, techniques, strategies, and environmental set-ups would work best for your child.

Step 2

Now go back over the Plan. This time circle or highlight one or two items in each section that you feel comfortable trying at home. Also note a couple of items that you might be willing to talk to the teacher about.

Step 3

Fill out the Areas for Growth section. These are *general* areas, for example: Producing skills, Word-Language Reasoning skills, Math skills, and so on. In Chapter 11 you will learn how to work on *specific* skills such as spelling and memorizing math facts.

Step 4

Fill out the Life Goals section. Again, these are *general* goals: become a veterinarian, own my own business, teach ballet. In Chapter 11 you will learn how to work on *specific* learning goals

such as increasing the score on spelling quiz, memorizing the 3×
table, etc.

TALK TO YOUR CHILD

How do you talk to your child about learning style? Very simply!
Share with your child what you have learned in this book. Talk
about the benefits of learning about oneself and how this knowledge can help at school, at home, and at the workplace. Talk
about the importance of respecting each person's unique gifts
and style of learning. Explain that each of us has different talents, dispositions, interests, environment needs, and
modality strengths. We are all smart in our own ways and we all
learn differently. Teach your child that the information about her
learning style can help her in many learning situations and can
also help point the way to possible career choices.

You can also tell your child that most classrooms are set up
to basically teach one type of learner—one who has the Producing Disposition and Auditory Modality strength. If this is your
child's style and she is already doing well in school, explain that
applying some of the other learning style information can make
studying even easier. Also explain that there are aspects of her
learning style that probably are not being addressed by the
school program, and that you can
help her tap into those areas in other
ways. If your child is *not* the Producing Disposition–Auditory Modality
type, and she *is* having difficulty in
school, explain that her teacher is
doing the best he knows how with
the system he has to work with.
Offer to make as many changes as
possible at home and help her come
up with strategies to cope with
school. Assure her that no matter
what, you know that she is smart and
capable and talented.

> **Teach your child that the information about her learning style can help her in many learning situations and can also help point the way to possible career choices.**

Also tell your child that learning style information is *not* meant to be used as an excuse to get out of something you need to do, or as a reason to give up on something that is difficult. The information is meant to be used in a positive way, to help a person be successful and move forward. Learning style information also helps us to better communicate and cooperate with others as we become aware of *their* individual styles as well.

As children participate in the learning style process they become more proficient at meeting their own learning needs. Do not keep the results to yourself and file them away! Refer to the Profiles often, have family discussions, talk about the differences among the members of the family, think about ways to apply the information to make learning easier. In Chapter 11 you will find more ideas for applying learning style information, including how to graph scores; suggestions for family meetings, discussions, and individual meetings with each child; and how to use strengths to overcome weaknesses.

> **L**earning style information also helps us to better communicate and cooperate with others as we become aware of *their* individual styles as well.

 ## TALK TO THE TEACHER

In many cases, you will be the first to approach your child's teacher with information about learning style. You might feel awkward speaking to a professional, and not very confident. In Chapter 14 you will find suggestions to help you.

 ## DOES THIS WORK FOR REAL FAMILIES?

Okay, you're thinking, I understand all of this. But I'm still not sure what to *do*. How does it work in real life? Does this learning style stuff work for real families?

> *Many people don't realize that the word* genius *actually means "to be born" or "to come into being." In ancient times all persons were believed to possess a personal genius . . . that was given to them at birth and that governed their fortunes in life and determined their essential character.*
>
> —Thomas Armstrong

Let's take a look at some real families who have used the Learning Style Profile: why they were interested in learning style assessment; how each family applied the results of the assessment; and the differences it made for the children and their families.

Greg's Story

Greg was in seventh grade in a private school. He couldn't seem to keep up with the class work and the assignments. He had difficulty comprehending the material in several subject areas and did not do well on tests. It was suspected by the school and his parents that Greg had a learning disability that affected areas of comprehension, retention, organization, and written expression.

I tested Greg. In most areas he seemed to perform in an age-level appropriate manner. He could probably use a few tricks to help him learn how to organize material to study for a test or write an essay. His comprehension was fine; his spelling was a "problem."[1] His parents wondered, Should he be in special education classes?

Results of Greg's Profile

As you read this section refer to Greg's Learning Style Portrait (see Figure 10.1).

In the Disposition section of the Profile, Greg scored highest in Invent and second highest in Relate/Inspire, indicating that he learned best when he was able to take his time thinking things through, and that bouncing ideas off other people was also helpful. Jumping from subject to subject was not his style. He did better when he could concentrate on one project for awhile. Discussions, field trips, and time to explore, reflect, and discover could all be helpful to Greg's learning.

Greg's Learning Style Portrait

Disposition

Needs: Score

Time to _____ ____ ✪ Performs
think alone

                              ____ ✪ Produces

Bounce ideas off _____ 42 ✪ Invents
of others

                       25 ✪ Relates/Inspires

_____ ____ ✪ Thinks/Creates

Interests

Science

History

Modality

Visual - Picture

T/K - Hands-On

Environment

Quiet

Alone sometimes

Able to move around

Discussion groupings

Color: Green

Bright, natural light

Talents

Mechanical Reasoning

Spatial

Goals	Strategies
To increase learning retention	Charts, Graphs, Posters
To increase organization & writing skill	Visual strategies & Information mapping
To spell better	Computer games, Visualization "tricks," Hands-on word analysis

Figure 10.1 Greg's Learning Style Portrait

In the Modality section he chose a combination of Visual (Picture) and Tactile (Hands-on). This indicated that the use of charts, graphs, and posters could increase learning and retention; visual strategies such as information mapping could increase his organization and writing skills; computer games, visualization "tricks," and hands-on techniques for analyzing words could help him to be a better speller.[2]

In the Talent section Greg scored highest in Mechanical Reasoning and Spatial Talent. His Interests included science and history. The information in both these sections gave us further insight into the disposition and modality results. For example, Greg's Inventing Disposition will probably tend toward physical science and possibly engineering. His interest in history is probably tied in to the Relating Disposition but could also be linked to his disposition for exploring and discovering (Inventing).

We also found out that Greg needed a quiet setting where he could be alone part of the time. Ideally he would be allowed to get up and move around and to periodically engage in discussion to help him better understand a lesson. His favorite color, green, could be chosen for pens, pencils, notebooks, beanbag chair, and so on. Bright, natural light helped him stay focused, so working next to a window could be beneficial.

As we began to integrate the five parts of the Profile, Greg's parents were able to see, for the first time in Greg's school life, all of his strengths, gifts, and abilities. A picture began to emerge of a very capable, unique individual with many positive attributes! Options and possibilities for goals and careers became evident. Now, by taking action based on the results of the Profile, we could take advantage of his strengths and give him the tools to handle the subject matter he was struggling with at school. This would build up his confidence and lead to more successes.

As we discussed the results of Greg's Learning Style profile, another aspect was uncovered. Greg's family realized that Greg was the only Inventing–Relating Disposition in the family. The rest of them were Performing people!—always on the go, very athletic, energetic, noisy . . . No one could understand why Greg didn't fit in, why he didn't want to go to game after game, why he became upset and edgy and crabby. Now they under-stood. He needed quiet, reflective time . . . time to just be alone with his thoughts . . . time to invent and create.

What Happened Next?

Greg recognized himself in the descriptions of the Inventing and Relating styles. Instantly, his facial expression, his smile, and his body language told me that this made sense to him. He wasn't stupid or lazy or disobedient or contrary or disabled! He had a wonderful learning style of his own—*and* he was smart and cre-ative. He understood that he was in a learning situation that did not allow him to make use of his abilities or learn the way he was born to learn. He realized that he was being forced to operate in a way that was contrary to his makeup.

Greg's family began to allow opportunities at home for Greg to have quiet, reflective time amidst the frenzied atmo-sphere. They also gave him some choice about whether or not he would accompany them to all of their activities and outings. With respect to schoolwork, his parents talked to his teachers about the Profile results and also encouraged Greg to use the informa-tion about his disposition, modality strengths, talents, and other learning style areas when doing homework assignments and studying for tests.

Did the teachers change anything for Greg? Actually, no. One of them wasn't really interested; the other was sympathetic, but she had a large class and she didn't think there was much she could do other than acknowledge and encourage him.

What did Greg do? He did not turn into the perfect stu-dent. But his attitude changed. He understood that sometimes we are stuck in a learning or job situation that is less than ideal. He realized that there was nothing wrong with him; rather, the system was a problem. He stopped feeling stupid and inadequate and angry. And he actually started to improve! All by himself, he began applying the information that he learned about his best ways to learn. He also was more willing to cooperate with the teachers and the system now that he knew this "problem" was not his fault.

What Really Happened Here?

The teachers didn't change, the parents changed a little, but mostly Greg changed! Often, merely acknowledging a child's unique characteristics and talking with him about his Profile results is enough to produce feelings of self-worth and major changes in attitude. Remember the C.A.R.E.S. principles discussed in Chapter 3: When we begin working with *them*, they begin working with *us* and themselves.

> **T**here is simply no substitute for self-confidence rooted in acceptance and appreciation.

I am amazed each time I experience this. Greg's reaction is not a rare one; I have seen this happen over and over after discussing learning style results with a child. Whether or not the school program is changed, the kids feel better and act differently just knowing that someone has bothered to find out what they are like, and that their results describe a competent, valued person. There is simply no substitute for self-confidence rooted in acceptance and appreciation.

What Else Could Have Happened?

Even though Greg made gains on his own, think about the possibilities if his learning style information had been used by his teachers and implemented in his school program. The Profile information was a powerful tool waiting to be used and applied by his teachers to create the best possible learning situation for Greg.

Ann's Story

As you read this section, refer to Ann's Learning Style Portrait (see Figure 10.2). Ann was in first grade. She was a bundle of energy and loved to talk. She was having trouble staying at her desk, keeping quiet, and paying attention to directions. She loved recess and the other kids, and she liked to swing and build and dance and play the musical instruments. She seemed to be

Ann's Learning Style Portrait

Disposition

Needs:

To move

To do

Games

Variety of Activities

Quiet, alone time

Score

37   Performs

  Produces

  Invents

  Relates/Inspires

28   Thinks/Creates

Interests

Playing drums	Legos
singing	dancing
crafts	dogs
computer games	

Modality

Visual - Picture

T/K- Whole Body

Auditory - Verbal

Environment

Other people around

Able to move around

Frequent snacks

Dim lights

Talents

Spatial

Body Coordination

Interactive-Others

Interactive-Animals

Humor

Goals	Strategies
To improve math skills	Touch Math, Can Do Exercise, Math Videos
To memorize facts	Make rhymes, sing, dance
To do homework	Study with music in background, Breaks & snacks
To spell better	Combine drawings with letters, visualize
Sit at desk at school	Get a timer - How long can she stay quiet?

Figure 10.2 Ann's Learning Style Portrait

doing okay in reading, but she wasn't getting math at all. Her parents wondered, Was there something they could do at home?

Results of the Profile

Ann scored highest in the Perform and Think/Create Dispositions. The Modality section showed Visual (Picture), Tactile-Kinesthetic (Whole Body), and Auditory (Verbal) strengths. Her Environment needs included having other people around, being able to walk around, having frequent snacks, and dimming the lights. Her Talents showed up in the categories of Spatial, Body Coordination, Interactive-Others, Interactive-Animals, and Humor. Her Interests included playing the drums, building with Legos, singing and dancing, doing crafts, playing with her dogs, and playing computer games.

> *The child's true constructive energy, a dynamic power, has remained unnoticed for thousands of years.*
>
> *—Maria Montessori*

It was obvious from the Profile results that Ann needed to move. She did her best learning when people were around, when she could talk about the material being presented, and when she could involve her whole body in a learning experience.

Since math was the immediate concern, suggestions were made to help Ann at home. A program called *Touch Math* and the *Can Do* exercise math videos (also mentioned in Chapter 9) were recommended. The *Touch Math* program involved Ann's tactile sense and she quickly grasped the concept of addition. The *Can Do* videos made it fun to memorize math facts because she could sing along and exercise with the kids in the video. Her parents also provided two computer math programs that taught math thinking-skills through mazes and games. Once Ann caught on, math was a breeze. (See Appendix II for information about where to obtain these materials.)

What About Ann's Behavior at School?

Ann continued to have trouble sitting at her desk quietly and completing worksheets during the school day. The classroom was simply not conducive to her style of learning. However, when I spoke to the teacher, she told me that even though her behavior wasn't "perfect," for the first time Ann was bringing in completed homework assignments and she was demonstrating that she really understood math.

Ann's parents continued to apply what they had learned from the Profile results. At home they allowed Ann to do homework with music in the background, take frequent movement breaks, and snack as needed. They helped her to make rhymes and sing and dance when she had to memorize science terms. If she had difficulty with a spelling word, they encouraged her to draw silly pictures around the "problem" letters, then picture the words in her mind. And they recognized that she needed to talk things out, rather than work quietly by herself. Suddenly, learning became fun and easy—for Ann *and* her parents.

Ann's parents talked to her about the difference between the home and the classroom. They explained that the teacher cared about Ann and was doing her best. They helped her to come up with ways she could challenge herself to stay in her seat or complete a worksheet when it was boring. Ann had a watch with a timer and she made a game out of timing herself. How long could she stay quiet? How fast could she complete a worksheet? Could she break her record? The teacher realized that Ann was putting forth an effort to comply with the classroom "rules" and began praising her for her "improved" behavior. Ann was pleased and so were her parents.

Is This Really What It's About?

You might be thinking, Isn't this just like "playing the game"? Are we doing Ann a service or disservice? First we are showing her what a great learning style she has and teaching her about how she learns best. Then we are telling her to come up with ways to conform, fit in, and act that are contrary to her learning style.

One can look at this several ways. From one point of view, if you don't have a schooling option and your child must attend a traditional school, you don't want her to miss out on learning basic skills simply because the school isn't teaching to her learning style. You can use the information from the Profile to show

> **T**he more you allow children to work through their learning styles, the better equipped they are for the "real world."

her ways to understand and remember and learn that she will use for a lifetime. In addition, the "tricks" that she learns to help her deal with less than preferable situations will lay the foundation for an attitude of positive problem solving—that is, using creativity to find solutions. You will learn more about this in Chapter 12.

From another point of view, it might be time to consider other schooling options for Ann. Many families make the decision to homeschool because they want to tap into their children's highest potentials. Actually, the more you allow children to work through their learning styles, the better equipped they are for the "real world." They still learn how to deal with less than preferable situations, *and* they develop and learn in ways that are not possible when their natural talents and dispositions are stifled.

I am giving you both sides of the story here. It could be that you are in a position to change your child's schooling situation. If you are not, you still have plenty of great tools to give your child, and your own attitude of support will be most important. Remember, you are your child's first and most influential teacher. (In Part III you will also learn how to be your child's learning-success coach.)

What Else Might Happen?

The teacher might change! As Ann's parents continued to share all of the techniques they were using and their successes, and as Ann "improved," the teacher was more open to suggestions. She gave permission for Ann to wear a visor in class when the classroom was too bright for Ann, and she began experimenting with turning on music for the whole class. She was also open to Ann listening to music with earphones, since this helped Ann tune out what was going on around her and allowed her to focus on the task at hand. This teacher was learning about learning style from these parents. Your child's teachers can learn from you, too!

COMBINING ALL ASPECTS OF LEARNING STYLE

These stories show how the different aspects of learning style are put together to get the whole picture. Dispositions, Talents, Interests, Modality, and Environment interact in various, unique ways for each individual child. Two children can score about the same in a particular disposition but learn very differently because of the unique combinations of all the other aspects of their learning style.

Let's say two children score the highest in the Performing Disposition. Child A scores 45 and Child B scores 32. Already there is a difference. Child A's highest score is higher than Child B's highest score. Child A probably has more of the Performing characteristics than Child B. Then we look at the second highest score. Child A doesn't really have one—all the other scores are in the teens and about the same. But Child B scores 29 in Relate/Inspire. We are beginning to get the picture of two very different children. When we look at the other sections we find more differences. Child A is Visual and Tactile-Kinesthetic; has talents for building models, telling jokes, and dancing; and works better with music and a space in which he can move and stretch often. Child B is Auditory-Verbal; has talents for working with people, playing guitar, and playing sports; and needs a quiet workplace with other people around. Child A loves woodshop and acting, and Child B has a passion for photography. Child B also likes to draw, even though he scored low in Think/Create and doesn't have a particular talent for art. If drawing is an interest, it can be incorporated into teaching strategies for this student—it's okay to use whatever works.

Now that you have learned more about how to put all of the learning style information together, take another look at the Summary form. Notice that it is organized so that you can easily access the results of all five aspects of learning style. Now go back to the Plan form and fill it out if you have not already done so. This form will help you organize the specific learning techniques you gather from each chapter (5 to 9) about the various aspects of learning style. As suggested earlier, plan the "ideal" program for your child, based on the recommended methods and strategies. Then think about the options, choose a few, and get started!

Make Life Easier

Don't worry about coming up with the "perfect" program. Realize that it will take some experimenting on everyone's part. You might make some mistakes. Keep a sense of humor while you and your child explore different options.

You Will Be Appreciated

When children's learning needs are acknowledged and respected, they respond with an amazing eagerness to do their best even in less than satisfactory conditions. In other words, even a little willingness on your part to make some changes will go a long way. Your child will appreciate what you are trying to do. Include her in the "strategy" sessions. Discuss her unique combination of needs and the conditions that will help her learn best. She will probably surprise you by offering to handle those circumstances that cannot be changed easily.

> **W**hen children's learning needs are acknowledged and respected, they respond with an amazing eagerness to do their best even in less than satisfactory conditions.

Accept Your Child's Uniqueness

Remember that the most important part of this whole process is getting across the message that your child is a wonderfully gifted and capable human being, who has a unique life purpose to share with the world that no one else has. Her value does not depend on being a great speller or on understanding parts of speech. When your child feels this *inside,* she will be confident in moving forward. Often it seems that miracles happen. The side benefit is that she *can* learn the parts of speech and her spelling *will* greatly improve when she is taught through strategies that fit her learning style and make her feel competent!

 ## KEEP IT SIMPLE

In developing the Learning Style Profile, every effort was made to use category names (such as Perform, Invent, Visual-Picture) that people could identify with. However, the terminology is not as important as the message. In other words, if you can't remember the names of the different dispositions, the talent categories, or the modality types, don't worry! If you haven't grasped all of the information about learning style, relax. You don't have to understand it all in order to make it work. Most of us don't know how computers, microwave ovens, and VCRs work, but we use them anyway!

As you continue to work with the Profile and your family's results, the language and concepts will become more familiar to you. Refer often to the Profile chapters, the teaching suggestions, and the charts provided in this book. Eventually, you will integrate the information and will be able to talk about it naturally and automatically, just like when you learned to ride a bike. Remember that it's okay to use common, everyday language to describe how your child learns best: He needs to act things out, draw pictures, watch videos, etc.

> Remember that the most important part of this whole process is getting across the message that your child is a wonderfully gifted and capable human being, who has a unique life purpose to share with the world that no one else has.

The important thing is that you are now aware of all the different aspects that make up learning style; that you continue to observe and listen to your child, and ask questions to further clarify what works best; and that you are willing to provide the opportunities that will help make your child a successful, eager, self-motivated learner!

Follow-Through Activities

This chapter gives you several simple ways to continue to use the Learning Style Profile to contribute to your child's learning-success in the months and years to come. It contains activities to help you learn more about how to use the Profile information.

ACTIVITY 1:
KNOW WHERE YOU WANT TO GO

The process of raising a child to become an eager, self-directed student is given purpose and direction when you take the time to determine what learning behaviors you would like to see in your child. In your opinion, what does a successful learner do? If you were looking through a window into your child's classroom, what would you like to see him or her doing? List these, then put a check mark by the things she does in class already.

_____ _____

_____ _____

_____   _____

_____   _____

_____   _____

_____   _____

_____   _____

Now take a few minutes to write down general characteristics that you would like to see in your child as an adult.

_____   _____

_____   _____

_____   _____

_____   _____

The characteristics you chose reflect your goals for your child.

What are you doing to promote the learning or life goals that you stated above?

_____

_____

_____

_____

_____

With your goals identified you can check now and then to see if your actions actually support them. When your actions are in alignment with what you want to accomplish, there is little that can get in the way of progress in your chosen direction.

ACTIVITY 2:
TAKE THE PROFILE YOURSELF

I recommend that all of the adults who have responsibility for your child take the Profile, including grandparents, child-care providers, and teachers. In the spirit of working together to develop a positive learning team, everyone can contribute by increasing their understanding about learning style.

> **W**hether we intend to or not, we see our children through the filter of our own learning style.

Whether we intend to or not, we see our children through the filter of our own learning style. For example, you may have been a whiz in math, and you might think that your child's low grades in math show that he isn't "trying hard enough" or that he isn't paying attention in class. You may be impatient with his inability to memorize math facts or because he's asking the same questions over and over again. On the Profile your skill in math shows up as 10 in Math-Logic Reasoning Talent. Your child's score is 2. Your differences are obvious, and they are an integral part of each of you. Some of the difference has to do with your experience, of course. However, a great deal of the difference has to do with your individual talents. With the Profile information, you are able to move on to problem solving about what can be done to give your child the foundation he needs in math—staying focused on a *solution* rather than worrying or feeling frustrated.

> **"** *Most of us do our best work when attempting to improve our own performance, not when trying to surpass the performance of others. Yet, in classrooms we have established the dynamic wherein each child wishes to see his classmates fail.*
>
> —Richard D. Lavoie **"**

Similarly, you might not understand why your child wants to spend so much time in her room studying. Until you take the Profile and compare scores with your child, you might think that this is a problem. Perhaps you are worried, perhaps her brother and sister have begun to tease her about it. Maybe she is beginning to feel guilty. Your Profile might show a score of 45 in the Relating/Inspiring Disposition. Your need for interaction is likely to be the filter through which you are seeing your child. Let's say your child scored –3 in the Relating/Inspiring Disposition. Obviously you and your daughter aren't likely to want the same amount of socializing. You are opposites in your desire to be with others. This is an opportunity to see your child without the filter of your bias and to move on to solution-focused problem solving as soon as possible. Chapter 12 will show you how to do this.

ACTIVITY 3: GRAPH TALENT AND DISPOSITION RESULTS

Graphing the scores for talents and dispositions is another way to get information from the Profiles. The graphs are easy to read, and children as young as eight and nine years old enjoy sharing their observations. (See Figures 11.1 and 11.2.)

Graphing Dispositions

Find the Disposition scores on the Summary form. Transfer the scores to the Disposition Graph. Do this for each member of the family, using a different colored pencil for each person. If you used the preschool version, multiply each score by 5 before graphing.

Graphing Talents

Find the Talent scores on the Summary form. Graph the scores on the Talents Graph. Do this for each member of the family, using a different colored pencil for each person. (Note that the Talent section of the preschool Profile is set up differently and cannot be graphed.)

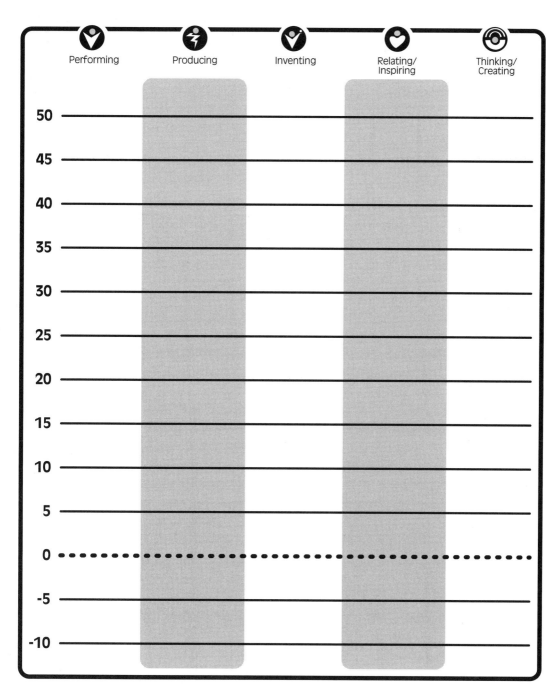

Figure 11.1 Dispositions Graph

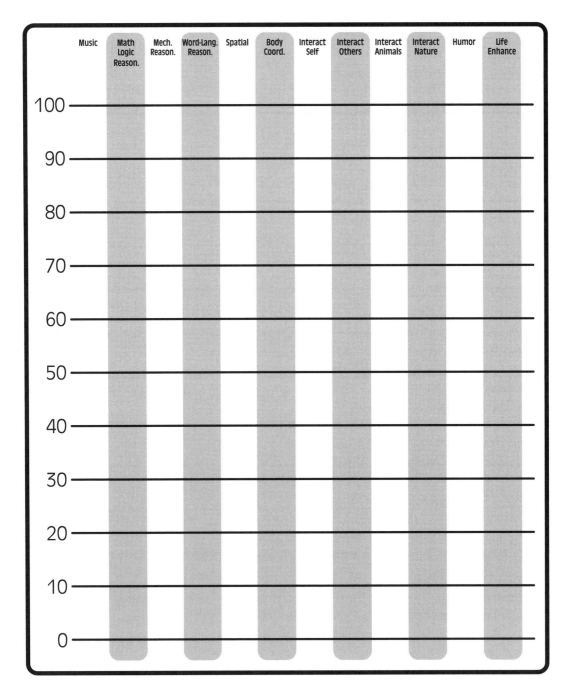

Figure 11.2 Talents Graph

ACTIVITY 4: THE FAMILY MEETING

Share Profile Results

Family meetings are a great way to share all kinds of information, make plans, problem solve, etc. With the Profile results in hand you can set an appointment to look at them together.

Put everyone's Summary forms and the Talent and Disposition Graphs on the table. Everyone can browse the results and share what they notice. You can derive information in many valuable ways. Here are some suggestions:

Look for Very High Highs

People with very high scores in specific talents or dispositions can take the lead in helping others learn to do what they do so well naturally. These people sometimes feel frustrated that others in the family don't understand them. They often have very high standards for the things that they do so well and can be critical of others who are less developed in those areas. Discuss ways to acknowledge each other and to share each person's strengths. Share your interest and delight in each person's gifts and abilities as well as your willingness to encourage their growth in these areas.

Look for Very Low Lows

A low score is an indicator that a specific talent or disposition is not an aptitude for that person. Lows can also be a sign of lack of exposure and opportunity. For example, a child who has no exposure to music and no opportunity to learn about it, is less likely to be able to check off any of the skills on the Music Talent assessment.

Sometimes people score very low in a talent or disposition because they have given up trying or competing with someone who is more skilled in that area. For example, if one member of the family is especially gifted with a talent for humor and has a Performing Disposition, other members of the family may feel that they can't compete in that arena, so they don't even try.

People with a Producing Disposition are often involved in this kind of bind. They want to share responsibilities with others; however, their high standards make participation difficult for other members of the family who feel that they aren't doing things the *right* way.

Explore possibilities for "trying out" activities in areas with low scores. Ask your children if there are areas that they would like to improve in. Accept the "no" responses as well as the "yes" ones.

Look for Clusters—
Places Where Everyone Is High or Low

Clusters are a group of similar scores. They are interesting because they usually are not unanimous for all members of the family. For example, one person with a high Producing Disposition is a stark contrast to the other members of the family clustered between –3 and 10 in the Producing Disposition. Or three out of four people might score 80 or above in Interactive-Nature Talent, and the fourth person scores low in that talent. This can be valuable information when you are planning the annual family camping trip and the child low in the Interactive-Nature Talent is kicking and screaming already. Think of how valuable the Profile knowledge can be! Now that you understand the reason for your child's reaction, you can sit down together, offer understanding for his point of view, and brainstorm ideas for making the camping trip less traumatic. Your child is likely to come up with his own solutions because you have acknowledged his feelings and needs.

> " *Treat your child as you would treat the person you would like him to become, and he will become that person.*
>
> —Dr. Haim Ginott "

Look for Gaps or Holes in the Clusters

Holes in the graph have a story to tell, too. For example, if no one in a family has a high score in the Producing Disposition, you may have more than your share of chaos and disorder at your house, *or* everyone may be sharing the practicalities of daily life equally. In the "real world," the former is more often true. Here is another example: Parents I worked with recently were surprised to find out that their child scored 0 in Math-Logic Talent. Furthermore, all five family members were clustered between 0 and 25, which is definitely on the low end of the graph. This is a hole. No one is high in the talent. This hole in the family profile means that probably no one in the family is suited for taking the lead in helping the child with math homework. In this case, outside help of some kind would be a good choice.

Look for a Person Who Has the Same Score in All Talents or Dispositions

Once in a while someone, usually an adult, scores in the middle range for most of the talents and the dispositions. Sometimes a person is drawn to all disposition possibilities and her scores are all about the same. Her line on a graph is nearly straight. This rarely occurs; however, when it does, it is worth noting and talking about. This person's characteristics might, indeed, be distributed evenly across the dispositions. In other cases, this could be the scores of someone who hasn't thought very much about herself and doesn't really know her own preferences.

Interpret for Learning-Success

When it is obvious which members of the family have particular dispositions and/or talents, it might be clearer who would be the best person to help Janice with her math homework and who would be best helping her with literature. That is, a parent who scores high in Math-Logic Talent is the best choice for helping with math homework, and a parent high in Word-Language Reasoning Talent is most naturally suited to help with literature. In either case, the willingness to work with the child's disposition needs *is as important as* having a talent for the subject. If there is no one who can work with your child's learning style at home, it is better not to try to help. Encourage your child to ask the teacher for help or get a tutor or friend who can work with him.

ACTIVITY 5: INDIVIDUAL MEETINGS

The family meeting is great for the overall picture. However, it's important to also have an individual meeting with each child. This is a good time to talk about strengths and determine how to develop them. It is also a good time to look at weaknesses and determine how to overcome them.

The graphs give you valuable information that can help you understand why you might be frustrated or ineffective in interacting with your child when it comes to homework or learning performance in general. When you separate your expectations, emotions, and preferences from your child's by using the Profile information, it takes the pressure off of both of you; no one is seen as a "problem." The Profile scores say, "This is the way it is. You are different from each other."

From this point on, you have choices about what you want to do with the information on your child's Profile. One choice is to make sure that your daily expectations are appropriate for the goals you have for your child. For example, in the goals you listed in Activity 1, let's say that you determined that you would like to see your child participate more in class discussion, join some clubs, and be more social. On the Profile you see that he scored very low in the Relating/Inspiring Disposition and the Interactive-Others Talent. Now you have some information to use in addition to your own thoughts, worries, hopes, and expectations. It isn't necessarily that your child is rude, a hermit, or on the road to a life of isolation; it could simply be that by nature he is not likely to seek out interaction with others. Now you can talk to your child about the importance of developing social skills and make a plan together for how to do that if he is willing to participate. In this way, you are respecting

> **W**hen you separate your expectations, emotions, and preferences from your child's by using the Profile information, it takes the pressure off of both of you; no one is seen as a "problem."

your child's style, getting his input, and moving forward by seeking solutions. You are modeling the solution-focused approach discussed in the next chapter.

Use Strengths to Overcome Weaknesses

Using a child's strengths to overcome weaknesses is an important component of the Learning Style Model. Young people are willing to participate in skill development when individualized and appropriate methods, materials, and activities are used. They begin to feel competent because they see that they *can* improve. Many kids don't improve because they are not being taught through their learning style. Using the same methods that didn't work in the first place gives them the impression that they *can't* succeed. Some *really* don't get it the way it is being taught, and they won't get it no matter how severe the punishment or how wonderful the reward.

Chapter 8 talks about the progress that can be made in reading when the child's appropriate learning modality is used to reach reading goals. This is an example of how skill can be developed by using appropriate methods, materials, and activities. Skill can be improved in any area. The Profile helps you and your child identify what you want to change. Instead of worrying or nagging, you can turn learning weaknesses into learning goals. Once learning goals are established, strategies that draw upon a child's strengths can be developed to achieve them. Step by step, the progression goes like this:

> **Instead of worrying or nagging, you can turn learning weaknesses into learning goals.**

1. Identify general weaknesses or areas for growth (refer to this section on the Plan form).
2. Turn weaknesses and areas for growth into specific learning goals, such as learning the '3' times table, complete homework assignments, learn five spelling words, etc.

3. Select Learning-Style appropriate methods, materials, and activities. (See Appendix II.)

Look at Ann's Learning Style Portrait in Chapter 10 (Figure 10.2). An identified goal for Ann is to improve math skills. By using her Spatial and Body Coordination Talents, her interest in movement, and her Performing Disposition, strategies can be put in place: math games, videos, and computer software all work through Ann's learning style to support reaching the identified math goal. (A blank portrait is provided on page 256 for you to fill out. Make several copies first.)

ACTIVITY 6: REASSESSING

Some people like to have their children retake the profiles every two or three years. It has been interesting to see the results of these reassessments. Generally, talents, modalities, and dispositions stay the same. Interests and environment are most changeable. Primary and secondary dispositions sometimes switch places. Usually this occurs when the gap between the two scores was small in the first place.

Once in a while, if there has been a dramatic event in a person's life, the learning style scores, especially for disposition, shift in a significant way. (See Chapter 5 for more information on this.)

ANOTHER STEP YOU CAN TAKE

You may or may not want to talk to your child's teacher about the Profile outcomes. If you decide to do so, having specific learning goals and strategies in mind can make it much easier to talk to a teacher because you are not only pointing to a concern but also offering appropriate suggestions. One thing is for sure, being prepared is your best bet, so consider taking copies of your child's Learning Style Profile and the Learning Style Portrait to the teacher. Chapter 14 gives more suggestions for how to make your case to a teacher in a way that is most likely to be heard.

PART 3

Coach for Success

Chapters 12 to 15 lead you through the process of becoming your child's learning-success coach. Chapter 12 discusses interaction techniques that make the application of Learning Style information more effective. Chapter 13 deals with concerns that many parents have about possible "learning problems," and Chapter 14 gives suggestions to help you share Learning Style information with your child's teachers. Finally, Chapter 15 suggests ways of looking at education that can help your child grow up to be a self-directed, eager learner for the rest of her life.

Now on to Part 3!

- **Read Chapters 12–15**
- **Do Exercises**
- **Fill out the Portraits**

Stay F.I.T.T.

Now that you've finished Part II of this book, you're ready to begin using the long-term learning-success coaching techniques that I myself have learned from families that I've worked with. Four interaction essentials help you keep F.I.T.T. as you continue to nurture the eager, self-directed learner in your child. Athletic coaches assist in accomplishing personal best, in taking a person to their next level of accomplishment. Your role as a learning coach is much the same, advancing one step at a time as your child is ready to take it.

The four Stay F.I.T.T. techniques are:

- **F**ocus on solutions,
- **I**dentify goals,
- **T**rack successes,
- **T**ake the pressure off.

 ## F—Focus on Solutions

Solution-focused kids are much more likely to feel capable in a learning situation, while blame-focused kids are often afraid and withdrawn or resistant and/or rebellious. Solution-focus keeps attention on how a problem can be handled in the present. Blame-focus brings up the past and tries to find out who or what caused the problem and what "should be done to" the person who caused the problem.

Kids who are raised with solution-focused problem solving instead of consequences or punishment develop the ability to keep going in the face of setbacks. Athletes are well trained at solution-focused problem solving. Every roadblock to the basket, the goal, or the finish line is faced positively and energetically to keep momentum going toward the goal. The belief is always that the roadblock is surmountable.

> **K**ids who are raised with solution-focused problem solving instead of consequences or punishment develop the ability to keep going in the face of setbacks.

When parents see their kids' school problems as surmountable—that there can be a positive way to work with them—they can stop negative patterns of interaction and teach their kids how to find win–win outcomes. They also put relationships with their kids on a footing that makes working with learning style not only more effective, but more fun.

A Parent–Child Interchange

Let's look at an example. If your child isn't turning in homework, a blame-focused approach would be to label the misbehavior, discover what your child did instead of doing homework, make threats, and determine some kind of consequence for the misbehavior. The interchange might go like this: "You are being so *irresponsible*. What are you doing during the time you say you're doing homework? You are never going to amount to anything if you

> *Students should be encouraged to concentrate on tasks that show what they can do instead of what they can't do.*
>
> —Richard D. Lavoie

don't learn how to play by the rules. I'm taking away your telephone privileges until you take care of this problem."

A solution-focused approach starts with the situation at hand, does not label or threaten, and invites the child to be part of the solution. The interaction might go like this: "When I heard that you weren't turning in your homework, I felt disappointed. You must be a little anxious yourself about getting behind in your work. What do *you* think could be done about the situation?" Your tone, facial expression, and posture are important; avoid sarcasm and indignation. If you are truly asking for participation in the problem-solving process, regardless of how old the child is, she will have useful ideas about how to do things differently. Sometimes the ideas can be quite silly and far-fetched. Accept those, too. If you collect four or five ideas from a child, add a couple of your own, and maintain the friendly tone throughout, you and your child are likely to come up with something that will work for each of you. A solution determined in this way has a longer lasting effect than a punishment does.

> **A solution-focused approach starts with the situation at hand, does not label or threaten, and invites the child to be part of the solution.**

Children who scored high on the Profile in the Relating Disposition or the Interactive-Others Talent will probably enjoy solution-focused problem solving the most. This kind of working together meets their needs for interaction, for talking things over, and for being part of a team. Producing children will probably enjoy this process, also, especially if you make lists of different solutions and check them off as you eliminate them. Young people with a Performing Disposition will enjoy problem solving if they can "ham up" their side, if it doesn't take too long, and if it can be *fun*. If your child has a Humor Talent, joking around is essential. Kids with Performing Disposition or a Humor Talent need to be acknowledged for their cleverness. Thinking/Creating and Inventing Disposition kids as well as kids with Spatial Talent are likely to want to draw or scribble during the problem-solving process. The Think/Create and Invent kids might even want time to think things over and make final decisions at another meeting.

Finding solutions together is an effective way to share responsibility for the outcomes of difficult situations. Don't be tricked into thinking that you must be in charge and know all of the answers for how to do things *right*. Don't be tricked into thinking that it is your job to find out who is *wrong* and who *should* be *punished*. As you work together with your child to find *solutions*, you will be pleasantly surprised at the changes that occur!

A Teacher–Class Example

To give you an idea of how this approach works in a classroom, consider a situation where some students are too noisy and the teacher has called a meeting to determine consequences. Students might suggest the following for those who are noisy:

Blame-focused consequences:

1. Write names on the board.
2. Make them stay after school.
3. Take away time from recess.
4. Take away recess privileges for a day.
5. Sit outside the classroom door.

Solution-focused ideas might be:

1. Have a buddy tap them on the shoulder to remind them to be quiet.
2. Students take turns as "noise monitors" and remind them to be quiet.
3. The teacher could ring a bell when it gets too noisy.
4. The teacher could turn off the light when it gets too noisy.

Unlike blame-focused consequences, solutions offered by kids are solutions they are willing to try and to support. When you practice solution-focus, your kids learn how to problem-solve from you. Their confidence will grow as they realize that they can learn from mistakes and affect outcomes.[1]

I—Identify Goals

Kids who have goals and can imagine a positive future for themselves are more eager learners than young people who are discouraged and don't see possibilities for themselves in the short or long term. Kids with goals have a reason of their own for all of the hard, daily work required in school. Kids with goals make a commitment to develop themselves. Goals are hopeful, forward looking, and convey the message to oneself that "I have someplace worthwhile to go." Without short-term and long-term goals, a child can be adrift. Goal setting opens up a world of choices, commitment, preferences, values, hope, and willingness to meet requirements.

Without goals of their own, kids are often *passive participants* in the goals that other people have for them. Other people's goals and expectations can feel to kids like demands, and it is a natural tendency to resist demands.[2]

If they don't have their own goals, kids have to rely on our judgment for twelve years about school's purpose and relevance, and that's a very long time. If we received a report card for our achievements in explaining the relevance of schooling, the grade should probably be a "D." The technique for passing on the importance of school studies is usually a long lecture followed by threats or horror stories of what will happen if a young person fails to study hard enough. To some, the whole presentation sounds more like a demand than an opportunity; they dig in their heels in resistance. Motivating by threats and fear seems to work in the short term. However, this is an illusion. Resentment builds in the child, and you end up finding out weeks, months, or years later that what you thought was a short-term solution definitely didn't work for the long-term. There's got to be a better way!

Setting aside twelve years for a young person to study is supposed to be an opportunity. How can you as a parent return

> **Without goals of their own, kids are often *passive participants* in the goals that other people have for them.**

to that original intention and make the school years an opportunity? Learning to help your child set goals can be helpful.

An Indirect Route to Life Direction

I remember my son's junior year of high school when he was thinking seriously about the profession he would pursue after graduation. He pored over the directory of U.S. colleges and universities for hours. Guided by his interests, talents, and imagination, he selected about twenty-five colleges to write to for information. In addition, he wrote to the Merchant Marines and the U.S. Coast Guard. Almost daily he was hatching new plans for yet another exciting career. Led by his imagination, he started with society's highest ranking professions. Law headed the list for a while. Then he began to think of his interest in sailing, which he had done every summer in Puget Sound, and the Coast Guard, Merchant Marines, and oceanography headed the list. Next he began to consider his obvious talent and love for drawing, design, and three-dimensional imaging and construction. (This kid designed with Legos until he was seventeen years old and could write manuals for constructing anything you could name.) Enthusiastically he shared each new scenario, and we talked over the pros and cons together.

Gradually, by his own processes and after months of research, with pounds of college catalogs stacked next to his bed, he decided that architecture was what he wanted to study. Choosing a school was the next step. He knew he wanted the challenge of living on the East Coast; that limited the field some. Eventually he chose six schools, some East Coast, some West Coast for back-up. Then began the visits to schools and the interviews. He went to Chicago, Rhode Island, New York, and Los Angeles. Everywhere is far away when you live in the most northwestern corner of the United States, as we did then. My husband and I had very little input into this process. Primarily we were there to act as sounding boards and to give support for his plans. He made all the contacts, arrangements, and visits while he was a senior in high school. He kept up with his classes and continued to set one goal after another for himself, motivated by a long-term goal that was getting clearer and clearer to him with each step. I witnessed my son grow in confidence with each challenge he met, with each short-term goal he reached. He had a great deal of practice setting goals and making choices all through junior high and high school, and the value of this was obvious as we watched him take hold of his future with such enthusiasm and confidence.

Real-World Motivators

Goals provide a strong motivation for doing what is needed, on a daily basis, to reach those goals. Finishing high school is an example of "doing what is needed." If finishing high school is linked to goals for the future that involve your child's talents and interests, and things that your child loves to do, then your child has a reason to complete her studies. When a child has her own reasons or purposes for doing years and years of hard work, the child becomes a self-motivated, eager learner. By teaching goal setting, you can help your child identify the reasons and purposes she needs to try difficult things and to persevere.

Goal setting has two distinct parts: 1) the outcome desired and 2) the means for reaching the outcome. To talk about goals to kids without consideration for *how* the goals can be reached leaves the outcomes dangling in midair with no steps leading up to them. We want our kids to be thinking about outcomes as well as the everyday steps they need to take to reach them.

> **B**y teaching goal-setting, you can help your child identify the reasons and purposes she needs to try difficult things and to persevere.

Goals are concrete outcomes that a person wants to achieve. With young kids it is extremely important to realize and be patient with the fact that their goals will change. If you can accept this fact early on, you will have more fun and less frustration listening to your child talk about his ideas for his future.

Even for older kids, long-term goals are going to change many times. Don't worry about this. Many of your child's goals for himself are related to age and stages of development. What matters is that kids are able to create some kind of picture of themselves as adults doing specific, constructive things. As a young person gets to know himself better by taking the Learning Style Profile, by pursuing interests, and by identifying role models, he will show a pattern of preferred activities. These activities eventually begin to resonate with livelihood possibilities and lasting goals. You must, however, trust the somewhat indirect process that many kids go through to sort out what they want to do, as my son's story about finding a college illustrated.

Goal-Setting Exercise I

An effective way to talk about goals is to have your child make a scrapbook of people she admires. She can use photos of relatives and friends. She can draw pictures. She can cut pictures from magazines and newspapers. As part of this activity, have her write, or you can write for her, what it is that she admires about these people. Talk about the principles that these people live by as well as the principles that you live by.

> **As a young person gets to know himself better by taking the Learning Style Profile, by pursuing interests, and by identifying role models, he will show a pattern of preferred activities.**

Somewhere in the book, encourage your child to set aside a page to draw or write about herself as an adult, what career she would like to pursue, where she thinks she might like to live, etc. If a young person is showing a strong interest in a certain career, a certain place she wants to visit, or subject she wants to study, work together on a scrapbook for that, too. Help your child gather as much information as possible on the people and subjects that interest her. Read library books together. Get information from the Internet. Find special picture books about a favorite subject. Take field trips. All of this provides special learning about something that is appealing to her at the time. This is when she is most receptive to learning.

Save some pages in the scrapbook for collecting ideas about how your child can reach his long-term goals. Take ideas from the lives of people he admires. Did these people go to college, take a job after high school graduation, study abroad, or start their own businesses? All of these ideas show your child the range of possibilities for reaching his goals.

When long-term goals are established, you can start talking about the short-term academic, social, and personal skills that support these long-term goals. When your child has long-term goals in mind, he has taken a major step toward becoming an eager, self-directed learner.

Goal-Setting Exercise II

From junior high school on it can be helpful to make an annual school-year plan. You can also make a plan to complete high school. When I discovered the importance of doing this goal-setting activity for my son, we started with a six-year plan. It is amazing to think back on how focused that plan kept us. My son has mentioned several times how important it was to him. Put the plan on paper. Include short-term goals such as trips you are planning to take; classes to be taken in school; classes to be taken in pursuit of interests, talents, and involvement issues; and other activities. Enter possible dates for reaching goals or completing projects on a calendar. Don't forget to include plans for celebrations of accomplishments.

Recruit for Your Child's Team

You can assist the goal-setting process by expanding the education team for your child. Your child can choose anyone he likes to be on his team to help him get through school—people he could call on for homework help, or for advice about a problem or an interest he wants to pursue, or who would take him on field trips at various times. These are people who would celebrate education milestones with you and your child. Such people can be helpful in many ways. You don't have to do it all yourself, and these friends, relatives, neighbors, and acquaintances are usually delighted to be asked to share their knowledge, skills, time, and wisdom.

> **E**nter possible dates for reaching goals or completing projects on a calendar. Don't forget to include plans for celebrations of accomplishments.

Spark Dreams

When my son was studying architecture he was fascinated by the work of a world-renowned architect. My husband and I told him to make the arrangements and we would pay his way to go see this architect in New Mexico. A one-hour appointment was set up at the architect's office, which turned into a two-hour meeting and a tour of his wonderful home that had been the spark for our son's interest in the first place. We can't afford *not* to encourage these kinds of vital connections for our children—connections that spark dreams and goals.

Maybe your child has some new goals to add to those on the Plan form that she filled out earlier. List them below. Notice that in addition to determining long-term goals she is asked to think of short-term steps to take to reach these goals. The secret of goal setting is to break the big goal into a series of small, doable steps.

Long-Term Goals	*Short-Term Goals to Support Long-Term Ones*
_____	_____
_____	_____
_____	_____
_____	_____
_____	_____
_____	_____

You might want to transfer some of these long-term goals to the Plan form.

T—TRACK SUCCESSES NOT FAILURES

Is it simply human nature to remember the pain of our failures more than the sweetness of our successes? You would think so, we do it so automatically. Conditioning, however, plays a major role in what we select to emphasize about ourselves. The conditioning to notice our failures starts young. Before children enter school, adults seem to be much better about keeping track of their children's successes rather than their failures. Preschool and kindergarten can also be quite supportive experiences for some children. However, as soon as teachers start sending home papers with smiling or frowning faces, stars, and red marks on them, the emphasis often turns to "tracking failures."

> **A**s soon as teachers start sending home papers with smiling or frowning faces, stars, and red marks on them, the emphasis often turns to "tracking failures."

Have you ever noticed how spontaneously we mark the wrong answers wrong rather than mark correct responses right? It's just as easy to make a capital "C" next to a correct answer as it is to put a check mark by a wrong answer. What if a paper covered with red marks was looked forward to because it was a record of all that had been done *right* instead of all that had been done *wrong*? Scores are usually written at the top of a page as –3 or –7. Why not a ratio such as: 17/20 or 20/20? Why not +17 or +13? Did you know that some teachers have a slide-rule-like device called an "EZ Grader" that automatically gives percentage scores based on the number of *errors* made? Why do all papers need to be scored anyway? Why not just comments and suggestions once in a while?

> **I** wonder what happens when a child hears a recitation of his failures day after day, year after year?

For better or worse, it is the "three wrong" that sticks in one's memory after the math test is returned, not the "seventeen right." I wonder what happens when a child hears a recitation of his failures day after day, year after year? Do you have a strong negative internal voice that is critical of yourself and others? Where did that voice come from? It is the result of our own up-bringings that tracked our failures rather than our successes. By the time we are eighteen years old, it is estimated that we have heard 180,000 statements reinforcing our limitations.

What if instead a child hears her successes recited day after day, year after year? "Wouldn't that make a child conceited, a spoiled brat, a tyrant?" you might be asking. On the contrary, that child grows up to be confident and goal oriented. Perhaps you've heard Albert Einstein's saying that it takes eleven positives to overcome one negative. To balance out the 180,000 negatives referred to above, it would take 1,980,000 positives. If you err on the side of recognizing successes, you are in no danger of falling into this kind of debt.

Fortunately, we have time to turn the situation around for children growing up now. When your child begins to have more learning-success as a result of your implementing the strategies in this book, emphasize even the smallest gains. "Wow! Look at that; your handwriting is so evenly spaced on this assignment." "You got eight right on your spelling test, two more than last week!" Stay descriptive, stay specific, stay accurate, and you will see confidence build. Your children will be more willing to try difficult things, to persevere longer, to share the results of their efforts, and, eventually, to challenge themselves with learning goals of their own.

> **B**y the time we are eighteen years old, it is estimated that we have heard 180,000 statements reinforcing our limitations.

Even if your child is having a positive school experience, it is important to track successes rather than failures. Many students do well in school because they are afraid they will "get in trouble" if they don't. Their parents are tracking failures also. These kids stew and fret and work late on their homework every night. As adults these people say, "I got good grades, but I don't remember a thing." Success tracking helps these conscientious learners take pleasure in their accomplishments rather than fear failure.

Be patient! The steps in the direction of better scores, more participation in classroom activities, or more enthusiasm for studies can be small. If you are consistent in acknowledging any progress toward learning-success, you will gradually see greater accomplishments. My husband and I came to realize while raising our son that, as my husband put in a poem, "*real change* often

> **E**ven if your child is having a positive school experience, it is important to track successes rather than failures.

happens at the corner of the eye and often in steps too small to measure."[3] So be on the alert for small successes and acknowledge them!

T—TAKE THE PRESSURE OFF

Kids under too much pressure are not able to focus on their studies because they are preoccupied with fears of failure. Two easy ways you can take pressure off of your child are: 1) give permission for your child to "not do" something that is extremely difficult, and 2) encourage your child to evaluate his own progress rather than rely on grades.

Give Your Permission to "Not Do" When Appropriate

If a child is having trouble with penmanship or spelling or reading, and it has been a problem for a long time, you can work wonders with the situation by giving your child permission to "not do" the troublesome activity and to focus on developing other skills. With repeated reminding about her inadequacies, a child becomes defensive and focuses on protecting herself. Children are painfully aware of many of their own inadequacies.

They don't need our continual reminding of what these are. In many cases they don't need our help to remedy them either. By letting go of your expectations for your child, you give her breathing room, and she can start to focus on her own approach to the problem.

> A person who engages in opportunity thinking focuses on constructive ways of dealing with challenging situations. A person who engages in obstacle thinking focuses on reasons to give up.
>
> —Christopher Neck and Annette Barnard

Sometimes a child has been hurried along in an area when he needed to develop better foundation skills. This often happens in reading. If a child's Modality is Visual-Picture and he has been given an Auditory or a Visual-Print approach to reading, it may take him longer to develop the foundation concepts. To be rushed when the foundation isn't in place can cause insecurity. Sometimes the feelings of inadequacy cause the child to shut down to the learning process entirely. If we can remove the pressure at home rather than make more pressure, the child gets enough relaxation from school requirements to find a renewed energy for getting back on track.

Within days or weeks of taking the pressure off by withdrawing your expectations or giving permission to "not do," a child usually starts to take responsibility for developing the weak area in his own way. His approach to the problem might be very different from yours. Trust what your child wants to do. His motivation to try is coming from the fact that he is being allowed to come up with his own solutions.

In the above example, even though school continues to have the expectation that your child will read, you can lighten his distress over the situation by using books-on-tape at home, reading to your child, and not expecting him to read to you for a while. At times we have to say, "What you are doing is 'good enough.'" In distressing situations, "C's" or sometimes "D's" can be "good enough" grades. In some cases, especially when it is a very weak subject for your child, what is important is that your child is *participating*.

Many of the students that I work with have difficulty with the physical act of writing. Taking notes and writing reports are a source of muscular pain and performance anxiety. To take the pressure off for these students, you can suggest to your child's teacher that your child tape-record some reports rather than write all of them. Your child can also use the tape recorder to tape lecture material rather than take notes. For older students who can type, a laptop computer might help the note-taking problem.

> **A**t times we have to say, "What you are doing is 'good enough.'"

The above are a few examples of when "not doing" could be appropriate. Many other areas respond to this approach, and you will begin to notice them quite easily as you work more with your child's learning style.

Remember, if the schools were following the Learning Style Model of Education, your child would not be experiencing this distress. Because schools generally do not follow the Learning Style Model, you need to take matters into your own hands and provide learning style support and teaching at home as well as advocating for your child's learning style at school when appropriate.

Encourage Self-Evaluation

Tests and grades are only one form of evaluation, although this is the primary form used by schools. For many students, grades are a discouraging form of evaluation. Once again *you* have an opportunity to give your child another view of herself. The Profile is a helpful tool to identify your child's strong and weak areas. Whether a subject is a strength or a weakness, learning to evaluate oneself is far more beneficial in the long run than trusting grades as the only form of evaluation we ever experience.

Over the years I have found that children who self-evaluate are harder on themselves than teachers or parents are. They are very aware of their learning processes, and, when asked, they can talk quite accurately about their efforts and progress.

They know how hard they have been trying. They know the kinds of frustrations they have faced. They know when they have been goofing-off. My experience is that they are quite willing to talk about all of it when they are asked and when they are assured that they won't get into trouble for what they say.

If you have developed a listening relationship with your child, you can sit down with her and hear her own assessment of exam scores and report cards. From her evaluation you will learn much more than a report card or a grade will ever tell you. You can ask her about what she knows now that she didn't know before or what new skills and vocabulary she has as a result of studying a subject. You can find out about her expectations for a class and whether or not they were met. You can ask her if she would recommend the course to someone else. If so, why? If not, why not? You can ask her about whether or not she thinks she will have a use for the information in the future. You can ask her about the effort she put into her work and what she might do differently next time. This type of follow-up gives you and your child far more valuable information about your child's thoughts, learning processes, and expectations than grades ever will.

> **T**he term "coach" has been chosen to describe your role. You might be more comfortable with advocate, guide, bridge-builder, or even learning mentor.

At home, you have no reason to compare your child with anyone else, and this does a great deal to relieve the pressure on students who are struggling. For students who do well in school already, self-evaluation and personal best takes the focus off of competing and puts it on themselves. Many excellent students have never stopped to think about what *they* would like to get from a course. No matter how young your child is, self-evaluation can be used with very good results.

 ## SUMMARY

I hope that you will use these supportive strategies to keep your child more fully involved in his learning process. I've no doubt that as you make progress in learning these interacting skills, they will translate into more confidence in your child, and you will benefit by staying F.I.T.T. for the many challenges that await you. Remember that change can be slow at first. It is your commitment to continue to work with your child's learning style and the learning style interaction philosophy that will make the difference.

The term "coach" has been chosen to describe your role. You might be more comfortable with advocate, guide, bridge-builder, or even learning mentor. All of these roles put the emphasis on assisting, supporting, and nurturing. Children *need* as much of these things in their lives as they can get.

What About Learning Disabilities?

If you've read the first twelve chapters in this book, you are now probably thinking one of two things:

1. My child doesn't have a learning disability—I can skip this chapter.
2. I still don't see how this book can help me and my child—my child has a learning disability.

If you are in the first group, I hope that you will not skip this chapter, because you can gain valuable insight from it.

If you are in the second group, your child has either been diagnosed as having a "learning disability" or you suspect a "learning disability." In my work with kids who have been diagnosed "learning disabled," I have seen families make great gains in understanding and dealing with their children's learning needs. They often come to me anxious and discouraged. Gradually, through a learning style approach, they begin to relax and see that their child's unique style is that child's gift. One mom described it this way:

> My son was in fifth grade, at what the school told me was a first-grade reading and writing level. The teacher constantly complained

that my son was disruptive, loud, and "like a spring ready to be sprung." I was having no problems with him at home, except when he had to read or write.

The Learning Style Profile was administered and this mom began applying the results at home.

Less than a year later, my son was reading airplane model instructions . . . In the following school year, he was reading aircraft flight manuals and repair books. Now, four years later, he can read anything . . . Best of all, he no longer thinks of himself as "dumb" and a "troublemaker." He knows he's smart, can do anything he wants to do, and no longer sees himself or his learning style as the problem.

I struggled with how to write this chapter so that I could give the parents of "learning disabled" children peace of mind about this topic. How can I unravel what seems to be a complex and frightening subject and bring you to a simple insight that will make a positive difference for you and your child and, literally, change your lives?

Before we begin discussing "learning disabilities," let's take a look at the series of events which generally occurs when a child begins school . . .

The Traditional School Model

The National Education Goals Panel, an independent executive branch agency of the federal government, has published a document entitled *National Education Goals: Building A Nation of Learners.*[1] This document presents eight goals for our nation's schools, to be reached by the year 2000. The first goal is: All children will start school *ready to learn*. And this is precisely where the trouble starts!

Prepared to Learn

Traditionally, "prepared to learn" has meant that the child arrives at school ready and eager to:

- sit in a desk and work alone quietly for long periods of time

- follow the teacher's sequential directions
- focus and listen to a lesson about phonics or adding numbers even when there is the ongoing noise of construction outside
- do worksheets instead of playing with toys
- be quiet for long periods of time
- listen to the verbal lesson and be prepared to answer the teacher's questions
- raise a hand for permission to speak and then stick to the topic being discussed
- organize and plan work time efficiently
- print and color neatly
- learn to read, write, and do math

The child who comes to school prepared to do the above is then labeled motivated, smart, eager to learn, and, most probably, above average, maybe even gifted. Now let's look at some different children. These children arrive at school ready and eager to:

- play at recess
- draw or fingerpaint
- tell imaginative stories
- entertain the teacher and other students
- experiment with the musical instruments in class
- tap on the desk with a pencil or any object, in the absence of musical instruments
- move around the room, exploring and discovering hidden "treasures"
- play, act and/or sing
- ask a lot of questions
- share their toys and play in class
- make forts out of the furniture

Teachers become concerned about these students because they do not behave or perform according to school expectations. Many of these children are labeled slow, unmotivated, immature, distractible, disruptive, or lazy. If problems persist, someone usually suggests testing to find out if there is a learning disability.

Testing and Labeling—Help or Hindrance?

What is the purpose of testing? What would you, the parent, like testing to do? Would you like to know your child's strengths and weaknesses, how your child learns best, and how to use this information to help develop the weak areas? Would you like to find out where your child's real talents lie, so that you can encourage and guide him in the best direction? Or would you like to know percentile rankings and IQ scores and the learning *label* that fits your child?

> " Testing may help . . . if it aims to uncover specific problems and strengths rather than to rank students as life's winners and losers.
>
> —Arthur Powell "

In reality, the typical school assessment provides the latter, and comes up with one of two conclusions:

1. There is nothing wrong with this perfectly "normal" or "average" or "bright" child—*motivation* or *interest* must be lacking. This is the parents' problem.
2. This child has a learning disability—a special program must be developed. This is the school's problem.

Either way the child loses. The first diagnosis implies laziness, stubbornness, rebelliousness, lack of effort. The second diagnosis implies deficiency. Let's look at how this affects a real child.

Jan is a twelve-year-old student. She is artistic and creative, physically active, and a great swimmer and runner. She holds appropriate conversations, loves animals, and is alert and friendly and enthusiastic. She is at "grade level" in math, *but,* she is a terrible speller, her writing skills are poor, and she doesn't like to read.

Notice that the *but* discounts all the previous statements about Jan. Her positive qualities and skills don't seem to count; all that is noticed are the one or two areas that are deficient.

Jan is tested in order to find out if she has a learning disability or if she is simply lazy or lacking in effort.

Either way, it will probably be concluded that Jan is spending too much time swimming or drawing and not enough practicing writing and memorizing spelling words. It will probably be recommended that swimming team or art classes be dropped until she brings her grades up in English.

> **It's time to confront the really big question: Do learning disabilities exist? Or is it all just a matter of learning style?**

If you were Jan, which label would you rather have? Would you rather be deficient and disabled or lazy and unmotivated? All of these labels are negative. Not one offers encouragement or sparks enthusiasm. Not one tells what kind of program would be helpful. Not one gives a direction for Jan and her talents.

What does labeling accomplish then? Aren't some learning disorders serious? What about dyslexia and ADD? It's time to confront the really big question: Do learning disabilities exist? Or is it all just a matter of learning style?

THE LEARNING STYLE MODEL

Earlier we discussed the National Education Goal, which states that *all* children will start school prepared to learn. Unfortunately, because schools generally set things up so that only one type of learner can be recognized as "prepared to learn," this goal is basically impossible to meet. It can only be met if programs are provided that respect what different learners are prepared to learn. Because the school traditionally decides *what* is supposed to be learned *when*, those kids who have natural abilities in these areas become the "gifted" ones and those who don't become the "learning disabled." Those who are unable to earn either of these distinctions are doomed to be "average," "below average," or "slow," as discussed in Chapter 2.

When the Learning Style Model of Education is applied, it is easy to see that *all* children arrive at school prepared to learn. It's just that they arrive eager and ready to learn different things in different ways, based on their own unique "hardwiring." With the Learning Style Model there is no need for testing and labeling; determining learning style is what's important.

Is My Talent Better Than Your Talent?

When I was in school, I was good at reading, writing, and math. I was very organized, did all of my work, and received mostly A's on my report cards. Today, I can't work the VCR, and computers give me all kinds of trouble. I also get turned around very easily and lose my sense of direction if I don't have a map to refer to. I don't swim well, I can't draw, and I have a terrible time figuring out blueprints and diagrams. Of course, all of these deficiencies were present when I was in school, but no one would have ever thought to label me with one of the "LD" (learning disabled) terms because I fit the description of the "good student."

> **A**ll children arrive at school prepared to learn. It's just that they arrive eager and ready to learn different things in different ways, based on their own unique "hard-wiring."

Why is it that no one said, "It's true she's great at reading and writing and studying for tests, *but* she's such a poor swimmer, and she can't follow a schematic diagram, and I don't think she'll ever understand how electricity works. And, oh, dear, her drawing skills! My goodness, we really need to get her tested so she can get help!"

Earlier, when we were discussing Jan, I mentioned that only the weak areas are noticed, even when a child obviously has many strengths. As you can see, this is not entirely true; our schools generally are only concerned when *certain* skills are weak—reading, writing, and math, mostly.

As adults, we are in awe of the great artist or musician, the person who can fix anything electrical or electronic, the talented mechanic, the creative landscaper, the gifted architect. But what did we do to these people when they were in school? Because, you see, these are the Visual–Tactile–Kinesthetic, Performing–Inventing–Creating people who needed to move and do and watch videos and experiment and invent and tap the desk and walk around the room and take things apart. Why did we tell them to stop doodling and quit daydreaming and stop fiddling, if that is what helps them to produce their best work?

Why isn't our educational system just as concerned when mechanical skills are weak? Or artistic and creative abilities? Or athletic skills? Or social skills? Why aren't we testing, diagnosing, and setting up programs to increase competence in these areas? Because these abilities, and many others, are considered to be talents, and we don't expect everyone to be proficient in all of them. In contrast, we don't consider reading, writing, and math to be talents, and we expect everyone to be proficient in them.

We apply labels to people who have difficulty with reading, writing, or math. We panic and worry and usually force "exercises" upon students, even though this has never worked, as is obvious by the number of adults who are "poor" readers, spellers, and writers or who can't balance a checkbook or figure out mileage.

Yet, as adults, we really don't care if the mechanic can diagram sentences—we want him to fix the car; when we hear a wonderful singer, we don't wonder how well he writes; and when we need an artist to design our brochures, it would never occur to us to give him a written exam. I know, personally, if I am stuck crossing the desert, it doesn't bother me that my traveling companion can't spell carburetor as long as he can fix it. And the fact that I can spell carburetor doesn't help me at all!

Am I saying that reading and writing are not important and that some people don't need to learn to read and write? Absolutely not! I am saying that this business of learning disabilities needs to be put into perspective. The bottom line, what this whole book is about, is still the same: Each student is unique, having different strengths and weaknesses and different learning styles. Learning styles aren't garments that kids can put on and take off. Their learning styles are who they are.

> **I know, personally, if I am stuck crossing the desert, it doesn't bother me that my traveling companion can't spell carburetor as long as he can fix it.**

Perhaps kids are labeled because it is easier to attach the blame to a "learning problem" than to search for the teaching method, the setting, and the materials that fit each child. Many

> **E**ach student is unique, having different strengths and weaknesses and different learning styles. Learning styles aren't garments that kids can put on and take off. Their learning styles are who they are.

"learning problems" are actually created because an individual child's unique learning timetable is not taken into account. Who said they should all learn the alphabet in preschool, start reading in kindergarten and first grade, do fractions in third, and so on? What's wrong with learning to play the piano in first grade, build a computer in second, draw faces in third? Who is to say whether one talent is superior to another talent or one way of learning is better than another? Jean Piaget, himself, cautioned about teaching reading or other academic skills too early, before concept development has taken place. He warned that formal detailed instruction given too soon can interfere with normal learning development.

As I've already discussed throughout this book, some kids need more time, some kids need a different program, and *all* kids need to be respected for their unique gifts. It's been said of Einstein that if he had listened to his teachers, he may not have become one of the greatest scientists of the twentieth century.

Assessing Abilities Rather Than Disabilities

When a child is having trouble in school, the following sequence of events usually occurs:

1. A "learning problem" is identified through testing.
2. A program is set up to "fix" the student.
3. The student's potential is seen as limited.
4. Excuses are made for the student's behavior and/or lack of accomplishments.

It is very interesting to me when the last event occurs. For example, a parent will say, "I can't expect him to behave in public, he has ADD." Or a teacher will think, "She probably won't accomplish much in English, she has such a limited vocabulary." Yet these same people often resist the idea of working with learning styles, because we shouldn't be "catering" to students—they have to follow "the program" like everyone else.

In contrast, what is accomplished when learning styles are assessed?

1. All aspects of learning style are identified, including talents and interests.
2. A program is set up to work *with* those learning style needs.
3. The student's potential is seen as unlimited.
4. Excuses are replaced with problem solving and collaboration.
5. Strengths are used to help overcome weak areas.

In other words, students are seen as capable rather than disabled. Their Talents and Interests are celebrated and encouraged. Their Dispositions, Modality, and Environment needs are taken into account. Appropriate materials and techniques are chosen to help them increase skills in weak areas. They are allowed to shine in areas of strength and are never made to feel deficient. Students are helped to discover the riches, potentials, and dreams inside each one of them. As a result, their skills in weak areas improve much faster and rise to higher levels, because they feel secure and competent instead of anxious and embarrassed, and are viewed by others as "smart" rather than "dysfunctional."

> " *"Fair" does not mean that every child gets the same treatment, but that every child gets what he or she needs.*
> —Richard D. Lavoie "

SO WHAT DO WE DO ABOUT DYSLEXIA AND ADD?

I know that you're still worried, especially if your child has been diagnosed dyslexic or ADD. Aren't learning problems of this sort serious? Everybody knows we need to intervene early so that we can correct the problems and prevent further deterioration.

Remember, we are not talking about cancer here. Sometimes, these labels are used as if they are diseases: Mary *has* dyslexia. Jim *has* ADD. We are talking about unique individuals who have incredible talents and gifts.

> **T**heir skills in weak areas improve much faster and rise to higher levels, because they feel secure and competent instead of anxious and embarrassed, and are viewed by others as "smart" rather than "dysfunctional."

If we continue to label students because their brains do not operate the way our educational system wants them to, we will continue to spread the idea that millions of brains are not as good as other brains, and perpetuate lifetime patterns of low self-worth, which affect future learning, career opportunities, and relationships.

The School Model of Education expects all students of the same age to learn the same things in the same way at the same rate. The Learning Style Model of Education expects *differences* in individual students: It is presumed that children learn through different methods at different times and at different rates. Let's take a look at some of the more familiar labels that are given to children to explain their "learning problems."

Learning Disability

According to the official general definition, "learning disability" means a disorder involving spoken or written language, which may show up as problems with reading, writing, math, speaking, or thinking. The definition excludes children whose difficulties are due primarily to physical handicaps, mental retardation, emotional disturbance, or cultural or economic disadvantage. A "learning-disabled" child is one who has "average" to "above average" intelligence but is not "performing up to his potential" in the basics of reading, writing, and math.[2]

Basically, this definition is talking about the "regular" kid who seems smart in so many ways, yet has so much difficulty at school. Often, behavior problems also develop because the child has trouble completing assignments, doing homework, following directions, or staying on task. Perhaps she is caught daydreaming, or talking to another child, or making a paper airplane, or drawing when she was supposed to do a worksheet. Maybe she is even becoming disruptive, inappropriate, angry, depressed, aggressive, negative, quarrelsome, timid, or discouraged.

> **If we continue to label students because their brains do not operate the way our educational system wants them to, we will continue to spread the idea that millions of brains are not as good as other brains . . .**

The Learning Style Model asks: What are this child's strengths? What are his interests? What makes him shine? What can we do to give him a great learning experience?

In the 1980s, Thomas Armstrong quit his job as a learning-disabilities specialist because he no longer believed in learning disabilities. He gives this advice:

It's time for the schools, and parents as well, to start focusing their attention on the inner capabilities of each and every child . . . the schools persist in labeling hundreds of thousands of children with perfectly normal brains as "minimally brain damaged" or "neurologically handicapped," when in fact teachers simply have not found a way of teaching them on their own terms, according to their own unique patterns of neurological functioning . . . The part of the brain that thrives on worksheets and teacher lectures probably takes up less than one percent of the total available for learning. More likely, these stale methods of learning are actually what educator Leslie Hart refers to as "brain-antagonistic"—they shut down potentials rather than open them up . . . It will end when parents decide to toss aside all of these labels and begin the task of understanding and nurturing their children's personal learning styles so that they can begin to learn in their own way.[3]

Dyslexia

Dyslexia is generally considered to be a specific "learning disability" and has become a popular label for those who have difficulty with reading. It is also a medical term used to describe a brain condition. Actually, the term "dyslexia" has been causing confusion for many years. In the 1970s the Reading Reform Foundation compiled a list of quotes regarding this subject: From *A Report from the National Academy of Education*, "There is little agreement about this term even among professionals."[4] From a college text, "Dyslexia . . . [a] term [that] implies specific brain defect . . . is misused by educators to indicate any reading difficulty . . . it is a specific medical definition that teachers should avoid."[5] From Jerry Pournelle, Ph.D., "[Dyslexia] is merely a word describing an obvious condition: the sufferer has trouble reading . . . The Michigan Reading Clinic has examined some 30,000 cases of 'dyslexia' and found precisely two children who could never learn to read."[6] And from Dr. Melvin Howards, "I have yet to meet what is described as the classic dyslexic. My experiments with thousands of children have never brought me to the conclusion that dyslexia explained anything or clarified anything or offered any corrective program."[7] More recently, Thomas Armstrong wrote, "Children get saddled with diagnostic terms such as dyslexia . . . and the like, making it sound as if they suffer from very rare and exotic diseases. Yet the word dyslexia is just Latin bafflegab, or jargon, for 'trouble with words.'"[8]

Definition

The word "dyslexia" literally means trouble with language. It usually refers to difficulties with learning to read and write. "Reversing" is the most familiar "symptom." People who are labeled dyslexic seem to have trouble recognizing words by sight, blending letter sounds, remembering the "rules," and keeping the letters in words in the right order. Frequently, they also have difficulty with the mechanics of writing (punctuation, sentence structure, spelling) and with organizing thoughts on paper. This is how the traditional School Model views them.

The Learning Style model asks: What is this child's strongest modality? What is the best approach for her disposition? How can we incorporate her talents and interests? Will it make a difference if aspects of the environment are changed?

Most people who are labeled dyslexic are Picture Learners. As discussed in Chapter 8, Picture Learners are often mistakenly treated as Print Learners. I am convinced that this misconception is the cause of the majority of reading problems

> *I asked them to do one thing for me: Please don't label kids. Because we are all "gifted," "average," and "slow," depending on the task at hand.*
>
> —Harry W. Forgan

among our students. It's true that the other aspects of learning style must also be taken into account for each student; however, modality is such a powerful component of the learning-to-read process, that changing this one aspect alone could make a huge difference for countless students.

According to Thomas Armstrong,

> These [children] often tend to be highly imaginative children with strong spatial intelligence. Because they regard letters as pictures they can't read them as symbols. As a result, they end up with the label dyslexic. What they need is an educational approach that will help them make the transition from image to symbol in a natural way.[9]

The creators of the Wilson Reading Program, the AVKO Spelling Program, and the Lindamood-Bell programs and materials understand the Visual Modality needs of these students. The Wilson and Lindamood programs also include a Tactile-Kinesthetic component, since many Picture Learners are strong in the Tactile-Kinesthetic Modality as well. As mentioned in Chapter 8, the books *The Gift of Dyslexia* and *Thinking in Pictures* are great resources which thoroughly explain the characteristics of the Picture Learner. (See Appendix II for more information on these books and programs.)

Reversals

What about reversals? Nothing seems to cause more panic in parents and teachers than to see a child reverse a letter! I was reading at four years of age and have never reversed a letter or word in my life. But I can never remember which is the backward and which is the forward slash for computer DOS commands, and I reverse them inconsistently. My friend can do whole strings of DOS commands perfectly, but is a terrible speller and inconsistently reverses letters and letter sequences. Are we *both* dyslexic? Or do we simply have talents in different areas?

A common misconception is that people who are "dyslexic" see letters backwards. When a child reverses a letter, such as a "b" or "d," it is not because she sees it backwards; it is because she cannot remember the abstract letter-sound label that distinguishes one from the other, just like I can't remember which label goes with which slash. Again, most likely, this child is a Picture Learner—with the appropriate memory strategy for her learning style she could easily eliminate reversals. (With the appropriate strategy for my learning style, I could easily stop reversing the slashes, but then I wouldn't be able to do demonstrations of my lack of ability at workshops!)

ADD and Hyperactivity

ADD and hyperactivity are often considered "learning disabilities" but they, too, are more properly described as medical conditions.

ADD stands for attention deficit disorder. This term generally means that a child is not able to focus attention on the task at hand. The child is too distractible and every little noise or movement diverts his attention away from his work. He can also be "distracted" by his own ideas! Often, this child is caught staring into space, or doodling, or fiddling with something.

"Hyperactive" is that magic label that first allowed us to put thousands of children on drugs (although, when ADD came along later, another reason was added). It, of course, refers to the inability to remain seated, quiet, and still. Like the ADD child, the hyperactive child seems unable to stay focused, pay attention, and complete assignments; but instead of daydreaming this child is busy fidgeting, moving about the room, or disrupting the class in various ways. Some children have the distinction of being ADHD—attention deficit combined with hyperactivity.

Even though ADD and ADHD are technically medical terms, and the conditions are supposed to be diagnosed by a doctor (they appear as psychiatric diagnoses in the Diagnostic and Statistical Manual of the American Psychiatric Association), these labels have become part of our everyday language. The most interesting description of ADD I have ever read appeared in an ad for an organization that works with children. It reads, in part,

> It [ADD] is often present at birth, but may not be diagnosed until the elementary years because the symptoms go unnoticed at home . . . But when sustained attention is required for boring, repetitive tasks in distracting settings like classrooms, the symptoms become easier to see. Sustained cartoon watching or video-game playing doesn't count. The behavioral symptoms are seen with boring, repetitive tasks in distracting settings.[10]

It then goes on to describe the testing that is available and the treatment options, including medication.

I often think, Don't the people who read this ad see anything strange about it? In the first place, why would I want my child to spend most of the day in a place where she is required to do boring, repetitive tasks? And if that is what school is all about, why on earth would I medicate a child to ensure that she does those boring, repetitive tasks? Sounds frighteningly like *Brave New World* to me . . .

In contrast, the Learning Style model asks: Does this child need less noise or more noise? Less movement or more movement? Are the lights too bright or too dim? What are his disposition needs and his modality strengths? Perhaps he needs a quiet corner. Perhaps he is bored and needs more challenge. Perhaps we need to let him lead with his talents and interests. Perhaps he needs to move to learn.

We are more tolerant of adults who exhibit "attention deficits." For example, when a parent in a workshop asks a question about something that I've just covered because he didn't "hear" it, do we immediately think, Oh, he must have ADD? What about when you get distracted and can't do your checkbook because your kids are making noise? Or a teacher at a meeting says, "I'm sorry, I didn't get what you said"? Don't we encourage taking breaks at the workplace, stretching at our desks at the office, getting up and moving around during a long seminar?

As adults, we make excuses: I can't concentrate because I have a headache, or the radio is too loud, or I'm worried about the roof leaking, or I'm so excited about my new home. I need to get up and move because my back hurts. . . . I didn't get enough sleep last night. . . . it's healthy to take stretch breaks. . . .

But kids are not allowed to have excuses or reasons, even when they are doing something really important in their heads, like inventing the next spaceship, or imagining the next award-winning special-effects movie. I suspect that the Wright brothers, Thomas Edison, and Albert Einstein could be among those who would have been labeled ADD. And let's not forget Steven Spielberg and George Lucas. As for hyperactivity—what better models than our beloved Huck Finn and Tom Sawyer! Priscilla Vail, in her book *Learning Styles*, sums it up perfectly:

> " *All too often kids are labeled because someone is confusing a need for a different teaching method with a "learning problem."*
> —Mariaemma Pelullo-Willis "

> A second grade boy who decides to study dust particles because he is bored by the lesson must not be labeled ADHD simply because his teacher likes children who maintain eye contact. Nor should normally active children be medicated because fate landed them under the control of Ms. Sitstillandlissen.[11]

Actually, if the term "ADD" is meant to describe the medical diagnosis of scattered thinking and extreme distractibility, it does not describe most of the children who have been given the label. The usual "ADD" child is not unfocused; on the contrary, she is very, very focused. She is focused on ideas, inventions, and possibilities that her imagination is constantly creating, some of which are triggered by the lesson or assignment that she is no longer paying attention to!

In terms of dispositions, it is the Thinking/Creating and Inventing children who are most often labeled ADD, and the

Performing children who are most often labeled hyperactive. The children in the first group are most at risk for depression and withdrawal, because they will retreat to their inner worlds in order to avoid the pain of being misunderstood and labeled as dysfunctional. When their unique abilities and skills are recognized and encouraged, these people often are the ones who become great artists, inventors, and creative thinkers. The children in the second group are the most at risk for dropping out of school or getting into trouble, because of their needs for movement and action. When their energies are channeled, these people often become entrepreneurs, adventurers, and risk-takers.

In his book, *The Myth of the ADD Child*, Thomas Armstrong says,

> Children who were once seen as "bundles of energy," "daydreamers," or "fireballs," are now considered "hyperactive," "distractible" and "impulsive": the three classic warning signs of attention deficit disorder. Kids who in times past might have needed to "blow off a little steam" or "kick up a little dust" now have their medication dosages carefully measured out and monitored to control dysfunctional behavior . . . I wonder whether there aren't hundreds of thousands of kids out there who may be done a disservice by having their uniqueness reduced to a disorder and by having their creative spirit controlled by a drug.[12]

Perhaps a shift in thinking would help us give new meaning to the terms we have been discussing. In most instances, people who have been labeled "LD" are learning deceived—that is, they have grown up believing that they are deficient and their own natural abilities are not worth much. In my opinion, ADD more aptly refers to Attention to Dreams and Discoveries, and ADHD describes Alert to Daydreams and Humorous Diversions—in other words, the Performing, Inventing, and Thinking/Creating Dispositions! And, lastly, I will admit that there is some truth to ADD standing for attention deficit disorder—there is a definite *deficit* in the kind of *attention* that our young learners receive; therefore the *disorder* is with those schools who are labeling our children!

OTHER ISSUES

It is important to distinguish between what are commonly called "learning disabilities" and certain physical and biological conditions that can affect learning and behavior. When a true disorder exists which impairs a child's learning abilities, this must be diagnosed and treated correctly, not labeled a "learning disability." Just as much of an injustice is done to a child when a real disorder goes undiagnosed, as when a nonexistent condition is labeled as one.

> **In most instances, people who have been labeled "LD" are learning deceived . . .**

Some physical impairments are obvious, such as vision or hearing difficulties. Those listed here are not so familiar to the general population; being aware of them could make a big difference for your child, if you suspect that something other than Learning Style might be involved in his learning difficulties.

Scotopic Sensitivity

Scotopic Sensitivity Syndrome (SSS) is an issue related to light. Some children are extremely sensitive to light and brightness in any form and exhibit symptoms ranging from headache and nausea to reading difficulties and perceptual distortions that can affect coordination and energy levels. Black print on glaring white paper can be especially troublesome. In the 1980s Helen Irlen discovered that colored overlays greatly alleviated these symptoms. She eventually developed a system for testing and prescribing colored lenses, which has completely changed the lives of countless children and adults. Many people with reading difficulties, including those diagnosed as dyslexic or ADD, have been found to have scotopic sensitivity, which when corrected, eliminated the reading problems. You can get more information regarding SSS by contacting the Irlen Institute at 800-55-Irlen, 5380 Village Rd, Long Beach, CA 90808, or reading Irlen's book, *Reading by the Colors*.[13]

Neurological Problems

Some children have legitimate neurological problems that need to be diagnosed by a doctor. For these children, the neurological basis for problem behaviors or difficulties in the classroom may require specific medical treatment including medication. Your pediatrician knows the signs that indicate the possibility of neurological problems. While it is extremely important to diagnose dysfunctions of a neurological nature, it is just as important not to label a child neurologically impaired, simply because the child is very active or because the child appears to daydream. Learning styles are not neurological impairments and shouldn't be treated as such.

> **I will admit that there is some truth to ADD standing for attention deficit disorder—there is a definite deficit in the kind of attention that our young learners receive; therefore the disorder is with those schools that are labeling our children!**

Biochemical Imbalances

Some children have allergies or chemical imbalances that affect their abilities to concentrate and think clearly. A child might be extra sensitive to certain foods or have imbalances of vitamins, minerals, and other nutrients. Allergies and chemical imbalances can cause erratic behavior, impulsivity, scattered thinking, depression, mood swings, and many other problems. A healthful diet free of sugars, processed foods, and chemical additives, which emphasizes whole grains and fresh vegetables, is always best to support optimum brain functioning. (Check the books listed in Appendix II for more information on this topic.)

 ## FAMOUS FAILURES

If the school has already labeled your child, is there still hope?

Yes! Begin implementing the ideas in this book. Talk to your child about Learning Style. Encourage her natural talents and interests. Make her feel great! Read about people who became successful in spite of obstacles and share the stories with your child. Books such as *Chicken Soup for the Soul* and *Celebrity Setbacks* have many such stories. Here are a few:

Learning styles are not neurological impairments and shouldn't be treated as such.

Les Brown was labeled educable mentally retarded when he was in school and he believed that he was. It took the words of a teacher to help him change his image of himself; he is now a gifted motivational speaker.

Albert Einstein did not speak until he was four years old. He had trouble learning to read. A teacher described him as "mentally slow, unsociable, and adrift forever in foolish dreams." He was expelled and was refused admittance to the Zurich Polytechnic School. And, of course, we consider him a genius.

Thomas Edison's teachers said he was too stupid to learn anything.

Leo Tolstoy, author of *War and Peace*, flunked out of college. He was described as both unable and unwilling to learn.

Described as the worst pupil in the school, the sculptor Rodin failed three times to secure admittance to the school of art.

Isaac Newton did very poorly in grade school.

Robin Williams was voted least likely to succeed in high school.

Charles Schulz, creator of the Peanuts cartoon strip, failed all subjects in the eighth grade, and flunked algebra, Latin, English, and physics in high school.

Jay Leno's fifth grade teacher said, "If Jay spent as much time studying as he does trying to be a comedian, he'd be a big star." [14,15]

A very special person graduated with honors from Radcliffe College in 1904. It's true, she wouldn't fit the official learning disability definition because she had physical problems—she was deaf, blind, and mute—and, if she had been tested for IQ, she would have scored below average. Fortunately, her teacher was not involved in testing and labeling, in trying to figure out whether Helen Keller was LD or retarded. Anne Sullivan simply did not give up until she discovered the method that worked, beginning the process that allowed Helen to develop as a highly gifted person.

> Unable to use her sense of sight or hearing, Helen Keller learned first through touch. And the good news is that modern breakthroughs have now provided the tools for all of us to "switch on" to easier learning, even those who may have been labeled "backward" or "slow." Almost a century after Keller's graduation, her message to the world is still clear: everyone is potentially gifted—in some way . . . This is not to deny that some people have learning difficulties. But labeling them "learning disabled" must rank with IQ tests as one of the great education tragedies of the century. The very act of labeling has added to the stress. *Our research convinces us that any person can learn—in his or her own way. And those ways are many and varied.*[16]

If any person could be labeled "disabled," it would be Helen Keller. Her story demonstrates what can happen when a label is not allowed to limit a person's potential or interfere with natural gifts and talents.

CAPABLE VERSUS DISABLED

The Learning Style Model of Education views students as creative, bright, and capable. The school program that flows out of this model is one that

- matches methods and programs to students' learning styles
- provides curriculum flexibility to meet each student's needs
- displays patience and allows learning to take place at its own pace
- instead of comparing students, encourages them to work together and share talents

- truly values, appreciates, and acknowledges each student's gifts
- helps students to learn about themselves, develop talents, and reach potentials

When this happens we will no longer need to offer excuses for a child's misbehavior or inability to "perform" or "get the job done." All students will be encouraged to become problem-solvers and to use the information about how they operate to take charge of themselves and be accountable for their behaviors. They will learn to take responsibility for their actions and to take a major role in decision making.

There is no reason for an "ADD" child to run wild in public, and no reason for any student to fail any subject based on a "disability." If Helen Keller could accomplish what she did, then certainly we can do our children the favor of seeing them as capable, providing the right tools and techniques for them to "switch on," and allowing them the dignity of becoming responsible for their own learning and behaviors.

> **So if your child has been labeled by the school system, get on your child's team, drop the labels, see the possibilities, and coach for success!**

Until all schools are ready to follow this model, it is up to the parents to work as closely as they can with teachers, and to do as much as they can at home to help their children learn. Parents will find many teachers who welcome this view of the child as capable rather than learning disabled, and who will gladly put Learning Style information to use in their classrooms.

So if your child has been labeled by the school system, get on your child's team, drop the labels, see the possibilities, and coach for success!

How to Talk to
Your Child's Teacher

Next to you, your child's teacher is the most influential person in your child's life. It is possible to partner with a teacher—to be on the same team—for the important job of educating your child. Partnering can be your opportunity to share what you have discovered about your child and the Learning Style Model of Education.

Your child's teacher might already be familiar with learning styles, multiple intelligences, modality, and other terms having to do with individualizing curriculum, since these terms are talked about a great deal in education circles. She might have attended workshops on these topics and even implemented one or two ideas. She might be convinced that working with each child's Learning Style is the best way to teach. Yet she might also believe that it isn't possible to put into practice what is presented at workshops—there's a big difference between the real classroom and the workshop setting. Your child's teacher might feel overwhelmed and not know how to apply learning style principles to an entire classroom of students. Even in the new, smaller classrooms, we're still talking about twenty kids!

According to a poll taken by the Association for Supervision and Curriculum Development, when asked what they need, teachers said:

1. practical, hands-on ideas for their classrooms
2. management strategies for *diverse students*
3. teaching behaviors that promote positive learning environments[1]

Since the Learning Style Model of Education addresses and provides solutions for these issues, your child's teacher might welcome the information you have to share because it has application beyond your child's individual needs.

HOW A TEACHER PERCEIVES OBSTACLES

The more you are able to address a teacher's classroom concerns and needs, the better your chances are of partnering and having your ideas taken seriously. It's not easy for a teacher to rethink the way he's been conducting his classroom for many years. Even when he knows in his heart that it's the right thing to do, there are many administrative, financial, environment-related, and emotional obstacles to making changes that incorporate learning styles.

> *Teachers are amazing people! We are faced with situations that would throw most people into a tailspin! Have you ever imagined what it would be like to place a high-salaried politician, doctor or lawyer in front of a class of 25 first graders? My prediction is that the majority of them would run for the door after the first thirty minutes!*
>
> —Esther Wright

Administration

When a teacher wants to make a change in the classroom, administration is likely to be concerned that some parents won't understand or support changes in policy. Administration will also want to be assured that a shift in policy will at least maintain standardized test scores if not improve them. Teachers are under great stress because standardized test results are often interpreted by administration as a reflection of their teaching abilities. Principals tell them to do whatever needs to be done to improve test scores. In other words, they are not apt to get many rewards for taking a learning styles approach to teaching unless it guarantees immediately improved test scores.

Class Size, Learning Environment, and Finances

Teachers on the whole want to do what is best for each child. They realize that they are limited in their ability to give the personal attention that they would like to give because they are responsible for too many young people at one time. Teachers are often under attack for not using more individualized instruction even though they are required to work with large groups of young people. It takes specialized training, a specialized environment, and the support of parents and administrators to "individualize" a classroom. Financial and environment-related considerations come into play when a teacher wants to increase the number of hands-on materials for some learners and provide different furnishings for the classroom—bookshelves for the new materials, new desks for new kinds of seating arrangements, and so on.

> Teachers are often under attack for not using more individualized instruction even though they are required to work with large groups of young people.

Fear of Change

Last, but far from least, are the emotional considerations. When I was a classroom teacher I remember coming to an impasse with some of my students. I had invented many techniques to work with kids who had different learning styles; however, I still wasn't reaching certain kinds of learners. I remember when I realized that I needed to find help—that I needed to go beyond my usual ways of organizing and conducting a classroom. I felt afraid and vulnerable. I didn't want to see my shortcomings, let alone take charge and do something about them. The thought of it was overwhelming to me. It was a gradual process from realizing that I needed to make a change, to finding the courage to do it, to taking steps toward making new contacts with people who could help me.

To partner with a teacher for change in the classroom means understanding the obstacles to change that a teacher has to overcome. A little bit of empathy for *their situation* goes a very long way, and is the best strategy for eventually getting your child's learning style needs met.

SOME TIPS FOR TALKING TO YOUR CHILD'S TEACHER

If you decide to talk with your child's teacher, the time you put into laying a foundation will be worth it. Review the guidelines below carefully if you want a good chance of having your voice heard.

Cultivate Your Relationship First

If you already have a good relationship with your child's teacher, it will be much easier to talk to her than it would be otherwise. Whether you have a good relationship or not, think about the *teacher's* learning style. What might her interests, talents, and dispositions be? What is she apt to value? She organizes her classroom the way she does for specific reasons. What might they be? When you can see the teacher's point of view and talk with her about it, you are more likely to be heard. If you think about your child's teacher in this way, you can make a good relationship even better, or you can make a positive relationship where you didn't have one before.

Be Prepared

To help you organize your thoughts and present them in a succinct way, a blank version of the Learning Style Portrait used to explain

Greg's and Ann's stories in Chapter 10 is included here for your use (see Figure 14.1). (Be sure to make lots of copies of the blank; you'll need them.)

- Refer to the Summary Form to fill in the Dispositions, Talents, Interests, Modality, and Environment information.
- With your child, decide on a few goals.
- Refer to the Plan Form to fill in Strategies.

Maybe the most valuable thing that you need to know about teachers is that time is precious—they *never* have enough of it. The time you take in advance to get important information, goals, and strategies on paper will save the teacher hours of racking his brain to come up with ideas appropriate for your child. At the same time, you'll be demonstrating that you are willing to contribute to a partnering relationship. You and your child can fill out the Learning Style Portrait together in preparation for a meeting with the teacher. When your child's teacher sees how carefully thought out your ideas are, he is likely to be much more open to listening.

> *What children need as much as computers or books is relationships with caring adults.*
> —James Comer, Associate Dean, Yale University School of Medicine and Director of School Development Program

Go Slowly

It may take two or three meetings to say all of what you have to say. The first time you get together you might find out how much the teacher knows about learning styles. Perhaps you could tell her that you are reading a book about learning styles and wonder if she would be willing to talk with you about it at some point. During an informal talk you can

Maybe the most valuable thing that you need to know about teachers is that time is precious—they never have enough of it.

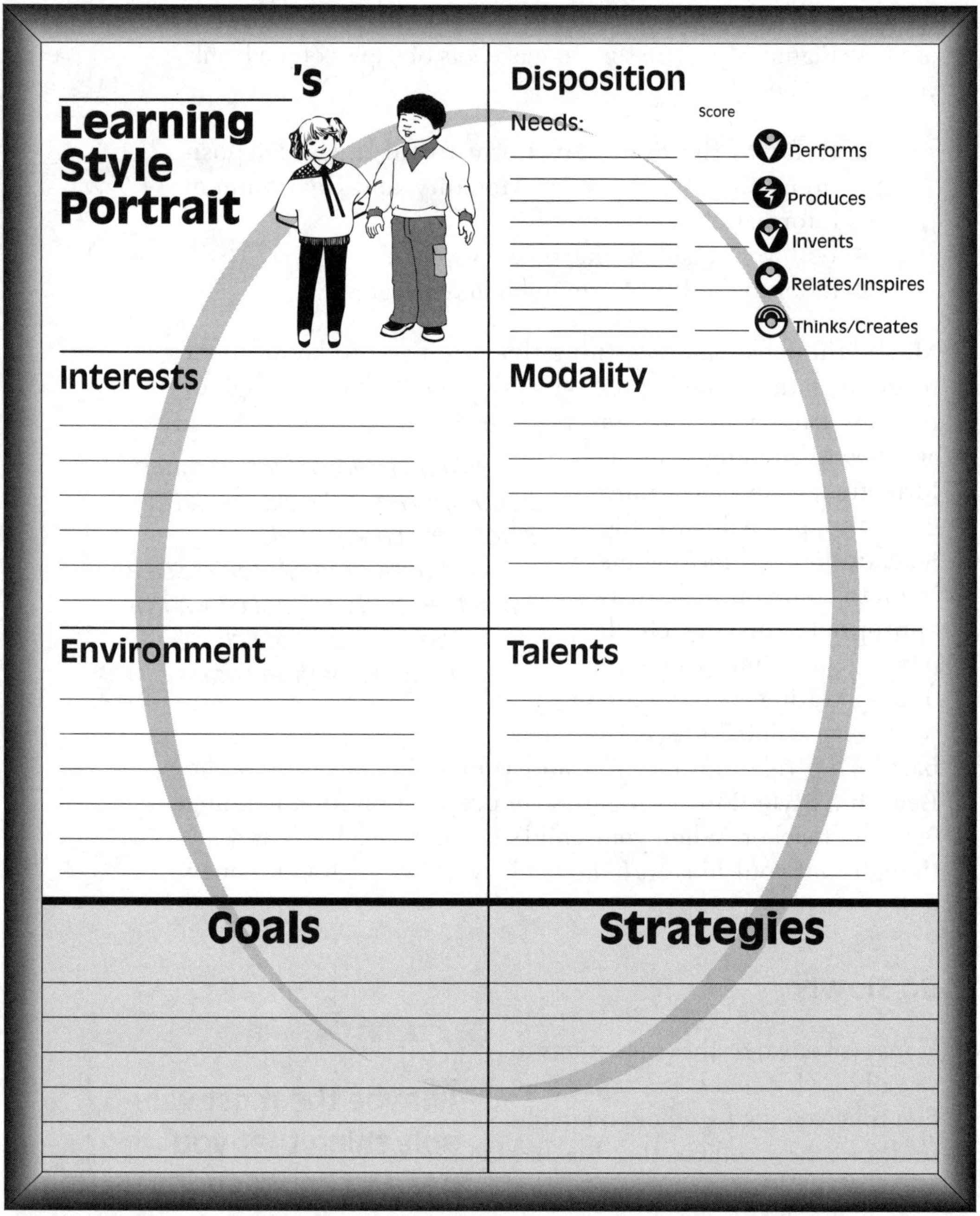

_____'s

Learning Style Portrait

Disposition

Needs: Score

_____   _____ Performs

_____   _____ Produces

_____   _____ Invents

_____   _____ Relates/Inspires

_____   _____ Thinks/Creates

Interests

_____

_____

_____

_____

_____

Modality

_____

_____

_____

_____

_____

Environment

_____

_____

_____

_____

_____

Talents

_____

_____

_____

_____

_____

Goals

_____

_____

_____

_____

Strategies

_____

_____

_____

_____

Figure 14.1 Learning Style Portrait Form

determine what her attitude is about learning styles. It might not be until the third meeting that you talk about your child specifically. Looking for quick results can be seen as a threat and is likely to undermine your efforts to be heard.

Take Your Child to the Meeting

Kids need to be involved in the processes that concern them whenever possible. When discussing your child's learning style needs with a teacher it is important that your child attend the meeting also. Your child can learn a valuable lesson about how to ask for what she needs while you provide support. Be sure to notify the teacher in advance that your child will be attending the meeting.

Talk About One Concern at a Time

Before your meeting, brainstorm a list of learning goals and prioritize them. Make many copies of the Learning Style Portrait referred to above (Figure 14.1) and fill out one Portrait for each learning goal that you and your child identify—working from the top down on the prioritized list. A teacher approached with a barrage of requests is likely to feel overwhelmed and unreceptive. Start by filling out one or two Portraits that identify specific areas for growth and goals.

 ## ACTUAL RESULTS OF USING LEARNING STYLES IN CLASSROOMS

Some teachers need to feel assured that the Learning Style Model actually works. Some excellent publications you could refer your teacher to include *How to Implement and Supervise a Learning Style Program* by Rita Dunn, *How to Change to a Nongraded School* by Madeline Hunter, *Learning Styles* by Priscilla Vail, and *Circles of Learning* by David Johnson, Roger Johnson, and Edythe Holubec.

Perhaps some stories about how the Learning Style Model has worked for parents and education professionals would help as background if you need to provide more assurance to your child's teacher.

In the words of Francine Burns, a sixth-grade teacher at Holy Cross School in California:

> "Last semester, I was taking an art course and decided to apply some of the learning style techniques to teach a course to my students. I applied the techniques to facilitate their comprehension of the artists and their histories. I was amazed at what a good job they did with the project that I assigned. I decided that their work was so good that I wanted my 6th graders to present it to my college class, so I submitted *their* presentations as *my* final! What took me by surprise was that one of my peers asked me if I was teaching a gifted class! I looked at my students and with a smile I said, 'It's not a gifted class *per se*, but, yes, they are pretty special!' Since using the learning style techniques in my classroom, I have seen my students grow and learn in wonderful ways. I know that the Learning Style Model works!

A fifth-grade teacher in a private elementary school in Ojai, California, gives the Learning Profile to her new students every year. She reports that it is the best activity she has ever done. She even has the parents of her students take the Profile so that they can learn how to work more effectively with their child at home.

The principal of a parochial school has commented several times, "I keep telling my teachers that using learning style methods works every time." And the vice principal mentioned earlier says, "First, the grades have got to go! Then we have to start teaching in the ways kids learn best."

In her book *How to Implement and Supervise a Learning Style Program*, Learning Style pioneer Rita Dunn tells about the wonderful successes among educators across the country when they implemented her learning style programs:

> Sherrye Dotson, Director of Secondary Instruction, Jacksonville, Texas, explains, "Our summer learning style program offered only eighteen days of instruction, but many students accomplished goals that they hadn't mastered through years of traditional education."
>
> Duane Alm, a principal in Aberdeen, South Dakota, says, "In every classroom, the achievement gains of the children using learning styles have convinced teachers to become advocates."

Penny Todd Claudis, Curriculum Supervisor, Shreveport, Louisiana, provides assurance for some of the more controversial aspects of the Learning Style Model for Education when she says, "In the beginning parents express concern about kids learning on the floor and snacking while studying. Once they understand the program, they help redesign the room, make tactile materials, and ask to have their other children tested for learning styles."[2]

Finally, here's a report from one of my clients, the parent of an eighth grader:

> *The classroom, like a fine orchestra of instruments with various sounds and textures, awaits the great maestro to bring out the best of each instrument—while directing the lovely harmonies and melodies we call learning.*
>
> *—Esther Wright*

My thirteen-year-old son's grades were slipping. We received his progress report and were astonished as well as disappointed to see his first D. Social studies had numerous dates and events to memorize. I knew his continued reading and re-reading about these events wouldn't be enough to help him "try" to remember.

This child was brought in for a Learning Style assessment and taught a technique that fit his learning style. His mother reported:

> Within two and a half weeks of learning this valuable technique, my son brought his grade up to a C⁻ and is on his way to bringing it up to a B before too long. Best of all, he feels proud, confident, and excited about learning again. Thank you for your insight, compassion, and valuable training.

Three weeks later this mom called to report that her son had received A's on his last two social studies tests.

Learning style success stories could fill an entire book. I hope that your confidence (and your child's teacher's) in using the learning style method to create learning-success is increasing as you read about real people using learning style assessments and techniques.

WHAT IF A TEACHER CAN'T MAKE ANY CHANGES?

If your child's teacher is unable to apply the Learning Style Model, you might have planted some seeds anyway. You never know what will sprout in a few weeks or months. In any case, your child knows that the two of you tried to make a difference at school. What you have learned can still be implemented at home. Sometimes the fact that someone is working with your child and acknowledging her is all that it takes for the child to feel encouraged because she knows that somebody really is on her team. After all, unless a child feels encouraged, she isn't going to be willing to take any steps to becoming an eager, self-directed learner.

If you prepare yourself for the meeting with your child's teacher, if you keep the obstacles to classroom change in mind, and if you are willing to go one step at a time (while staying true to your child's Learning Style needs), you and your child are most likely to be heard.

Regardless of how it actually turns out with the teacher, I hope that if you had to choose between a confident, self-directed, eager child and a child who gets "good" grades, you would choose the former knowing that these wonderful attributes are the most important ingredients for success in life. I hope that regardless of how your meeting turns out with the teacher, you will continue to acknowledge and celebrate your child's talents, interests, and skills now that you have the knowledge and the means to develop a confident, self-directed, eager learner.

Educating for
the Real World

Recall that in the Introduction you were asked to keep two questions in mind: What is a successful learner? and How can I help my child become a successful learner?

Have you become clearer about the answers to these questions? Do you have educational goals for your child and, if so, are they compatible with his unique gifts and what he loves to do? That is, are they in line with his learning style—his talents, interests, dispositions? Most importantly, can they be summarized as one basic goal—giving your child the foundation, tools, and confidence to develop his own set of educational goals, which will lead to a fulfilling future?

What about the schools? What are their goals for our children? Is it likely that schools will be looking at methods for teaching that are compatible with the needs of different learners? Can you, the parent, partner with your child's school to help her develop her interests and talents, encouraging her toward a rich and successful future?

The answers to these questions have to do with how we define *success*, how we define *education*, and what we want for our young people in the real world.

SUCCESS AND EDUCATION IN THE REAL WORLD

What makes a person successful in the real world? Does success in school, as measured by grades, determine success in life? This is an interesting question. As discussed in Chapter 3, schools try to convey the message that unless students "shape up" and do well, they won't get anywhere in life. Yet some very successful people dropped out of high school, and some very unsuccessful people did well in school and even have doctoral degrees.

What Is Success?

Back to our questions about success in life. Is success measured by money, career, happiness? Many books have been written on this subject. The common theme that seems to surface over and over is this: Although each person has to define what success means for himself, generally success seems to involve having a passion, loving what you do, using your unique talents and interests to give back to the world, and having a life purpose. Furthermore, achieving success has more to do with self-knowledge, positive thinking, goals, and confidence in one's abilities, than with grades.

> **A**chieving success has more to do with self-knowledge, positive thinking, goals, and confidence in one's abilities, than with grades.

An educational system that measures learning with testing and grades, discounts individual abilities and needs, and compares students with one another, has a powerful influence over the confidence levels of adults who learned as children that they just weren't very "smart." Many adults don't recognize the talents that are hidden within them, or don't realize what they could achieve if they set their minds to it and learned some strategies for success.

Bookstore shelves are filled with books that advise adults to forget what they were told in school and go for their dreams. The way to do this, the authors say, is to rediscover one's natural talents and interests, which are the clues to one's direction and life purpose. We are told to forget the mediocre grades we got in school, which led us to believe that we weren't good enough to go for what we want, or even the good grades, which might have steered us away from paying attention to what we really love.

> Each second we live is a new and unique moment of the universe, a moment that will never be again . . . And what do we teach our children? We teach them that two and two make four, and that Paris is the capital of France. When will we also teach them what they are? We should say to each of them: Do you know what you are? You are a marvel. You are unique. In all the years that have passed, there has never been another child like you. Your legs, your arms, your clever fingers, the way you move. You may become a Shakespeare, a Michelangelo, a Beethoven. You have the capacity for anything.
>
> —Pablo Casals

I recently met a successful attorney who was very unhappy. With the help of a career counselor, this woman realized that what she really wanted was to own a small restaurant. Her people-oriented personality, talents, and interests were pulling her in that direction. She changed careers and loves her new life. Is this what we call midlife crisis? I call it midlife *celebration* when someone finally finds what she is truly meant to do with her life!

Adults seeking life direction and guidance are finding it in books such as *Do What You Love—The Money Will Follow*, *I Could Do Anything If I Only Knew What It Was*, *What Color Is Your Parachute?*, *How To Find Your Mission in Life*, *Straight A's Never Made Anybody Rich*, and *Seven Strategies to Wealth and Happiness*. Seminars and workshops are retraining adults at the workplace in principles of self-awareness for increased efficiency, goal setting, and positive thinking, because these are the real skills needed to thrive in the real world.

The point is, companies and individuals are paying lots of money to learn about the kinds of learning techniques and success strategies that are presented in this book. If these principles are so valuable, why not teach them to our children in the first place? Most students who graduate from high school have no idea what their talents are, long ago forgot about their interests, and don't know what they want to do with their lives. Many go on to college, hoping they will find something there. Others grab the first job they can get and begin the daily cycle of getting up, going to work, coming home, going to bed. For most students, the years they spent in school (and the assignments they were required to do), and what they end up doing in the real world have no connection.

> **M**any adults don't recognize the talents that are hidden within them, or don't realize what they could achieve if they set their minds to it and learned some strategies for success.

The Learning Style Model of Education helps you start your child off in the right direction from the very beginning. Your child can grow up understanding how to make the best use of his learning style—how to set goals and plan for the future, how to move toward his life purpose.

Education: Are We Drawing Out or Piling Upon?

In Latin, the word "educate" means to *draw out* and the word "instruct" means *systematic piling upon*. As Chris Brewer and Don Campbell so succinctly put it, "When we pile upon, we do not honor the creative process . . . When we instruct, we merely provide facts and answers. Educating implies a drawing out, an active participation in creating intelligence, and an awakening of inner thought processes."[1]

Ways of Piling Upon

Since many schools rely solely on tests to determine the success of students, mostly what happens in classrooms is a lot of systematic "piling upon." Memorizing hundreds of bits of information to take a quiz or test, then promptly forgetting everything as soon as the test is over in order to begin cramming information for the next test is "piling upon." Almost everyone who has gone through elementary school has been assigned the task of memorizing the states and capitals, the Declaration of Independence, and the definitions of the parts of speech. How many people can still recite these as adults? A few can to be sure but most of us can't, don't care, and furthermore do not have a reason for using any of this information in the real world.

Is there any value to memorizing information that most students don't really grasp but hold in their minds just long enough to pass a test? Is there a value to memorizing history facts, science precepts, math formulas, or excerpts from literature in the first place? Many people believe this is valuable. E. D. Hirsch, in his book *Cultural Literacy*, writes about his concern that our children are growing up without committing to memory those bits of information that *are* a part of our culture—the bits of information that make a person well-rounded and well-educated. The question is, is this common cultural foundation best achieved through memorizing isolated pieces of information in order to pass tests?

> *Outside of school we simply never think of people in terms of where they fall on the normal curve. Indeed, we seem to be far more comfortable with people's complexity outside of the context of the classroom . . . Except when facing their driver's license or civil service tests, what adults ever think of test scores at all?*
>
> *—James Alan Astman*

I believe there is merit to the broad, liberal arts education that aims to give a common foundation to all of our citizens. In theory, we are exposing all the nation's children to the same basic information, so that everyone has a foundation for 1) treating each other humanely—with compassion and a spirit of collaboration; and 2) pursuing "unlimited" opportunity in the real world—to choose occupations and to be successful adults. Isn't that the American dream? The intention is good but what are the actual results?

Education for All?

In reality, our school system is strangling opportunity for millions, because this common foundation and liberal arts education is *not* available to *all*. It is not available to *all* because the information is not presented in a way that all children can absorb. Those who don't are banished to the ranks of slow, average, or learning disabled. The message is conveyed to them early on that they won't do well in life (recall the awards ceremony in Chapter 2). Those who are labeled above average, smart, or gifted don't necessarily fare any better. These children learn to play the game, to memorize for good grades; but what do they really *know* that will be useful in the real world? Perhaps some are learning to "win" at the expense of others and even their own integrity. Since the school system thrives on accentuating differences, ranking, and doling out privileges and punishments, we are kept in constant competition with one another—not a setting that fosters compassion and collaboration, at school or in life.

Somewhere along the line the system went haywire, launching a frenzied, unexamined attempt to transfer information bits, and high test scores became the standard goal. More and more information is piled upon students with little regard for their learning needs and at the expense of developing their natural gifts and abilities. The assumption is that we are educating for the real world of "unlimited" opportunities; however, this goal is far from being reached for the majority of our kids. For the young people who decide that this goal is unreachable, discouragement and even cynicism are common responses.

Who Is Left Out?

David D'Arcangelo, a financial and marketing consultant, in-demand public speaker, author, and host of the television talk show "Money Talk," tells the story of his school experience. He talks about not doing well with rote learning. Yet his goal was to go to college even though he would be the first one in his family to do so. When he took the college entrance exam he received a low score. He was especially disconcerted over questions like, If two trains leave from two destinations at the same time, traveling at such and such speeds, at what time will they meet? (you know the kind!). He couldn't believe that his "fitness" for college was being determined on the basis of being able to answer such questions. He knew he was smart but this test didn't show it, and it was limiting his opportunity. After several phone conversations, one college he applied to recognized his creativity, determination, and commitment. Not only was he accepted, he also received a scholarship. He went on to become an all-American football player and athletic hall of famer and to successfully graduate. Today, he owns several companies and is considered America's home-based business expert.[2] Somehow, D'Arcangelo was able to achieve all this in spite of the messages he received in school about his "inabilities." Most people, unfortunately, accept the limitations placed on them during the school years and give up, not realizing how capable they really are.

Skills Versus Content

According to Hirsch, children who are not acquiring the information that *he* considers essential, which he has compiled in his books, "are being cheated, with the best of intentions, by, among other things, wrong-headed theories about the primary importance of teaching skills rather than traditional content—theories that have dominated instruction in American schools in the past few decades."[3] But the fact is that content is not a problem when children are given the tools they need to acquire it. Right now, schools are set up to deliver content only to those children who are skilled at rote learning. Those who learn in other ways are not being served. Once again, note Rita Dunn's conclusion after years of working with Learning Styles—"Most children can master the same content, *how* they master it is determined by their individual styles,"[4] and David Elkind's advice—"It's not that we shouldn't have expectations and standards, but we need to recognize that children don't all learn in the same way at the same rate."[5] Dunn further recommends, "Rather than eliminating testing, it seems sensible to require that teachers teach using learning styles and then give the students opportunities to demonstrate how well they learn. We should strive to transform all of our schools into learning style schools."[6]

For the real world we need skills *and* content so why not provide both? Rather than simply piling on information, and giving the A's and B's to those who have a facility for "memorizing for the test," the Learning Style Model helps *all* children learn—*whatever* content our nation decides is important—by drawing upon the inherent intelligence of each child.

> **T**he Learning Style Model helps *all* children learn—whatever content our nation decides is important—by drawing upon the inherent intelligence of each child.

Since most of our schools are not following the Learning Style Model of Education at this time, it is extremely important that you, the parent, become knowledgeable about learning styles, in order to ensure that your child is an eager, self-directed, successful learner, not only for school but, more importantly, for real life.

THE CONFIDENCE TO SUCCEED

For real-world education to take place, learning must occur from the inside-out and not the outside-in, as discussed in Chapter 3. This means, among other things, that kids need to be allowed to practice and experiment without fear of punishment for making mistakes. It also means that they need people behind them who will support, guide, and advocate for their learning processes.

Practice Leads to Learning

A person learns the most when mistakes are viewed as lessons to learn from, rather than failures. Thomas Edison himself did over 9,999 experiments trying to invent the lightbulb, with no luck. On the ten-thousandth try he got it right. When asked how he could continue after experiencing so many failures, he assured the inquirer that he had not experienced a single failure; he had merely learned all of the ways that didn't work, bringing him closer to the solution.

In the real world, we create opportunities for ourselves when we believe that certain outcomes are possible. The real world depends on learning from mistakes as the source of motivation to take the next step. If our schools are to educate for the real world, they must give kids the opportunity to be tested without fear of mistakes, learn from these tests, and be given the opportunity to be retested. What's the point of giving a weekly test, marking the grade, and moving on? How is one supposed to learn from this system?

What if kids could take tests without anxiety? We are completely devoted to practice when it comes to sports, music, and dance—why not for academics? If no grades were attached to daily quizzes and weekly tests, students could practice and learn, and they could go back over the material they missed to find out what they don't understand, or what they still need to memorize. Learning to memorize is actually a very useful tool that one can take into adulthood. If we taught each child to memorize by using her Learning Style, she would not only learn the *content*, she would also be learning the *skill* of memorizing. In this case, memorizing would no longer be an exercise in futility—a short-term objective to get a grade—but would be transformed into a valuable technique to be used throughout one's life (see techniques and materials discussed in Chapters 5 through 10).

Using testing to *teach* rather than *label* helps all kids to learn content while they are also learning about how they learn. Instead of grading the *tests*, a child could be assigned a grade based on his effort and final outcome, *after learning the material.* With this system, a common foundation based on a liberal arts education does become possible for all children. In addition, each child's natural intelligence is valued and encouraged and each child experiences success. Experiencing many successes leads to confidence—which spills over into real life and sets the stage for experiencing accomplishments as adults.

Mentoring

Books and tapes such as *The Power of Positive Thinking, The Greatest Salesman in the World, The Aladdin Factor,* and *It's Possible* make it clear that self-knowledge, confidence, determination, and strategies for positive thinking are the ingredients for success. Athletes seem to know this principle to a greater degree than the rest of us. Star athletes, those who break records for wins, are also the ones who break records for losses—in other words, the only reason they're winners is because they're willing to lose, too! Bonnie St. John Deane, Silver Medal winner for skiing in the 1984 Disabled Olympics, (who, by the way, has one leg), has said that when winners fall down they get back up, and Gold Medal winners get up faster! Michael Jordan has missed more than 9,000 shots in his career and has lost almost 300 games. He has failed over and over and over again, and that is why he succeeds.

What gives people the confidence to believe in their own abilities and potentials and to keep going? One of the key ingredients is being surrounded by mentors and coaches who believe in them. Les Brown was able to eventually break out of the "educable mentally retarded" category, because in high school a teacher commented that he should never let other people's perceptions of him create his reality. This was the beginning of a new belief in himself, about who he was and what he could do.

We've forgotten the value of mentoring in this country. Some high schools and colleges are rethinking the idea of apprenticeships and programs that allow students to interact with community businesses to either explore careers or begin their real-world experience in their chosen careers. The Learning Style Model encourages parents to seek out mentoring relationships that nurture and draw out their children's natural talents and interests.

> "
> *What is desired is that the teacher cease being a lecturer, satisfied with transmitting ready-made solutions—his role should rather be that of a mentor stimulating initiative and research.*
>
> —Jean Piaget
> "

The process of building confidence and self-direction begins in childhood. When children's learning needs are respected, and when parents and teachers take the time to help children learn about themselves and how they learn best, kids feel valued. When Modality and Disposition are taken into account for lessons and assignments, and when Talents and

Interests are encouraged, kids feel competent. When students evaluate themselves, set goals, and track accomplishments, they learn about determination and positive thinking. When kids have people on their team (see Chapter 12) who cheer them on and coach for learning-success, they feel supported. Kids who know their strengths and how to work with their weaknesses, who feel competent and successful, become successful learners for a lifetime.

EDUCATING FOR THE FUTURE

Most parents would agree that we place a high value on education because it has the power of profoundly affecting a child's future in the real world. Precisely because we are educating our children for their futures, we need to continually question which aspects of our present system of education contribute positively to their futures and which do not. Part of this process involves deciding what is useful and what is useless. Sometimes, because kids learn to play the "game," success in school is a false or deceptive success, which does not prepare a child for real success in the real world. The parent's job as a learning-success coach is to help the child stay on track and move in a forward direction toward her goals and aspirations.

The Bottom Line

Now that you've come to the end of this book, you are ready to think about everything that goes into making a successful learner. What is the bottom line? What happens when the "school world" and the real world seem to conflict? Read Bob's story below and then do the final exercise.

Bob's Story

Bob loves science, is a natural at exploring and inventing, and has a goal of becoming a physicist. His knowledge of science far exceeds that of his classmates. In most of his classes, including science, A's are dependent on memorizing facts in order to get high test scores. Even when Bob uses techniques that work best for his Learning Style, he still has to put in several hours a night because of the quantity of material required to be memorized. This student has the opportunity to be mentored by a physicist who can draw out his natural scientific abilities. The physicist can meet with Bob several days a week after school. Should Bob's parents insist that he spend the time memorizing to get the high grade or is it all right to be satisfied with B's or even C's so that Bob can spend his time doing real-life learning with his mentor? What would you do if you were Bob's parents?

There is no easy answer to this question, nor to the many issues that you and your child will face regarding her education. Whatever the situation or problem, use everything you've learned to help you and your child decide *together*. Recall what prompts a child to be an eager, self-directed learner. Think about the C.A.R.E.S. principles. Review the information about Dispositions, Talents, Interests, Modality, and Environment. Go over the Plan form. Think about the principles for helping your child stay F.I.T.T. as a learner. Reread the sections in this chapter titled "Success in the Real World" and "The Confidence to Succeed." Then answer the following questions:

What is a successful learner?
What do I want for my child?

Learning Styles 2000

In answering the question How important will Learning Styles be in the year 2000, Rita Dunn states:

Learning styles are likely to become a mandated prerequisite for schooling within the next decade. It will only take one class-action suit, led by one small group of angry parent advocates, whose non-traditional children have been demoralized by the imposition of traditional schooling, to cause that change. And it will happen, because learning style is not something that affects other people's children. In every family . . . learning styles are dramatically different from each other . . . In most families, one child does extremely well in traditional schooling and another considers academics dull and uninteresting. A third child may be extremely different from the first two . . . Style affects everyone. Whether or not we acknowledge that we each learn differently, certain resources, approaches, and teachers are right for some—and very wrong for others.[7]

Whether or not schools are forced to begin teaching through Learning Styles as Rita Dunn predicts, I encourage you, the parent, to take the information in this book and help your child become a successful learner by getting on your child's team and coaching for success.

EPILOGUE: SOME LAST THOUGHTS

In an article in *The Educational Therapist*, an educator quoted an elementary school principal: "After 24 years of teaching, I can tell you that when parents bring their kids in for the first day of kindergarten, they'll either say, 'Oh, he's sharp as a pin,' or, 'This one's a real devil, you'll have your hands full.' Not one ever comes in saying, 'My kid is just average.' But oh, how fast we make them average."[1]

We hope that this book has given you the knowledge and confidence to view learning, education, and your child in a different way. We hope you have been assured of your child's natural abilities. We hope you believe that your child is truly gifted, that *all* children are gifted, regardless of whether they have been labeled gifted or not.

Learning Style Profile Assessments

DISPOSITION ASSESSMENT

Allow young people to answer the questions by themselves, without prompting. Of all the sections in the Profile, this is the one that sometimes results in inaccurate information because the child's or adult's responses can be based on how they wish they were or how they think they "should" be. So encourage students to respond according to what <u>they</u> think.

Instructions:
For the following questions write one 5, one 4, and one 1.
You will have two blanks.
5 = I am like this the most!
4 = This is a lot like me.
1 = This is the least like me.

For example:
I like
__5__ games.
___ workbooks.
__4__ experiments.
__1__ group projects.
___ wondering and thinking.

1. I...
A ___ am fun to be with.
B ___ get things done,
C ___ ask questions.
D ___ help others.
E ___ think a lot.

2. Learning is best when it...
A ___ is exciting.
B ___ happens step by step.
C ___ involves discovering things.
D ___ is done with others.
E ___ comes from my own ideas.

3. Assignments need to be...
A ___ short.
B ___ on time.
C ___ interesting.
D ___ done in groups.
E ___ important to me.

4. I like...
A ___ games.
B ___ workbooks.
C ___ experiments.
D ___ group projects.
E ___ wondering and thinking.

277

5. In classes or workshops, I like…
A ___ to move.
B ___ to listen quietly.
C ___ to explore alone.
D ___ to make friends.
E ___ to watch or think.

6. I like to do things…
A ___ now.
B ___ on a schedule.
C ___ for as long as I want.
D ___ when it works for everyone.
E ___ when it feels right to me.

7. Schedule…
A ___ keep me from being free.
B ___ keep order.
C ___ take time away from projects.
D ___ are OK if fair.
E ___ don't make sense to me.

8. I like to…
A ___ take things apart.
B ___ finish things I start.
C ___ figure things out.
D ___ talk to people.
E ___ use my imagination.

9. I think about…
A ___ what I'm doing now.
B ___ planning ahead.
C ___ my projects.
D ___ people
E ___ ideas.

10. I feel best when I'm…
A ___ spontaneous.
B ___ organized.
C ___ inventing new things.
D ___ helpful.
E ___ thinking or creating.

Transfer the Disposition scores to the Summary form. Total the scores horizontally by adding 4s and 5s and subtracting 1s. The highest score is the Primary Disposition. The next highest score is the Secondary Disposition.

For example:
Questions 1 and 2 - Record your responses as follows:

	1.	2.
Performing	4	0
Producing	0	1
Inventing	5	4
Relating/Inspiring	1	0
Thinking/Creating	0	5

TALENT ASSESSMENT

In the lists below, check all of the things that are easy for you. Then add up the check marks in each group, multiply by ten, and transfer these scores to the appropriate spaces on the Talent section of the Summary form.

1.

☐ playing music in my head
☐ playing an instrument
☐ whistling or humming
☐ keeping with the beat or rhythm
☐ singing
☐ learning to play new music
☐ collecting records or tapes
☐ memorizing words to songs
☐ making up songs
☐ composing music

TOTAL CHECKS ⬤ ×10= ⬤

3.

☐ guessing what's wrong with something
☐ fixing things
☐ taking apart/putting together
☐ inventing
☐ running machines
☐ taking care of cars
☐ building things
☐ figuring out how things work
☐ being handy with tools
☐ doing household repairs

TOTAL CHECKS ⬤ ×10= ⬤

2.

☐ with numbers
☐ games like chess, checkers
☐ science or math projects
☐ working with money
☐ working with computers
☐ doing experiments
☐ logic puzzles
☐ using calculators
☐ doing math problems
☐ playing with numbers in my head

TOTAL CHECKS ⬤ ×10= ⬤

4.

☐ spelling
☐ reading
☐ talking
☐ writing or telling stories
☐ memorizing names and facts
☐ word games like Scrabble, crossword puzzles
☐ thinking in words
☐ writing plans, outlines, lists
☐ explaining ideas
☐ getting the point when I read

TOTAL CHECKS ⬤ ×10= ⬤

5.

- ☐ drawing or copying pictures, designs
- ☐ thinking in pictures
- ☐ jigsaw puzzles or mazes
- ☐ remembering what I see
- ☐ reading maps or charts
- ☐ knowing where things are
- ☐ direction (finding my way)
- ☐ painting pictures
- ☐ doodling
- ☐ creating an imaginary world

TOTAL CHECKS   **x10=**

6.

- ☐ baseball, basketball, or tennis
- ☐ dancing
- ☐ biking, skating, working out
- ☐ typing or sewing
- ☐ hiking or running
- ☐ hammering or sawing
- ☐ doing models or crafts
- ☐ skateboarding, snowboarding, skiing
- ☐ swimming or surfing
- ☐ writing neatly

TOTAL CHECKS   **x10=**

7.

- ☐ being alone
- ☐ giving my opinion
- ☐ being independent
- ☐ looking my best
- ☐ taking care of myself
- ☐ having hobbies
- ☐ making up my own mind
- ☐ working by myself
- ☐ thinking about my life
- ☐ making plans for what I want

TOTAL CHECKS   **x10=**

8.

- ☐ making friends
- ☐ helping others
- ☐ group games or projects
- ☐ being fair
- ☐ baby-sitting
- ☐ settling arguments
- ☐ understanding people
- ☐ making others feel good
- ☐ solving people problems
- ☐ leading groups or meetings

TOTAL CHECKS   **x10=**

9.

- ☐ raising or caring for animals
- ☐ training pets
- ☐ grooming pets
- ☐ calming down an animal
- ☐ playing with animals
- ☐ getting animals to trust me
- ☐ communicating with animals
- ☐ protecting animals
- ☐ rescuing animals
- ☐ teaching others about animals

TOTAL CHECKS   **x10=**

10.

- ☐ hiking or backpacking
- ☐ exploring nature trails
- ☐ exploring tide pools
- ☐ observing wildlife
- ☐ camping
- ☐ protecting the environment
- ☐ recycling
- ☐ watching/charting stars and planets
- ☐ climbing trees
- ☐ learning about nature

TOTAL CHECKS   **x10=**

11.

☐ laughing
☐ doing funny things
☐ playing practical jokes
☐ making people laugh
☐ mimicking others
☐ using my imagination for fun
☐ making things fun for others
☐ telling jokes
☐ teasing
☐ being clever, tricky

TOTAL CHECKS [   ] ×10= [   ]

12.

☐ cooking
☐ doing yard work, growing plants
☐ coordinating clothes and fashion
☐ cleaning
☐ decorating, painting, or wallpapering rooms
☐ organizing rooms
☐ organizing people
☐ organizing paperwork/materials
☐ budgeting or organizing money
☐ planning or organizing time

TOTAL CHECKS [   ] ×10= [   ]

INTEREST ASSESSMENT

Interest Priority Scale   List your Interests on the priority scale: 10 = most interested, 1 = least interested. You can include favorite subjects and activities in or out of school. Transfer your choices to the appropriate columns (1–4 or 5–10) of the Interest section on the Summary form.

10. _____

9. _____

8. _____

7. _____

6. _____

5. _____

4. _____

3. _____

2. _____

1. _____

Involvement Issues   Answer the following questions, then note a few of your ideas in the Involvement Issues column of the Interest section on the Summary form.

What do you really care about?

at home:

_____

in the neighborhood:

_____

at school:

_____

in your town:

_____

in the world:

_____

How can you help take care of the things you care about?

_____

_____

_____

_____

What things do you want to do some time during your life?

_____

_____

_____

_____

MODALITY ASSESSMENT

PART I. In each set of statements, circle one choice. Then transfer the scores to the Modality Part I section on the Summary form.

1. I prefer to:
- **(A)** Hear a story
- **(B)** See a movie
- **(C)** Play outside

2. I prefer to:
- **(A)** Listen to music
- **(B)** Read a book
- **(C)** Walk or run

3. I prefer to:
- **(A)** Listen to the radio
- **(B)** Watch television
- **(C)** Play a game

4. The best way for me to remember is to:
- **(A)** "say it over and over" to myself.
- **(B)** "make a picture" in my head.
- **(C)** "just do it."

5. I understand instructions better when:
- **(A)** someone explains them to me.
- **(B)** I can read them or see pictures.
- **(C)** someone shows me how.

6. When I am thinking, I:
- **(A)** talk to myself.
- **(B)** see pictures in my head.
- **(C)** need to move around.

7. **(A)** I remember what people say.
- **(B)** I notice how things look; I like colors and designs.
- **(C)** I often play with coins and keys in my pocket or objects on the table.

8. I am a:
- **(A)** listener, not a watcher or doer.
- **(B)** watcher, not a listener or doer.
- **(C)** doer, not a watcher or listener.

TOTAL ITEMS CIRCLED:

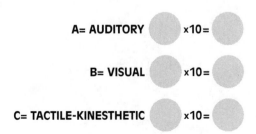

A= AUDITORY   ×10=

B= VISUAL   ×10=

C= TACTILE-KINESTHETIC   ×10=

PART II. Suppose you are learning about how the lungs work. Which of the following would be the easiest way for you to learn about this subject? Number your choices, 1, 2, and 3 for your first, second, and third choices. On the Modality Part II section of the Summary form record 1, 2, 3 next to the items that correspond to your choices.

I learn best when I:

_____ listen to someone talk **(LISTENING)**

_____ listen to a tape **(LISTENING)**

_____ talk in a group **(VERBAL)**

_____ talk aloud to myself **(VERBAL)**

_____ see pictures **(PICTURE)**

_____ watch movies or slides **(PICTURE)**

_____ look up information in reference books **(PRINT)**

_____ read about the lesson **(PRINT)**

_____ have a model to touch, take apart, or put together **(HANDS-ON)**

_____ act out the lesson **(WHOLE BODY)**

_____ draw a picture of the lesson **(SKETCHING)**

_____ write about the lesson **(WRITING)**

ENVIRONMENT ASSESSMENT

PART I. What helps you to study, do school work, or do paperwork? (Check <u>one</u> in each category.) Transfer your responses to the appropriate spaces on the Environment section of the Summary form.

SOUND
☐ quiet
☐ noise (like cars or street noise)
☐ music
☐ people talking

BODY POSITION
☐ sitting at a desk or table
☐ sitting on the floor
☐ lying on the bed, floor, or couch
☐ standing at the board or a tall table

INTERACTION
☐ being by myself with the door closed
☐ being with other people who are quiet
☐ being with other people who are talking or doing things
☐ being with a pet

LIGHTING
☐ bright light
☐ low light
☐ sunlight (outdoors)
☐ light from a window
☐ the kind of light doesn't matter

Parent's observations about the child's lighting needs:

_____

PART II. Check the statements that describe you the best. Then transfer your choices to the appropriate spaces on the Environment section of the Summary form.

TEMPERATURE
☐ I get cold easily.
☐ I get hot easily.
☐ I like the windows open.
☐ I like to keep the windows closed.

☐ I often need my sweater or sweatshirt.
☐ I would rather wear shorts most of the time.
☐ The temperature is usually fine for me.

Parent's observations about the child's temperature needs:

_____

FOOD

☐ I get hungry before lunchtime.
☐ I get hungry between lunch and dinnertime.
☐ I am usually hungry when I get home from school.

☐ I get hungry between dinner and bedtime.
☐ I get thirsty a lot.
☐ I usually don't feel hungry or thirsty.

Parent's observations about child's food needs:

_____

PART III. Fill in your answers below, then transfer them to the appropriate spaces on the Environment section of the Summary form.

Color

My favorite or best color is: _____

My least favorite or worst color is: _____

Time

My best time of day when I have a lot of energy is: _____

My worst time of day when I have no energy is: _____

Learning Style Summary

Name: _____ Date: _____

Disposition

Disposition Questions—Add 4's and 5's, Subtract 1's

		1	2	3	4	5	6	7	8	9	10	TOTALS	Activities
A	Performs												**Move:** skits, shows, demos, games, audiovisuals, sports, "real" life
B	Produces												**Organize:** schedules, outlines, workbooks, reading, writing, portfolios
C	Invents												**Discover:** projects, portfolios, debate, brainstorm, computers, "labs"
D	Relates/ Inspires												**Interact:** group projects, people stories family trees, discussion
E	Thinks/ Creates												**Create:** art, music, nature, poetry, math theory, day dreaming, philosophy, portfolios

Talents

1. _____ Music
2. _____ Math-Logic Reasoning
3. _____ Mechanical Reasoning
4. _____ Word-Lang. Reasoning
5. _____ Spatial
6. _____ Body Coordination
7. _____ Interactive-Self
8. _____ Interactive-Others
9. _____ Interactive-Animals
10. _____ Interactive-Nature
11. _____ Humor
12. _____ Life Enhancement

Interests

1-4 on the Interest Priority Scale

_____
_____
_____
_____

5-10 on the Interest Priority Scale

_____
_____
_____
_____

Involvement Issues

_____
_____
_____
_____

Modality

PART 1

_____ **Auditory** Hear/Talk

_____ **Visual** See/Read

_____ **Tactile-Kinesthetic** Touch/Do

PART 2

_____ **Listening:** Audio tapes, books-on-tape, music, rhyming, songs, stories, computers, live lectures, oral / duet reading
_____ **Verbal:** read aloud, discuss, verbalize to self, read w/books-on-tape, interactive video / computer programs, tape reports/assignments, present orally, sing info or set to music, work with another or in a small group

_____ **Picture:** Videos; computers; picture time lines, cues, diagrams / charts; picture note-taking, info mapping; live performances
_____ **Print:** reading, research, word diagrams/charts, time lines, word note-taking/info mapping, highlight printed material

_____ **Hands-On:** touching, assembling, taking things apart, manipulating objects, textured materials, models, Legos, blocks
_____ **Whole Body:** acting out, moving, dancing, exercising, build large things / construct, walk-on materials
_____ **Sketching:** drawing, coloring, doodling, picture note-taking, picture information mapping
_____ **Writing:** writing, tracing, copying, workbooks, research, outlines, word notetaking / information mapping

Environment

Sound _____   Lighting _____   Color_____
Body Position _____   Temp _____   Time _____
Interaction _____   Food _____

Preschool Assessment Page 1   Name: _____   Date: _____

Section A: Disposition

Read through each section and check the items that best describe the child most of the time. Count the total number of checks in each section and record the totals. Circle the 2 highest scores and record their Disposition names in the Summary Section.

Performing

__ Active

__ Moves from thing to thing

__ Likes to be the center of attention

__ Likes to be "fun"

__ "Charges" into a group

__ "Entertainer"

__ Likes games/competition

__ Takes things apart for fun

__ Likes to laugh and joke

__ Takes risks/puts on a show

Total _____

Producing

__ Organized

__ Plays quietly for a long time

__ Likes to be a helper, wants to get things done

__ Likes to do things "right"

__ Observes a group to be able to fit in

__ "Rule Keeper"

__ Likes to color & look at books

__ Puts things away, is neat and orderly

__ Likes schedules and routines

__ Careful, purposeful, sometimes bossy

Total _____

Inventing

__ Focused

__ Engages in "experiments"

__ Likes to be with others who like to "invent"/"explore"

__ Likes to ask questions

__ Shies away from groups

__ "Little Scientist"

__ Likes to collect/tinker

__ Takes things apart to discover

__ Gets lost in projects

__ Prefers to be alone or with adults

Total _____

Relating/Inspiring

__ Sensitive to others' feelings

__ Thrives on group interaction

__ Likes to be friends

__ Likes to talk and be social

__ Looks for "warm" frienships

__ "Diplomat"/"Mediator"

__ Likes cooperative projects

__ Shares activities & belongings

__ Likes to be read to/cuddle

__ Expresses feelings and is hurt easily

Total _____

Thinking/Creating

__ Pensive/Reflective

__ Watches others play/work

__ Likes to be quiet and alone

__ Likes to daydream/create

__ Warms slowly to a group, or stays on the edge

__ "Creator"/"Dreamer"

__ Likes to observe, imagine, wonder

__ Gets involved in arts, crafts, music, or dancing

__ Notices beauty in nature

__ Often seen as witdrawn or shy

Total _____

Section B: Modality
Total the check marks in each column. Note the highest score and record Modality name in Summary Section.

Visual
__ Likes picture books, puzzles
__ Is drawn to colors, shapes, patterns
__ Likes to color and draw
__ Remembers what has been "seen"
__ "Watches" to learn things
__ Keeps things neat and clean
__ Prefers table games to outside play

Auditory
__ Likes tapes and music
__ Tunes in to sounds and noises
__ Likes to be read to
__ Remembers what has been "heard"
__ "Listens" to learn
__ Talks to self when playing
__ Prefers talk to motor activity

Tactile/Kinesthetic
__ Likes running, climbing, jumping
__ Touches everything
__ Likes to play with sand
__ Remembers what has been "done"
__ "Mimics" to learn
__ Doesn't mind getting dirty
__ Prefers outside play to table games

Totals _____   Totals _____   Totals

Section C: Environment
In Summary Section, record items checked.

When doing chores or at play (s)he likes:
__ quiet
__ noise
__ music
__ having others around
__ being alone

Section D: Interests
Record in Summary Section.

Favorite Toys:

Favorite Colors:

Favorite Pastimes:

Section E: Talents
In Summary Section record Items checked.

Check talent areas:
__ Language/Verbal
__ Artistic/Visual
__ Music
__ Numbers
__ Mechanical
__ Logic/Reasoning
__ Coordination
__ Social
__ Humor
__ Life Skills

Section F: Inner Clock
Record times in Summary Section.
Time of day when most:
Active: _____   Cooperative: _____
Productive: _____   Tired: _____

Comments: _____
_____
_____

Summary

Section A. Disposition
1. _____
2. _____

Section B. Modality

Section C. Environment

Section D. Interests

Section E. Talents

Section F. Inner Clock
Active _____ ("play time")
Cooperative _____ ("teaching/task time")
Productive _____ ("teaching/task time")
Tired _____ ("rest/break time")

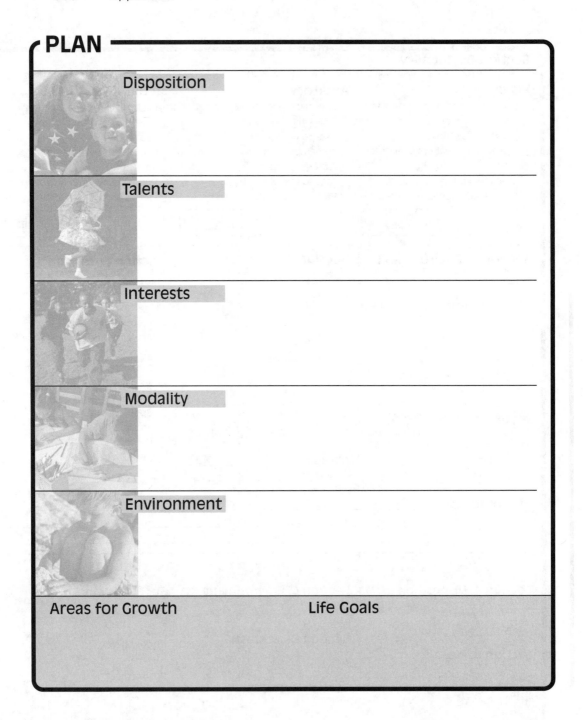

PLAN

Disposition

Talents

Interests

Modality

Environment

Areas for Growth   Life Goals

Plan Form

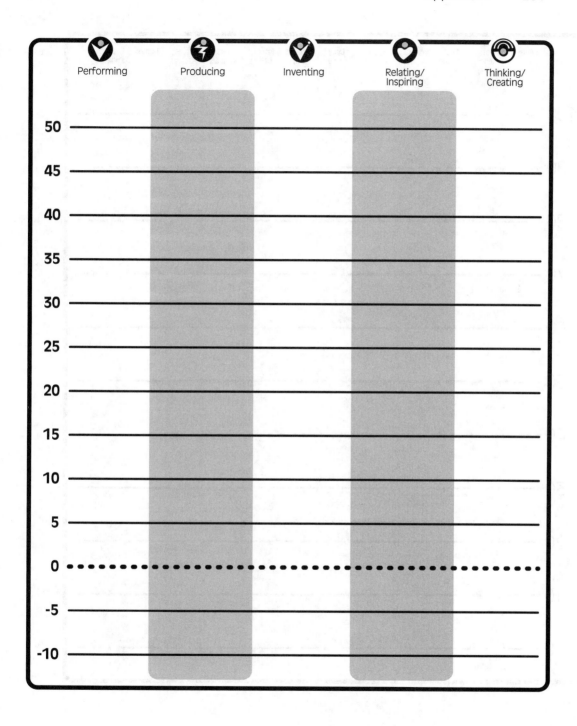

Dispositions Graph

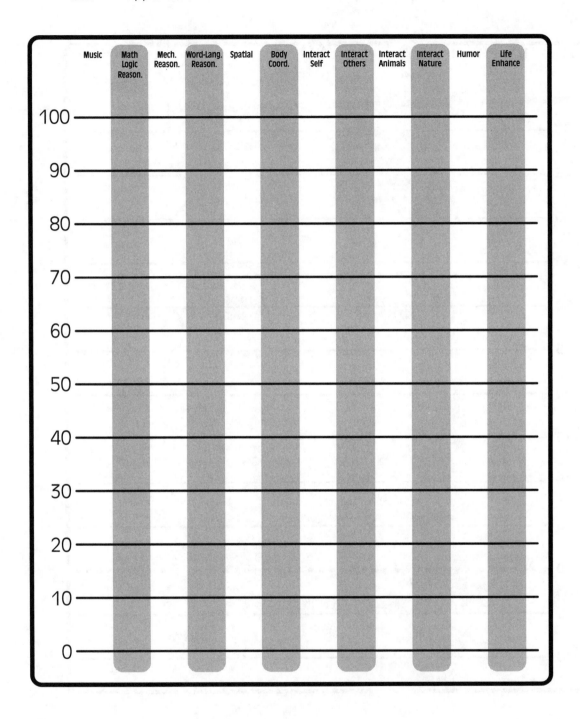

Talents Graph

_____'s
Learning
Style
Portrait

Disposition

Needs: Score

_____   _____ ⓥ Performs

_____   _____ ⚡ Produces

_____   _____ ⓥ Invents

_____   _____ ♥ Relates/Inspires

_____   _____ ◉ Thinks/Creates

Interests

_____

_____

_____

_____

_____

_____

_____

Modality

_____

_____

_____

_____

_____

_____

_____

Environment

_____

_____

_____

_____

_____

_____

_____

Talents

_____

_____

_____

_____

_____

_____

_____

Goals

Strategies

APPENDIX II—RESOURCES

Materials Mentioned in Text (listed alphabetically)

Abacus Math Program, Activities for Learning, 21161 York Rd., Hutchinson, MN 55350, 612-587-9146.

About Teaching Math—A K–8 Resource, by Marilyn Burns, Cuisenaire Co. of America, Inc., 800-237-3142.

Arithme-toons, CM School Supply, 800-464-6681.

Art with Children, by Mona Brookes, available at bookstores.

Audio Memory Publishing: grammar, geography, math set to music, 800-365-SING.

AVKO, 810-686-9283.

Backyard Scientist, Excellence in Education, 818-357-4443.

Boomerang, magazine on cassette, 800-333-7858.

Bornstein Memorizer math cards, L.A., CA 310-478-2056, 800-468-2058.

Build A Doodle, The Learning Works, available at bookstores.

Can Do Videotapes, exercise and learn math facts, 800-286-8585.

Cartoon Guide series: *Cartoon History of U.S., Cartoon Guide to Physics, Genetics*, etc., available at bookstores.

Coloring Book series: *The Anatomy Coloring Book, The Zoology Coloring Book, The Geography Coloring Book,* etc., available at bookstores.

Color the Classics, available at bookstores.

Daily Grams, Creative Home Teaching, 619-263-8633.

Dorling Kindersley books and computer programs, 805-482-5144.

Drawing with Letters and Numbers, Scholastic, available at bookstores.

Draw Write Now, drawing/writing course, Barker Creek Pub., 800-692-5833.

Family History Project, J & K Schooling, 612-479-2286.

Family Math, K–8, Jean K. Stanmark, et al., University of California, Berkeley, Lawrence Hall of Science, 1976. Available at bookstores or Creative Home Teaching, 619-263-8633.

Geography Rummy, available in educational supply stores.

Geography Songs, see Audio Memory Publishing.

GeoSafari, 800-933-3277.

Gizmos and Gadgets, computer program, available in educational stores.

Grammar Songs, see Audio Memory Publishing and New Each Day.

Graphic Organizers, Scholastic, 800-325-6149.

Historical TimeLine, J & K Schooling, 612-479-2286.

Historical TimeLine Figures, J & K Schooling, 612-479-2286.

History Through Art, CD ROM, Zane Pub., 800-460-8923 or AMEXPO, 619-720-1010.

How Things Work, computer program, available in educational stores.

Information Mapping: *What To Do When They Don't Get It*, M. Pelullo-Willis, 805-648-1739.

It's Alive and Kicking, Prufrock Press, 800-998-2208.

Janice Van Cleave's Spectacular Science Projects, Excellence in Education, 818-357-4443.

Key Curriculum: *Fractions, Decimals, Percents, Algebra I, Geometry*, P.O. Box 2304, Berkeley, CA 94702, 800-338-7638.

Lyrical Life Science, Effective Education, 3586 Prince St., Escondido, CA 92025, 800-454-6284.

Mastering Mathematics, by topics not grade level, Mastery Publications, 90 Hillside Lane, Arden, NC 28704.

Math for the Real World, Merrill Publishing, Glencoe, CO, 800-334-7344.

Math Mystery Theater, videos, CM School Supply, 800-464-6681.

Math Shop, Scholastic Educational Technology catalog, 800-541-5513.

Math Strategies, computer games, Pixel Graphics, Inc., 800-GAME-345; for demo: www.pixelgraphics.com.

Math Trivial Pursuit, Good Apple Inc., P.O. Box 299, Carthage, IL 62321; also see Creative Home Teaching (under Great Catalogs).

Mathematics, high-school video/computer program, 505-523-6789, also available at Price Costco.

Multiplication Rock Video, Hands on History catalog, 201 Constance Drive, New Lenox, IL 60451.

National Geographic videos/software, 800-368-2728.

New Each Day: grammar, languages set to music, 800-477-4372.

New Practice Reader, Phoenix Learning Resources, 800-221-1274.

Number Mat: *What to Do When They Don't Get It,* Pelullo-Willis, 805-648-1739.

On Cloud Nine, Lindamood-Bell Learning Processes, 800-233-1819.

Pen Pal Newsletter, P.O. Box 2920, Big Bear City, CA 92314.

Phonics in Song Cassette, Leon Metcalf, Homeschooling Book Club, 810-685-8773.

Phonics Tutor, computer program, 800-231-3570.

Play N Talk, 800-472-7525.

Portfolio Assessment, Getting Started, Alan De Fina, available at bookstores.

Presidential Card Game, J & K Schooling, 612-479-2286.

Real Life Math Mysteries, Prufrock Press, 800-998-2208.

Recipe for Reading, Nina Traub, Farnsworth Books, 800-540-4097.

Rhyme Tymes, Carol Picard, M.A., P.O. Box 1015 NB, Niwot, CO 80544.

Science by Mail, Museum of Science, Science Park, Boston, MA 02114, 800-729-3300.

Science Trivial Pursuit, Creative Home Teaching, 619-263-8633.

Sim City, computer program, available in educational stores.

Sing/Spell/Read/Write, 800-321-TEACH.

S'Math, a board game similar to Scrabble but with numbers, available in toy stores.

Star Trek Series, Globe Fearon, 800-848-9500.

Stories and Plays Without Endings, Globe Fearon, 800-848-9500.

Studentreasures, "publish" own book, 800-867-2292.

Super Workbooks, ESP Pub., 800-643-0280.

Switch On Electronic Circuit Kit, 206-747-7766.

The Great Series, Steck Vaughn, 800-531-5015.

TNT™ Fact Kit, games/picture stories for multiplication/division, 909-276-0989.

Touch Math, Innovative Learning Concepts, Inc., 800-888-9191.

Ultimate Phonics, computer program, Spencer Learning, 800-755-9818, 619-455-9818.

Usborne books, available at bookstores.

Video Tutor, basic math through algebra/geometry, 800-445-8334.

What About Series, Steck Vaughn, 800-531-5015.

What Do You Think?, The Learning Works, available at bookstores.

What to Do When They Don't Get It: A Guide to Great Teaching Techniques, M. Pelullo-Willis, 805-648-1739.

Wilson Reading Program, 162 W. Main St., Millbury, MA 01527, 800-899-8454.

Wonder Number Game, Interactive Dimensions, 805-526-7335.

All materials and resources mentioned in the text are listed below by category. This listing also includes additional resources not previously mentioned.

EDUCATIONAL MATERIALS

Beginning Reading (sequential phonics approach)

Phonics in Song Cassette, Leon Metcalf, Homeschooling Book Club, 810-685-8773.

Phonics Tutor, computer program, 800-231-3570.

Play N Talk, 800-472-7525.

Recipe for Reading, Nina Traub, Farnsworth Books, 800-540-4097.

Sing/Spell/Read/Write, 800-321-TEACH.

Ultimate Phonics, Spencer Learning, San Diego, CA, 619-455-9818.

Wilson Reading Program, 162 W. Main St., Millbury, MA 01527, 800-899-8454.

Reading/Study Helps/Language Arts/Literature

Critical Thinking Press and Software Catalog, P.O. Box 448, Pacific Grove, CA 93950, 800-458-4849.

Franklin Learning Resources Catalog, electronic language/writing helps, 800-525-9673.

Graphic Organizers, Scholastic, available at bookstores.

The Great Series, Steck Vaughn, 800-531-5015.

Information Mapping: *What To Do When They Don't Get It: A Guide to Great Teaching Techniques,* M. Pelullo-Willis, 805-648-1739.

Memorizing Made Easy, Mort Herold, available at bookstores.

New Practice Reader, Phoenix Learning Resources, 800-221-1274.

Phonics Tutor, computer program, 800-231-3570.

Reading by the Colors, scotopic sensitivity syndrome, Irlen Institute, Long Beach, CA, 310-496-2550.

Riggs Dictionary, Riggs Institute, 503-646-9459.

Short Classics, Steck Vaughn, 800-531-5014.

Spellbinders, Globe Fearon, 800-848-9500.

Star Trek Series, Globe Fearon, 800-848-9500.

Stories and Plays Without Endings, Globe Fearon, 800-848-9500.

Studentreasures, "publish" own book, 800-867-2292.

Study Smarts: How to Learn More in Less Time, J. Kesselman-Turkel and F. Peterson, available in bookstores.

Super Workbooks, ESP Pub., 800-643-0280.

Test Taking Strategies, J. Kesselman-Turkel and F. Peterson, available in bookstores.

Thinking It Through: Exercises in Critical Thinking, Globe Fearon, 800-848-9500.

Ultimate Phonics, computer program, Spencer Learning, San Diego, CA, 619-455-9818.

Wilson Reading Program, 162 W. Main St., Millbury, MA 01527, 800-899-8454.

Writing

CoWriter, Write Out Loud, software, Don Johnson Developmental Equipment, 800-999-4660.

Franklin Learning Resources Catalog, electronic language/writing helps, 800-525-9673.

Graphic Organizers, Scholastic, available at bookstores.

A Journey Through Grammar Land, The Great Editing Adventure Series, Daily Grams, Grammar Songs, Major Punctuation, Creative Home Teaching, P.O. Box 152581, San Diego, CA 92195, 619-263-8633.

Studentreasures, "publish" own book, 800-867-2292.

Math

Abacus Math Program, Activities for Learning, 21161 York Rd., Hutchinson, MN 55350, 612-587-9146.

About Teaching Math—A K–8 Resource, Marilyn Burns, Cuisenaire Co. of America, Inc., 800-237-3142.

Arithme-toons, cassettes, CM School Supply, 800-464-6681.

Baseball Math, Basketball Math, The Drinking Gourd, 800-TDG-5487.

Bornstein Memorizer math cards, L.A., CA 310-478-2056, 800-468-2058.

Can Do Videotapes—Multiplication March, Addition Adventure, learn math facts while exercising, 800-286-8585.

Family Math, K–8, Jean K. Stanmark, University of California, Berkeley, Lawrence Hall of Science, 1976. Available at bookstores or Creative Home Teaching, 619-263-8633.

Grocery Cart Math, Family Learning Center, 800-953-2762.

It's Alive and Kicking, Prufrock Press, 800-998-2208.

Key to Curriculum: Fractions, Decimals, Percents, Algebra I, Geometry, P.O. Box 2304, Berkeley, CA 94702, 800-338-7638.

Mastering Mathematics, by topics not grade level, Mastery Publications, 704-684-0429.

Mathematical Reasoning Through Verbal Analysis, The Drinking Gourd, 800-TDG-5487.

Mathematics, high-school video/computer program, 505-523-6789, also available at Price Costco.

Math for Smarty Pants, Marilyn Burns, The Drinking Gourd, 800-TDG-5487.

Math for the Real World, Merrill, Glencoe, CO, 800-334-7344.

Math Mystery Theater videos, CM School Supply, 800-464-6681.

Math Safari, 800-933-3277.

Math Shop, computer program, Scholastic Educational Technology catalog, 800-541-5513.

Math Strategies, computer games, Pixel Graphics, Inc., 800-GAME-345; for demo: www.pixelgraphics.com.

Math Trivial Pursuit, Good Apple, Inc., P.O. Box 299, Carthage, IL 62321; also see Creative Home Teaching (under Great Catalogs).

Multiplication Rock Video, Hands on History catalog, 201 Constance Drive, New Lenox, IL 60451.

Number Mat: *What To Do When They Don't Get It*, M. Pelullo-Willis, 805-648-1739.

On Cloud Nine, Lindamood-Bell Learning Processes, 800-233-1819.

Real Life Math Mysteries, Prufrock Press, 800-998-2208.

Rhyme Tymes, Carol Picard, M.A., P.O. Box 1015 NB, Niwot, CO 80544.

S'Math, a board game similar to Scrabble but with numbers, available in toy stores.

TNT™ Fact Kit, games/picture stories for multiplication/division, 909-276-0989.

Touch Math, Innovative Learning Concepts, Inc., 800-888-9191.

Video Tutor, basic math through algebra/geometry, 800-445-8334.

Wonder Number Game, Interactive Dimensions, 805-526-7335.

Music/Art

Art Lessons for Children on Video, Creative Home Teaching, 619-263-8633.

Art with Children, Mona Brookes, available at bookstores.

Audio Memory Publishing: grammar, geography, math set to music, 800-365-SING.

Build A Doodle, The Learning Works, available at bookstores.

Coloring Book series: *The Anatomy Coloring Book, The Zoology Coloring Book, The Geography Coloring Book,* etc.

Color the Classics, available at bookstores.

Drawing for Beginners, Sure Curriculum, Box 30101, Amarillo, TX 79120.

Drawing on the Right Side of Your Brain, Betty Edwards, available at bookstores.

Drawing with Letters and Numbers, Scholastic, available at bookstores.

Draw Write Now, drawing/writing course, Barker Creek Pub., 800-692-5833.

History Through Art, CD ROM, Zane Pub., 800-460-8923, or AMEXPO, 619-720-1010.

New Each Day: grammar, languages set to music, 800-477-4372.

Phonics in Song Cassette, Leon Metcalf, Homeschooling Book Club, 810-685-8773.

Studentreasures, "publish" own book, 800-867-2292.

The Music Game, music theory, 505-672-1619.

Science

Animal Addresses, Creative Home Teaching, 619-263-8633.

Backyard Scientist, Excellence in Education, 818-357-4443.

Beakman's Book of Dead Guys and Gals in Science by Luann Colombo, *Blood and Guts* by Linda Allison available at educational bookstores.

Cartoon Guide series: *Cartoon Guide to Physics, Genetics*, etc., available in bookstores.

Coloring Book series: *The Anatomy Coloring Book, The Zoology Coloring Book,* etc., available in bookstores.

Gizmos and Gadgets, available in educational supply stores.

How Things Work, available in educational supply stores.

Janice Van Cleave's Spectacular Science Projects, Excellence in Education, 818-357-4443.

National Geographic videos/software, 800-368-2728.

Science by Mail, Museum of Science, Science Park, Boston, MA 02114, 800-729-3300.

Science Trivial Pursuit, Creative Home Teaching, 619-263-8633.

Sim City, available in educational supply stores.

Switch On Electronic Circuit Kit, 206-747-7766.

Timeless Treasures Catalog, minerals/fossils, 602-488-3708.

What About Series, Steck Vaughn, 800-531-5015.

Zane CD catalog, (800) 460-8923.

Social Studies

American Girls History Program, crafts, cooking, theater kits, 800-481-3466.

Boomerang, magazine on cassette, 800-333-7858.

Cartoon Guide to U.S. History, available in bookstores.

Family History Project, J & K Schooling, 612-479-2286.

Famous Black Americans, Steck Vaughn, 800-531-5015.

The Geography Coloring Book, available in bookstores.

Geography Rummy, available at educational supply stores.

Geography Songs, Audio Memory Publishing, 800-365-SING.

GeoSafari, 800-933-3277.

Historical TimeLine, J & K Schooling, 612-479-2286.

Historical TimeLine Figures, J & K Schooling, 612-479-2286.

History Through Art, CD ROM, Zane Pub., 800-460-8923.

Jean Fritz's American History series: *And Then What Happened, Paul Revere? What's the Big Idea, Ben Franklin*, Beautiful Feet Books, 800-889-1978 or Bluestocking Press, 916-621-1123.

Multicultural Biographies, Globe Fearon, 800-848-9500.

National Geographic videos/software, 800-368-2728.

Pen Pal Newsletter, P.O. Box 2920, Big Bear City, CA 92314.

Presidential Card Game, J & K Schooling, 612-479-2286.

U.S. Kids History, Brown Paper School Pub., stories, plays, poems, songs, crafts, cooking, more, available at bookstores.

What Do You Think?, The Learning Works, available at bookstores.

Yo Millard Fillmore, presidents, Scholastic, 800-325-6149.

Software

ASLAN Software Catalog, 800-395-4194.

Davison and Associates, Inc.: *Word Attack Plus, Spell It Plus, Math Blaster,* algebra, geometry, writing, science, ecology, social studies programs, 800-545-7677.

Discovery Educational Software, 800-919-1191.

Don Johnson Developmental Equipment, 800-999-4660.

Dorling Kindersley Family Library, 7800 Southland Blvd. #200, Orlando, FL 32809, 407-857-5463.

Educational Resources, 800-624-2926.

The Edutainment Catalog, 800-338-3844.

Great Wave Software: *Reading Maze, Kids Time, Number Maze, American Discovery*, 800-423-1144.

Gizmos and Gadgets, available in educational supply stores.

How Things Work, available in educational supply stores.

M&M Software, public domain and shareware library, 800-642-6163; email: mmsoft@aol.com.

MECC: *Word Munchers, Number Munchers,* geography programs, 800-228-3504.

Mindplay Software Catalog, 800-221-7911.

National Geographic Educational Technology catalog, 800-368-2728.

Nordic Software: *Preschool Pack, Turbo Math Facts, Word Quest, Word Search*, 402-488-5086.

Pride's Guide to Educational Software, Mary Pride.

Scholastic Educational Technology catalog, 800-541-5513.

Sim City, available in educational supply stores.

Special Times Software, special learning needs, 800-637-0047.

Ultimate Phonics, computer program, Spencer Learning, San Diego, CA, 619-455-9818.

Zane CD catalog, (800) 460-8923.

Great Catalogs

Brain Store, 800-325-4769.

Creative Home Teaching, P.O. Box 152581, San Diego, CA 92195, 619-263-8633.

Dorling Kindersley books and computer programs, 805-482-5144.

Globe Fearon, 800-848-9500.

High Noon Books, 800-422-7249.

National Geographic videos/software, 800-368-2728.

Phoenix Learning Resources, 800-221-1274.

Prufrock Press, 800-998-2208.

Scholastic, 800-325-6149.

Steck Vaughn, 800-531-5015.

Zephyr Press, 520-322-5090.

RESOURCE BOOKS

(Everything listed below available in bookstores, except where noted)

Learning Styles/Education

Awakening Your Child's Natural Genius, Thomas Armstrong.

Awareness Through Movement, Moshe Feldenkrais.

Circles of Learning, D. Johnson, R. Johnson, and E. Holubec.

Dumbing Us Down: The Hidden Curriculum of Compulsory Schooling, John Taylor Gatto.

Emotional Intelligence, Daniel Goleman.

The Exhausted School, John Taylor Gatto.

The Gift of Dyslexia, Ronald D. Davis.

Help Yourself: How to Take Advantage of Your Learning Styles, Gail M. Sonbuchner.

How to Talk So Kids Will Learn, Adele Faber and Elaine Mazlish.

In Their Own Way, Thomas Armstrong.

Learning Styles, Priscilla Vail.

The Myth of ADD, Thomas Armstrong.

Nurturing Intelligences, Brian A. Haggerty.

Portfolio Assessment: Getting Started, Allan De Fina.

Reading by The Colors, scotopic sensitivity syndrome, Irlen Institute, Long Beach, CA, 310-496-2550.

Schools Without Failure, William Glasser.

Smart Kids with School Problems, Priscilla Vail.

Switching On, Paul Dennison.

Thinking in Pictures, Temple Grandin.

Unicorns Are Real, Barbara Meister Vitale.

What To Do When They Don't Get It: A Guide to Great Teaching Techniques, M. Pelullo-Willis, 805-648-1739.

Homeschooling

The Big Book of Home Learning, Mary Pride.

Christian Home Educators' Curriculum Manual, Cathy Duffy, Home Run Enterprises, 714-638-7956.

Family Matters: Why Homeschooling Makes Sense, David Guterson.

Homeschooling Almanac 2000, Mary and Michael Leppert.

Home Schooling the Child with "Learning Problems," M. Pelullo-Willis, 805-648-1739.

The Homeschooling Book of Answers, Linda Dobson.

The Link Homeschool Newspaper, free, 587 N. Ventu Park Rd. #F-911, Newbury Park, CA 91320; hompaper@gte.net.

The Unschooling Handbook, Mary Griffith.

Parenting

Beyond Discipline, Alfie Kohn.

Career Track cassettes: *Building Self-Esteem in Your Child; How to Raise Happy, Confident Kids,* 303-440-7440.

Different Children, Different Needs, Charles E. Boyd.

Discipline with Dignity, Richard Curwin and Allen Mendler.

Emotional Intelligence, Daniel Goleman.

How to Raise Parents, Clayton Barbeau.

How to Talk So Kids Will Learn, Adele Faber and Elaine Mazlish.

How to Talk So Kids Will Listen and How to Listen So Kids Will Talk, Faber and Mazlish.

Liberated Parents, Liberated Children: Your Guide to a Happier Family, Adele Faber and Elaine Mazlish.

Live the Love series, V. Kindle Hodson, 805-648-1739.

Logical Consequences, Rudolf Dreikurs, M.D. and Loren Grey.

Positive Discipline, Jane Nelsen.

Siblings Without Rivalry, Adele Faber and Elaine Mazlish.

Three Steps to a Strong Family, Linda and Richard Eyre.

Teaching

Accelerated Learning, Colin Rose.

Accelerated Learning Techniques, Brian Tracy and Colin Rose (audio), 800-323-5552.

Educational Leadership Magazine, ASCD, 800-933-2723.

The Everyday Genius, Peter Kline.

Good Morning Class—I Love You, Esther Wright.

Graphic Organizers, Karen Bromley et al.

How to Change to a Nongraded School, Madeline Hunter, 800-933-2723.

How to Implement and Supervise a Learning Style Program, Rita Dunn, 800-933-2723.

Introduction to Brain Compatible Learning, Eric Jensen, 800-325-4769.

The Learning Revolution, Gordon Dryden and Jeannette Vos.

Loving Discipline A to Z, Esther Wright.

The Mind Map Book, Tony and Barry Buzan.

Multiple Intelligences in the Classroom, Thomas Armstrong.

Portfolio Assessment: Getting Started, Allan De Fina.

Positive Discipline in the Classroom, Jane Nelsen.

Rhythms of Learning, Chris Brewer and Don Campbell.

What To Do When They Don't Get It: A Guide to Great Teaching Techniques, M. Pelullo-Willis, 805-648-1739.

Why Do I Have To Learn This?, Dale Parnell.

Why I Teach, Esther Wright.

Nutrition

Cooking with the Right Side of the Brain, Vicki Rae Chelf.

Feed Your Kids Right, Lendon Smith, M.D.

The Self-Healing Cookbook, Kristina Turner.

Sugar Blues, William Duffy.

Success in the Real World

Accelerated Learning Techniques, Brian Tracy and Colin Rose (audio), 800-323-5552.

The Aladdin Factor, Jack Canfield and Mark Victor Hansen.

Celebrity Setbacks, Ed Lucaire.

Chicken Soup for the Soul, Jack Canfield and Mark Victor Hansen (also *Chicken Soup for the Kid's Soul* and *Chicken Soup for the Teenage Soul*).

Do What You Love, The Money Will Follow, Marsha Sinetar.

The Greatest Salesman in the World, Og Mandino.

How to Find Your Mission in Life, Richard Bolles.

I Could Do Anything If I Only Knew What It Was, Barbara Sher.

It's Possible, video, Les Brown, if not available in bookstores, call (312) 829-5100.

Life Launch, Frederic M. Hudson and Pamela D. McLean.

Nonviolent Communication, Marshall Rosenberg.

The Power of Positive Thinking, Norman Vincent Peale.

The Seven Spiritual Laws of Success, Deepak Chopra.

Seven Strategies to Wealth and Happiness, Jim Rohn.

Straight A's Never Made Anybody Rich, Wess Roberts.

Think and Grow Rich, Napoleon Hill.

Three Keys to Greatness, video, Jim Rohn, if not available in bookstores, call (214) 401-1000.

Wealth Starts at Home, David D'Arcangelo.

What Color Is Your Parachute?, Richard Bolles.

Publications by Mariemma Pelullo-Willis or Victoria Kindle Hodson: *Getting Beyond Me Against You, Give It Your Best, Live the Love, Moods, Home Schooling the Child with "Learning Problems," What To Do When They Don't Get It: A Guide to Great Teaching Techniques.* Order from REP, 1451 E. Main St. #200, Ventura, CA 93001, 805-648-1739, 805-653-0261.

REFERENCES

Introduction

1. Thomas Armstrong, *Awakening Your Child's Natural Genius*, Jeremy P. Tarcher, 1991.
2. Armstrong, 1991.
3. David Guterson, *Family Matters: Why Homeschooling Makes Sense*, Harcourt Brace Jovanovich, 1992.
4. Jean Cowden Moore, "Fair to Provide College Education," *The Star*, Ventura, CA, April 14, 1999.

Chapter 1

1. Pedro Garcia, superintendent of Corona-Norco Unified School District, "Helping Our Children to be Successful," *Independent*, October 1998.
2. Alfie Kohn, *Punished by Rewards*, Houghton Mifflin, 1993.

Chapter 2

1. Cynthia Warger and Marleen Pugach, "Forming Partnerships Around Curriculum," *Educational Leadership*, February 1996.
2. Ernest Hilgard and Richard Atkinson, *Introduction to Psychology*, Harcourt Brace and World, 1967.
3. Henry Klugh, *Statistics: The Essentials of Research*, John Wiley and Sons, 1970.
4. Rita Dunn, Jeffrey S. Beaudry, and Angela Klavas, "Survey of Research on Learning Styles," *Educational Leadership*, March 1989.
5. Marge Scherer, "A Conversation with David Elkind," *Educational Leadership*, April 1996.

Chapter 3

1. Alfie Kohn, *Beyond Discipline*, ASCD, 1996 (quoting Arthur L. Costa, ASCD President).

2. Albert Bandura, Dorothea Ross, and Sheila A. Ross, "Transmission of Aggression Through Imitation of Aggressive Models," *Journal of Abnormal Social Psychology,* 1961, 63, 575–582.

3. Marsha Sinetar, *Do What You Love and the Money Will Follow,* Dell Publishing, 1987.

4. Daniel Goleman, *Emotional Intelligence,* Bantam, 1995.

5. Thomas Armstrong, *Awakening Your Child's Natural Genius,* Jeremy P. Tarcher, 1991.

6. Armstrong, 1991.

7. John Taylor Gatto, A *Short, Angry History of Modern Schooling: An Exorcism,* self-published, 1998.

8. Kohn, 1996.

9. John F. Covaleskie, "Discipline and Morality: Beyond Rules and Consequences," *Educational Forum,* 1992, 56, 173–183.

Introduction to Part 2

1. Thomas Armstrong, *In Their Own Way,* Tarcher/St. Martin's Press, 1987.

Chapter 5

1. Carol Ann Tomlinson and M. Layne Kalbfleisch, "Teach Me, Teach My Brain: A Call for Differentiated Classrooms," *Educational Leadership,* November 1998.

2. Victoria Kindle-Hodson, *Getting Beyond Me Against You,* Kindle Communication, 1993.

Chapter 6

1. Chris Brewer and Don G. Campbell, *Rhythms of Learning,* Zephyr Press, 1991.

Chapter 7

1. Greg Harris, "Delight Directed Home Schooling," *Our Family's Favorites*, Christian Life Workshops, 1992.

2. Linda Dobson, *The Homeschooling Book of Answers*, Prima, 1998.

Chapter 8

1. Mariaemma Pelullo-Willis, *What to Do When They Don't Get It: A Guide to Great Teaching Techniques*, Reflective Educational Perspectives, 1996.

2. Tony Buzan, *The Mind Map Book*, Penguin, 1993.

3. Karen Bromley et al., *Graphic Organizers*, Scholastic, 1995.

4. Gordon Dryden and Jeannette Vos, Ed.D., *The Learning Revolution*, Jalmar Press, 1994.

5. Dryden and Vos, 1994.

6. Peter Kline, *The Everyday Genius*, Great Ocean Publishers, 1988.

7. Linda S. Gottfredson, "The General Intelligence Factor," *Scientific American*, Winter 1998.

Chapter 9

1. Rita Dunn and Kenneth Dunn, *Teaching Students Through Their Individual Learning Styles*, Reston, 1978.

2. Rita Dunn, *How to Implement and Supervise a Learning Style Program*, Association for Supervision and Curriculum Development, 1996.

3. *American School and University*, "Top 10 Design Ideas for Schools of the 21st Century," Primedia Intertec, January 1998.

4. Eric Jensen, *How to Use Music in Teaching and Training*, Turning Point, 1995.

5. Eric Jensen, *Optimal Learning Environment*, Turning Point, 1994.

6. John Ott, *Health and Light*, Ariel Press, 1990.

7. Jensen, 1994.

8. Rita Dunn, Jeffrey S. Beaudry, and Angela Klavas, "Survey of Research on Learning Styles," *Educational Leadership,* March 1989.

9. Richard Simon, LA Times staff writer, "Do-Nothing Congress Doesn't Apply to State's Delegation," LA Times, July 18, 1999.

Chapter 10

1. Mariaemma Pelullo-Willis, *Homeschooling the Child with "Learning Problems,"* Reflective Educational Perspectives, 1993.

2. Mariaemma Pelullo-Willis, *What to Do When They Don't Get It: A Guide to Great Teaching Techniques,* Reflective Educational Perspectives, 1996.

Chapter 12

1. Jane Nelsen, *Positive Discipline in the Classroom,* Prima Publishing, 1997.

2. Marshall Rosenberg, Ph.D., *Nonviolent Communication,* Puddle Dancer Press, 1999.

3. Stanley J. Hodson, *Beside Ourselves with Calm,* in manuscript, 1983.

Chapter 13

1. *National Education Goals: Building a Nation of Learners,* National Education Goals Panel (federal agency), report, 1998.

2. Education for all Handicapped Children Act, Public Law 94-142, Part 200.1, 1975.

3. Thomas Armstrong, *In Their Own Way,* Jeremy P. Tarcher, 1987.

4. National Academy of Education, committee on Reading, Toward a Literate Society, McGraw-Hill, 1975.

5. Charles Child Walcutt, et. al., *Teaching Reading,* Macmillan, 1974.

6. Jerry Pournelle, Ph.D., Reading Reform Foundation Newsletter, Scottsdale, AZ, 1976

7. Dr. Melvin Howards, Director of Northwestern University's Center for Educational Development, Reading Reform Foundation Newsletter, Scottsdale, AZ, August, 1976.

8. Thomas Armstrong, *In Their Own Way,* Jeremy P. Tarcher, 1987.

9. Armstrong, 1987.

10. LDA Newsletter, a paid advertisement written by Children's Therapy Center, Inc., January 1997.

11. Priscilla Vail, *Learning Styles*, Modern Learning Press, 1992.

12. Thomas Armstrong, *The Myth of the A.D.D. Child*, Dutton, 1995.

13. Helen Irlen, *Reading by the Colors*, Avery, 1991.

14. Jack Canfield and Mark Victor Hansen, *Chicken Soup for the Soul*, Health Communication, 1993.

15. Ed Lucaire, *Celebrity Setbacks*, New York Prentice-Hall, 1993.

16. Gordon Dryden and Jeannette Vos, Ed.D., *The Learning Revolution*, Jalmar Press, 1994.

Chapter 14

1. Association for Supervision and Curriculum Development, reported in a letter sent to subscribers, March, 1999.

2. Rita Dunn, *How to Implement and Supervise a Learning Style Program*, ASCD Publications, 1996.

Chapter 15

1. Chris Brewer and Don Campbell, *Rhythms of Learning*, Zephyr Press, 1991.

2. David D'Arcangelo, *Wealth Starts at Home*, McGraw-Hill, 1997.

3. E. D. Hirsch, Jr., *A First Dictionary of Cultural Literacy*, Houghton Mifflin, 1991.

4. Rita Dunn, Jeffrey S. Beaudry, Angela Klavas, "Survey of Research on Learning Styles," *Educational Leadership*, March 1989.

5. Marge Scherer, "A Conversation with David Elkind," *Educational Leadership*, April 1996.

6. Rita Dunn, *How to Implement and Supervise a Learning Style Program*, Association for Supervision and Curriculum Development, 1996.

7. Michael F. Shaughnessy, "An Interview with Rita Dunn About Learning Styles," *The Clearing House: A Journal of Educational Research, Controversy and Practices*, Heldref Publications, Washington, D.C., January 1998.

Epilogue

1. James Alan Astman, Headmaster, Oakwood School, "No One Is Average," *The Educational Therapist,* February 1987, quoting from the comments of an elementary school principal, delivered at a meeting on critical thinking at Harvard University (Schwob, 9/5/84, p. L15).

INDEX

About the Authors

Victoria

Victoria Kindle Hodson was born and grew up in the Pacific Northwest. She attended Western Washington University and holds a Master's degree in Psychology, and a Bachelor's degree in Education. She is an educational consultant and has taught, developed educational programs, and conducted workshops for parents and teachers for more than 25 years.

Victoria has worked in many diverse educational settings that have provided experience with the needs of widely different kinds of learners. She has trained in special education, parenting, communication skills development, and Montessori education. Over the last 30 years she has been developing an alternative way of viewing children as learners. The learning techniques and strategies she encourages are based on her research, insight, and experience in psychology and education.

Mariaemma

Mariaemma Pelullo-Willis was born and grew up Southern California. She attended California State University, where she majored in Psychology. She holds a Master's degree in Education, and California Life Teaching Credentials for Regular and Special Education. She has been developing educational programs and conducting workshops for parents and teachers for more than 20 years.

Mariaemma was the director of a private school for children with 'learning disabilities' for eleven years, before going into private practice. She has also conducted training programs for literacy volunteers throughout Southern California, taught learning-success strategies in correctional facilities, and has developed assessment and teaching procedures for adult students.

Victoria and Mariaemma have worked with and spoken to thousands of children and parents as well as homeschooling families and classroom teachers—assessing learning styles, diagnosing school problems, designing customized curriculum plans, and teaching techniques and strategies that help children learn. They have developed and published *A Self-Portrait ™ Learning Style System* and several books for parents and teachers.

Mariaemma and Victoria can be reached by contacting:
Website: www.redp.com

Victoria Kindle Hodson, M.A.
P.O. Box 24246
Ventura, CA 93002
(805) 653-0261
vkhodson@bigplanet.com

Mariaemma Pelullo-Willis, M.S.
1451 E. Main St. #200
Ventura, CA 93001
(805) 648-1739
mepw1@aol.com